PUBLIC
SERVICES
DELIVERY

Introduction to the Public Sector Governance and Accountability Series

Anwar Shah, Series Editor

A well-functioning public sector that delivers quality public services consistent with citizen preferences and that fosters private market-led growth while managing fiscal resources prudently is considered critical to the World Bank's mission of poverty alleviation and the achievement of Millennium Development Goals. This important new series aims to advance those objectives by disseminating conceptual guidance and lessons from practices and by facilitating learning from each others' experiences on ideas and practices that promote *responsive* (by matching public services with citizens' preferences), *responsible* (through efficiency and equity in service provision without undue fiscal and social risk), and *accountable* (to citizens for all actions) public governance in developing countries.

This series represents a response to several independent evaluations in recent years that have argued that development practitioners and policy makers dealing with public sector reforms in developing countries and, indeed, anyone with a concern for effective public governance could benefit from a synthesis of newer perspectives on public sector reforms. This series distills current wisdom and presents tools of analysis for improving the efficiency, equity, and efficacy of the public sector. Leading public policy experts and practitioners have contributed to the series.

The first seven volumes in the series (*Fiscal Management, Public Services Delivery, Public Expenditure Analysis, Tools for Public Sector Evaluations, Macrofederalism* and *Local Finances, International Practices in Local Governance,* and *Citizen-Centered Governance*) are concerned with public sector accountability for prudent fiscal management; efficiency and equity in public service provision; safeguards for the protection of the poor, women, minorities, and other disadvantaged groups; ways of strengthening institutional arrangements for voice and exit; methods of evaluating public sector programs, fiscal federalism, and local finances; international practices in local governance; and a framework for responsive and accountable governance.

Fiscal Management

Edited by Anwar Shah

Public Expenditure Analysis

Edited by Anwar Shah

Tools for Public Sector Evaluations

Edited by Anwar Shah

Macrofederalism and Local Finances

Edited by Anwar Shah

International Practices in Local Governance

Edited by Anwar Shah

Citizen-Centered Governance

Matthew Andrews and Anwar Shah

PUBLIC SECTOR
GOVERNANCE AND
ACCOUNTABILITY SERIES

PUBLIC
SERVICES
DELIVERY

Edited by ANWAR SHAH

THE WORLD BANK
Washington, D.C.

ISBN-13: 978-0-8213-6140-5
ISBN-10: 0-8213-6140-6
eISBN: 0-8213-6141-4
DOI: 10.1596/978-0-8213-6140-5

Library of Congress Cataloging-in-Publication Data

Public Services Delivery / edited by Anwar Shah.
   p. cm. — (Public sector governance, and accountability series)
  Includes bibliographical references and index.
  ISBN 0-8213-6140-6 (pbk.)
   1. Government productivity—Evaluation. 2. Public administration—Evaluation. 3. Municipal services—Evaluation. 4. Medical care—Evaluation. 5. Education—Evaluation. 6. Public welfare—Evaluation. 7. Infrastructure (Economics)—Evaluation. I. Shah, Anwar. II. World Bank. III. Series.

JF1525.P67M43 2005
361.6'068'4—dc22

2005043246

Contents

Introduction to the Public Sector Governance and Accountability Series   ii

Foreword   ix

Preface   xi

Acknowledgments   xiii

Contributors   xv

Abbreviations and Acronyms   xxi

Overview   xxiii
by Anwar Shah

CHAPTER

Issues Associated with the Implementation of Governmentwide Performance Monitoring   1
by Alasdair Roberts
Current Efforts at Governmentwide Performance
    Monitoring   4
Difficulties in Execution   11
Prospects for Governmentwide Performance
    Planning   23
Annex 1.A: Outcome Measures in the Oregon Plan   30
Annex 1.B: Outcome Measures in the Florida Plan   31

Annex 1.C: Outcome Measures in the Alberta Plan   34
Annex 1.D: Outcome Measures in the
    Nova Scotia Plan   35
Annex 1.E: Draft Outcome Measures for the Canadian
    Government   37

2 A Simple Measure of Good Governance   39
by Jeff Huther and Anwar Shah

Measuring Governance Quality   40
Impact of Fiscal Decentralization on Governance Quality   46
Quality of Governance and Decentralization   52
Conclusion   54
Annex 2.A: Sources and Quality of Data and Explanations Regard-
    ing Development of Component Indexes   57
Annex 2.B: Composite Indexes   60

3 Assessing Local Government Performance in Develop-ing Countries   63
by Matthew Andrews and Anwar Shah

Evaluation Criteria   64
Evaluating Conformance to Legislation and Process   65
Evaluating Responsiveness   72
Evaluating Efficiency   75
Evaluating Accountability   77
Conclusion   80

4 Results Matter: Suggestions for a Developing Country's Early Outcome Measurement Effort   85
by Harry P. Hatry

What Is Outcome Measurement?   85
Why Measure Outcomes?   86
Obstacles to Outcome Measurement in
    Developing Countries   86
Basic Steps in Implementing an Outcome
    Measurement Process   88
Basic Outcome Measurement Procedures and Their Costs   93

Measurements of Extent of Corruption   98
Measurements of Response Time   99
Data Quality Control   100
Using Outcome Data   100
Final Note   102
Annex 4.A: Household Questionnaire   103
Annex 4.B: Trained Observer Procedures   107
Annex 4.C: Examples of Performance Indicators for Tracking
    Anticorruption Efforts   109

5

Delivering Local/Municipal Services   117
by Harry Kitchen
Public Sector Alternatives   117
Private Sector Provision   128
Public-Private Partnerships   139
Summary   145

6

**Assessing the Performance of Health Services
in Reaching the Poor**   153
*by Agnes Soucat, Ruth Levine, Adam Wagstaff, Abdo S. Yazbeck,
Charles C. Griffin, Timothy Johnston, Paul Hutchinson, and
Rudolf Knippenberg*
Channeling Resources to the Poor   156
Reaching the Poor: Equity of Coverage for Interventions Address-
    ing the Needs of the Poor   162
Equity and the Impact of Health Sector Financing   178
Conclusion   185

7

**Measuring Public Sector Performance
in Infrastructure**   193
by Hadi Salehi Esfahani
The Nature of the Problem   195
Choosing Performance Indicators   196
Evaluating Performance   206
Conclusion   207

FIGURES

4.B.1 Trained Observer Rating Scale   113
6.1   PRSP Framework—Determinants of Health Outcomes   154
6.2   DALYs Lost per 1,000 Population by Cause   158
6.3   Eight Steps to Effective Coverage for the Poor   163

TABLES

2.1   Components of Governance Index   41
2.2   Ranking of Countries on Governance Quality   44
2.3   Governance Index Correlation Coefficients   45
2.4   Correlation of Subnational Expenditures
      with Governance Quality Indicators   48
2.5   Omissions from Original Indexes   54
4.1   Outcome Indicators for Elementary and Secondary
      School Systems   88
4.2   Outcome Indicators for Youth Welfare   89
4.3   Outcome Indicators for Solid Waste Collection   91
4.B.1 Toronto Road Condition Rating Scale   112
5.1   Private versus Public Sector Delivery in Canada   131
6.1   Sources of Data for Assessing Coverage   164
6.2   Example of Determinants of Coverage with a Core Package
      of Activities   165
6.3   Summary of Major Questions to Be Answered in a Health
      Financing Assessment   185
7.1   Examples of Performance Measures for Power Infrastructure   198
7.2   Examples of Performance Measures for Telecommunications Infra-
      structure   199
7.3   Examples of Performance Measures for Transportation
      Infrastructure   200
7.4   Examples of Performance Measures for Water Infrastructure   201
7.5   Examples of Performance Measures for Sanitation
      Infrastructure   202

Foreword

In Western democracies systems of checks and balances built into government structures have formed the core of good governance and have helped empower citizens for more than two hundred years. The incentives that motivate public servants and policy makers—the rewards and sanctions linked to results that help shape public sector performance—are rooted in a country's accountability frameworks. Sound public sector management and government spending help determine the course of economic development and social equity, especially for the poor and other disadvantaged groups such as women and the elderly.

Many developing countries, however, continue to suffer from unsatisfactory and often dysfunctional governance systems including rent seeking and malfeasance, inappropriate allocation of resources, inefficient revenue systems, and weak delivery of vital public services. Such poor governance leads to unwelcome outcomes for access to public services by the poor and other disadvantaged members of the society such as women, children, and minorities. In dealing with these concerns, the development assistance community in general, and the World Bank in particular, are continuously striving to learn lessons from practices around the world to achieve a better understanding of what works and what does not work in improving public sector governance especially with respect to combating corruption and making services work for poor people.

This series advances our knowledge by providing tools and lessons from practices for improving the efficiency and equity of public services provision and for strengthening institutions of accountability in governance. The series highlights frameworks for creating incentive environments and pressures for good governance from within and beyond governments. It outlines institutional mechanisms for empowering citizens to demand accountability for results from their governments. It provides practical guidance on managing for results and on prudent fiscal management. It outlines approaches to dealing with corruption and malfeasance. It provides conceptual and practical guidance on alternative service delivery frameworks for extending the reach and access of public services. The series also covers safeguards for the protection of the poor, women, minorities and other disadvantaged groups; strengthening institutional arrangements for voice and exit; methods of evaluating public sector programs; frameworks for responsive and accountable governance; and fiscal federalism and local governance.

The *Public Governance and Accountability Series* will be of interest to public officials, development practitioners, students of development, and those interested in public governance in developing countries.

Frannie A. Léautier
Vice President
World Bank Institute

Preface

Globalization, localization, and information revolution are empowering citizens to demand accountability from their governments. For such accountability to be an effective tool, a framework for measuring government performance for public services delivery is required. This book provides tools of analysis for measuring performance for the whole of government and for various levels of government, as well as for important individual sectors such as health, infrastructure, and local and municipal services. The book also draws lessons from performance measurement systems in industrial countries.

The underlying framework presented in this book addresses two overarching issues: (a) whether the public manager is *doing the right things*—that is, delivering services consistent with citizen preferences; and (b) whether they are *doing it right*—providing services of a given quality at the lowest tax cost to citizens. To answer these questions, the book operationalizes the following empirical tests:

- *Efficacy test:* What is the extent to which the public programs meet stated goals?
- *Efficiency test:* Are public services being delivered in a least cost manner for a given quantity and quality of services?
- *Alternate service delivery test:* Is the access to public services being expanded with appropriate partnership or contractual relationships within and beyond government? What activities or programs could be outsourced in whole or in part to the private or voluntary sectors?
- *Money's worth test:* Are the public funds being put to their best use?

Applications of the above tests are expected to enable government managers to conduct self-evaluation of their achievements in creating public value and to provide other stakeholders with a frame of reference for judging government performance in delivering public services. Such a spotlight on government performance is expected to yield improved delivery of and access to government services in developing countries.

I am grateful to the Swiss Development Cooperation Agency for their support, and to the leading experts who contributed papers; together they have made this series possible.

Roumeen Islam
Manager, Poverty Reduction and Economic Management
World Bank Institute

Acknowledgments

The completion of this book has been made possible through a grant from the Swiss Development Cooperation Agency. The editor is grateful to the staff of that agency for their guidance on the contents of the book. In particular, he owes a great deal of intellectual debt to Walter Hofer, Werner Thut, Pietro Veglio, Gerolf Weigel, and Hanspeter Wyss. The editor is also grateful to senior management of the Operations Evaluation Department of the World Bank, the World Bank Institute, and CEPAL (the United Nations' Economic Commission for Latin America and the Caribbean) for their support. Thanks are, in particular, due to Juan Carlos Lerda and Roumeen Islam for their guidance and support.

The book has also benefited from comments received by senior policy makers at the CEPAL–World Bank joint workshop held in Santiago, Chile, in January 2001 and PREM (poverty reduction and economic management) seminars held at the World Bank. In addition, senior finance and budget officials from a large number of countries offered advice on the contents of the book. The editor is also grateful to leading academics who contributed chapters, and to Bank and external peer reviewers for their comments. Matthew Andrews, Azam Chaudhry, Neil Hepburn, and Theresa Thompson helped during various stages of preparation of this book and provided comments and contributed summaries. Agnes Santos prepared the book for publication. Finally this volume would not have been completed without the outstanding supervision and analytical contributions of Theresa M. Thompson.

Contributors

MATTHEW ANDREWS, a public sector management specialist at the World Bank, is a South African with a doctorate in public administration from the Maxwell School, Syracuse University, New York. He has worked at all levels of government in South Africa and has published on topics such as public budgeting and management, evaluation, and institutional economics.

HADI SALEHI ESFAHANI is a professor of economics at the University of Illinois at Urbana-Champaign. He has worked for the World Bank as a visiting staff economist and a consultant. He received his Ph.D. from the University of California at Berkeley. His research focuses on theoretical and empirical issues in the political economy of development. He has published numerous articles on the role of politics and governance institutions in the formation and outcomes of fiscal, trade, and regulatory policies.

CHARLES C. GRIFFIN holds a Ph.D. in economics from the University of North Carolina at Chapel Hill (1983) and a master's degree in public policy from Duke University (1981). He completed a two-year postdoctoral fellowship in economic demography at Yale at the Economic Growth Center (1984–86). His academic fields are economic development and public finance. Most of his professional work has been in health economics in developing countries. His World Bank operational experience and research work have been focused on "household economics," social sector finance, and the demand for services in health and education. Before joining the World Bank in 1992, he was an associate professor of economics at the University of Oregon in Eugene and a senior research associate at the Urban Institute in Washington, D.C. He also worked as a consultant, primarily on social sector financing and health economics in East and South Asia. He joined the World Bank in the Africa Region, where he worked on Eastern Africa. In September 1997, he transferred to the Latin America and Caribbean Region as lead specialist for Social Protection, and in December 1998, became sector manager for Health, Nutrition, and Population in the same region. He managed a portfolio of about $3 billion (financing about 30 projects). In March 2002, he became sector director for Human Development in the South Asia Region, leading Bank programs in education, health/nutrition/population, and social protection for Afghanistan, Bangladesh, Bhutan, India, the Maldives, Nepal, Pakistan, and Sri Lanka.

HARRY P. HATRY is director of the Public Management Program at the Urban Institute in Washington, D.C. He has many years of experience working on performance measurement and performance management with local, state, and federal agencies, and with nongovernmental organizations (NGOs). He has provided performance measurement assistance to Albania, Hungary, Indonesia, and Thailand. He has been a leader in developing performance measurement tools for a wide variety of public services. His recent book, *Performance Measurement: Getting Results,* has been widely used and is being translated into two other languages.

PAUL HUTCHINSON is currently an assistant professor of economics in the Department of International Health in the School of Public Health and Tropical Medicine at Tulane University. His main areas of interest focus on access to and demand for health care services in developing countries, on decentralization of health care services, and on issues of health care financing. For two years, he was based at the World Bank Resident Mission in Kampala, Uganda. Other projects have involved assessments of mortality decline in the 1990s and of the impacts of donor-funded projects on health status and health care–seeking behavior.

JEFF HUTHER is director of the Office of Debt Management at the U.S. Treasury. His office provides advice on the issuance and pricing of Treasury securities. His recent work has focused on expanding the Treasury inflation-protected securities (TIPS) market, improving the transparency of the Treasury's decision-making processes, and developing better measures of the Treasury's debt portfolio. His earlier projects at the U.S. Treasury included evaluation of the Treasury's buyback program, analysis of the implications of introducing a four-week bill, comparisons of the costs of alternative forms of short-term financing, and examination of the implications of suspending issuance of the 30-year bond. Before working at the U.S. Treasury, he spent two years at the New Zealand Treasury helping to develop an asset and liability framework for sovereign management of financial instruments.

TIMOTHY JOHNSTON is currently a senior human development specialist based in Burkina Faso, where he has been responsible for the World Bank's health and HIV/AIDS programs since January 2003. Formerly he was a senior evaluation specialist in the World Bank's independent Operations Evaluation Department (OED), working primarily on the health sector. In OED, he coauthored *Investing in Health: Development Effectiveness in Health, Nutrition, and Population* (1999) and was lead author of OED's *Annual Review of Development Effectiveness: From Strategy to Results* (2000).

HARRY KITCHEN is a professor in the Department of Economics at Trent University, Canada. He has published widely on public finances, local and regional government organization, and service delivery issues and has advised governments in both industrial and developing countries on a range of fiscal systems reform and local governance issues.

RUDOLF KNIPPENBERG is a doctor from the Netherlands and holds a Ph.D. from Johns Hopkins University. He is currently the principal adviser for health at UNICEF in New York, working on child survival acceleration and the Millennium Development Goals. He has worked extensively in Africa and East Asia, and in Brazil and India.

RUTH LEVINE is a health economist with 12 years of experience working on health and family planning financing issues in Eastern Africa, Latin America, the Middle East, and South Asia. She is currently directing a global health and population policy research program at the Center for Global Development in Washington, D.C. Before joining the Center, she designed, supervised, and evaluated health sector loans at the World Bank and the Inter-American Development Bank. Between 1997 and 1999, she served as the adviser on the social sectors in the Office of the Executive Vice President of the Inter-American Development Bank.

ALASDAIR ROBERTS is an associate professor in the Maxwell School of Citizenship and Public Affairs at Syracuse University. He is also director of the Campbell Public Affairs Institute. A native of Pembroke, Canada, Roberts holds a J.D. from the University of Toronto Faculty of Law, as well as a master's degree and a Ph.D. in public policy from Harvard University. From 1990 to 2001, he taught in the School of Policy Studies at Queen's University, Canada. He has also held visiting appointments at Georgetown University's Graduate Public Policy Institute and at the University of Southern California's Washington Public Affairs Center. He was a fellow at the Woodrow Wilson International Center for Scholars in 1999/2000 and an individual program fellow of the Open Society Institute, New York, in 2000/01. Roberts is a visiting fellow at the School of Policy Studies at Queen's University, a member of the Canadian Treasury Board Secretariat's Academic Advisory Council, and a member of the editorial boards of *Public Administration Review* and *Public Management Review.*

ANWAR SHAH is the lead economist and the team/program leader for Public Sector Governance with the World Bank Institute and a fellow of the Institute for Public Economics, Edmonton, Canada. He has previously served both the government of Canada and the government of Alberta, Canada, and held responsibilities for federal-provincial and provincial-local fiscal relations, respectively. He has advised the governments of Argentina, Australia, Brazil, Canada, China, Indonesia, Malaysia, Mexico, Pakistan, the Philippines, Poland, South Africa, and Turkey on fiscal federalism issues. He has lectured at the University of Ottawa, Canada; Quaid-i-Azam University, Islamabad, Pakistan; Duke University, Durham, North Carolina; Harvard University, Cambridge, Massachusetts; the Massachusetts Institute of Technology, Cambridge; Peking University, Beijing, China; Wuhan University, China; and the University of Southern California, Los Angeles. His current research interests are in the areas of governance, fiscal federalism, fiscal reform, and global environment. He has published several books and monographs on these subjects including *The Reform of Intergovernmental Fiscal Relations in Developing and Transition Economies,* published by the World Bank in 1994, and a 1995 Oxford University Press book titled *Fiscal Incentives for Investment and Innovation.* His articles have appeared in leading economic and policy journals. He serves as a referee and on editorial advisory boards for leading economic journals.

AGNES SOUCAT is a senior health economist at the World Bank and an author of the health chapter of the Poverty Reduction Strategy Paper (PRSP) sourcebook. She was a member of the WDR team that authored the *World Development Report 2005,* "Making Services Work for Poor People." Previously, she worked in the Africa Region on poverty and health issues, assisting countries in preparing the health content of their PRSPs. She is a doctor with a master's degree in nutrition and in tropical diseases from the University of Nancy, France. She received a Master of Public Health degree and a Ph.D. in health care financing from Johns Hopkins University. Before joining the World Bank, she worked for UNICEF, UNAIDS, and the International Children Center in Paris. She has worked extensively in East Asia (Cambodia, China, Mongolia, Myanmar, Thailand, and Vietnam) and Africa (Benin, Burkina Faso, Cameroon, Cape Verde, Côte d'Ivoire, Ethiopia, The Gambia, Guinea, Guinea-Bissau, Mali, Mauritania, Niger, Nigeria, Rwanda, and Senegal).

ADAM WAGSTAFF is lead economist in the Human Development Network and the Development Research Group at the World Bank. He was professor of economics at the University of Sussex (U.K.), where he is on long-term leave. He has researched extensively on poverty and health, has been involved in various training efforts on health and human development for World Bank staff and PRSP country teams, and has contributed to World Bank country work on health policy issues.

ABDO S. YAZBECK is a lead health economist at the World Bank Institute where he is the health and population program leader. He has a Ph.D. in health and labor economics and has a research focus on health economics and finance, health sector equity, health sector prioritization, and public-private collaboration. Before joining the World Bank in 1996, he taught economics at Rice University and Texas A&M University for five years and worked in the private sector for three years. His operational experience covers Africa, the Middle East, South Asia, and the former Soviet Union.

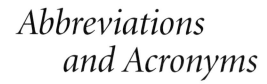

Abbreviations and Acronyms

DALY	Disability-adjusted life year
DOTS	Directly observed treatment, short course
GAO	U.S. General Accounting Office
GAP	Government Accountability to the People
GASB	Governmental Accounting Standards Board
GDP	Gross domestic product
GIS	Geographical information system
GNP	Gross national product
GQI	Government quality index
IGG	Inspectorate of Government
IMCI	Integrated Management of Childhood Illnesses
HDI	Human Development Index
IMF	International Monetary Fund
NGO	Nongovernmental organization
NSI	Next Steps Initiative
ODS	Ozone-depleting substances
OECD	Organisation for Economic Co-operation and Development
PPBS	Planning, programming, and budgeting systems
PPP	Purchasing power parity
PRSP	Poverty Reduction Strategy Paper
PUMA	Program on Public Management and Governance
SPRING	Systems and Procedures Rationalization in Government
TEQ	Toxic equivalent
UNDP	United Nations Development Programme
WHO	World Health Organization

Overview

ANWAR SHAH

Traditionally, public trust in public sector performance in delivering services consistent with citizen preferences has been considered weak in developing countries. The reason is that politicians and bureaucrats are typically observed to show greater interest in rent-seeking activities than in delivering services wanted by their citizens. The global information revolution of the late 20th century has further eroded this confidence. The information revolution empowers citizens to access, transmit, and transform information in ways that governments are powerless to block, and in the process it undermines authoritative controls. It also constrains the ability of governments to withhold information from citizens. Globalization of information—satellite TV, Internet, phone, and fax—enhances citizens' awareness of their rights, obligations, options, and alternatives and strengthens demands for greater accountability from the public sector. Thus, measurement of government performance has assumed topical importance in popular discussions and debates.

This book focuses on measuring government performance in the delivery of public services. For this purpose, the chapters in this book present ideas on the measurement of the whole of government performance and for selected sectors.

The underlying framework used in these chapters addresses two overarching issues: (a) whether the public manager is doing the right things—that is, delivering services consistent with citizen preferences; and (b) whether the public manager is doing them right—that is, providing services of a given quality in the least-cost manner. For the latter question, the following tests are used in the analysis:

- *Efficacy test:* Are the programs achieving agreed-upon objectives?
- *Efficiency test:* Is the public manager using resources economically?
- *Alternate service delivery test:* Does the public manager face the right incentives for forging appropriate partnership or contractual relationships within and beyond government? What activities or programs should or could be transferred in whole or part to the private or voluntary sectors?
- *Money's worth test:* Is the general public receiving the best value for its tax dollars?

The first section in this book is devoted to broad-gauge performance measurement. It draws lessons from performance measurement systems in industrial countries. It presents a simple measure of the quality of governance and offers a framework for assessing local government performance. The second section is concerned with the measurement of service delivery in developing countries for selected sectors.

The Whole of Government Performance

In the past several years many governments have restructured their public sectors in an attempt to deal with the twin problems of indebtedness and growing citizen disenchantment with government. In many jurisdictions, restructuring efforts have included an emphasis on the need to introduce a results-based or performance-based approach to management in the public sector. Typically, efforts at introducing results-based management have begun at the bureau or departmental level. However, several North American governments have begun experimenting with performance reporting at a very high level. The objective is to produce a governmentwide performance plan that links governmental activities to key social outcomes. The U.S. state of Oregon set up an independent board to develop and monitor measures of the social well-being of state residents (158 such measures in 1991, reduced to 20 in 1999). The U.S. state of Florida initially established 268 indicators dealing with progress in families and communities, safety, learning, health, economy, environment, and government. It has more recently abandoned this effort. The province of Alberta, Canada, has established 27 "measuring up" quality-of-life indicators. New Zealand reports on the net worth of the government. The United Nations (UN) publishes human development indicators.

The whole of government performance is addressed by the first three chapters in this book. In chapter 1, Roberts provides a review of experience in implementing such performance measurement in industrial countries. He describes current efforts and considers key challenges likely to be encountered in the adoption of this innovation. Huther and Shah, in chapter 2, develop a framework for measuring the quality of governance and present comprehensive indicators of the quality of governance for a sample of 80 countries. Chapter 3 by Andrews and Shah develops a framework for assessing the performance of local governments.

Lessons from Industrial Countries

Alasdair Roberts reflects on governmentwide performance measurement efforts in industrial countries and considers the challenges encountered in implementation. The goal of the new governmentwide performance monitoring is to (a) build consensus inside and outside government about priorities, thus making it easier for governments to make reallocation decisions in a period of retrenchment; (b) improve popular confidence in government; and (c) demonstrate the ineffectiveness of some government interventions, thus reducing popular pressure on governments to make irrational expenditure decisions.

There are four major challenges to the implementation of governmentwide performance monitoring.

- *Designing appropriate processes for selecting outcome measures:* This is inherently a political process. The quasi-independent commissions that have been used in some U.S. states are more independent of the pressures of the bureaucracy, but they have less legitimacy and their work is typically ignored by the legislature and the executive. In Canada, the indicators have been chosen by the governments, which have the legitimacy to do so, but they also may have a more difficult time making public statements about priority areas and may be reluctant to give attention to a few key social indicators for fear that they will have made explicit the criteria by which their performance should be judged in the future.
- *Collecting credible data on important dimensions of societal well-being:* It may be more difficult for smaller subnational governments to collect these types of data because of cutbacks and governmental restructuring. A related danger is the possible politicization of the statistical agencies.
- *Making causal connections between governmental activities and social indicators:* It is a difficult analytical exercise for officials to make clear causal links between their activities and higher-level outcomes because they must have the data needed to test whether the causal chain is working as

expected and must be able to discount the effect of exogenous factors appropriately.

■ *Using performance data to improve public debate about governmental responsibilities:* The media and legislative response to the new data has been muted. This is partly due to the skepticism about the credibility of information provided directly by government departments.

A review of industrial country experiences shows that governmentwide performance monitoring yields consultative processes that help polities make a rough ordering of priorities but do not lead to better assessment of the merits of alternative programs.

Alasdair Roberts concludes that governmentwide performance monitoring is more likely to be effective (a) when it is done in smaller, more homogeneous communities and (b) when the task of selecting outcomes to be measured is left to a body that is partly or wholly independent of government. In large jurisdictions a more prudent approach may be to emphasize the development of performance reporting on a sectoral basis and to promote the production of data that may be used by nongovernmental organizations (NGOs) to develop benchmarks of societal well-being. The sectorwide measures may make some of the methodological problems more tractable and reduce the political sensitivity of selecting targets.

A Simple Measure of Good Governance

Debates about the appropriate role, policies, and institutions of the state are often hampered by the lack of a definition for *good government*. To provide a quantifiable measure of good government, Huther and Shah (chapter 2) developed an index for the quality of governance for a sample of 80 countries. They apply the index to the debate on the appropriate level of fiscal decentralization.

In measuring the quality of governance, the authors developed indices for the government's ability to achieve the following:

■ *Ensure political transparency and a voice for all citizens:* The citizen participation index measures political freedom and political stability.
■ *Provide effective public services efficiently:* The government orientation index measures judicial and bureaucratic efficiency and the absence of corruption.
■ *Promote the health and well-being of its citizens:* The social development index measures human development and equitable distribution of income.

▦ *Create a favorable climate for stable economic growth:* The economic management index measures outward orientation, independence of the central bank, and an inverted debt-GDP ratio.

In relating the index of governance to the degree of fiscal decentralization for the 80 countries, Huther and Shah are not astonished to find a positive relationship between fiscal decentralization and quality of governance. However, the strength of the correlation is surprising.

Assessing Local Government Performance

Andrews and Shah (chapter 3) tackle two important questions faced in developing countries:

▦ What does good local government look like in the developing world?
▦ What factors should one consider when evaluating local governments?

The importance of such questions derives directly from the fact that decentralization has become increasingly common in developing countries over the past 15 years. Local governments are increasingly required to play larger roles in providing services, alleviating poverty, and facilitating development. Given the important role that local governments are being called to play, central governments and development organizations are starting to ask how well they are doing and how they can be improved, but resources for conducting such evaluations remain limited.

Andrews and Shah attempt to identify criteria for evaluating local governments in developing countries. The chapter takes a mixed practice-theory approach to identifying such evaluation criteria. The practice element builds on existing evaluations practice at the local level in developed countries such as the United States, which typically focus on issues of legal conformance and fiscal health. The theory dimension introduces concerns about responsiveness, efficiency, and accountability, where the potential for gains in these areas are the dominant underlying arguments in favor of decentralization and local-level governance. The approach recognizes that local governments in developing countries face their own special issues, and that evaluation criteria identified for use in such settings must be easily accessible, facilitating an observation-based analysis and requiring limited resources.

The first area in which the authors suggest that evaluation is vital relates to legislative and process conformance. Local governments face legislative and process requirements related to setting up and upholding bylaws, - generating and collecting revenues, following specific steps in resource disbursement, and providing services. Evaluating conformance to these requirements is important for ensuring the legality of local governance as well as for providing guidance as to temporal limitations and complexities and even inconsistencies in the institutional setting in which local governments find themselves. This knowledge can help evaluators in determining why the local government is performing as it is and in providing appropriate advice for remediation or improvement.

The second evaluation area is fiscal health. This area is important for evaluators because local governments are generally required (by national or provincial/state governments) to manage their fiscal matters carefully, ensuring that they do not overspend and that their expenditure is in line with their mandate as it is generally represented in the budget or as it is stipulated in national-level policy documents or legislation. The most fundamental criterion for assessing fiscal health is the net worth of the government that incorporates its cash flows, its revenues and expenditures, and its assets and liabilities. This criterion can be derived from standard financial statements and budgets: High and sustained deficits and debt, poor allocations (with significant resources going to administration rather than to capital maintenance, for example), and a disjunction between planning allocations and implementation. These fiscal health evaluation criteria are also only as reliable as the budget and financial reporting process that determines financial figures, however. Because of this, evaluators are directed to examine not only the figures reflecting fiscal health on the expenditure side, but also the processes by which expenditures are reported. Furthermore, because the literature stresses that fiscally healthy local governments should have their own reliable revenue sources, a fiscal health evaluation should analyze the size of the local revenue base (that is, the potential local resources available to the government) and the revenue effort on display (or the actual local resources raised as a percentage of the potential).

Andrews and Shah suggest responsiveness as a third area in which local government evaluations should focus, arguing that decentralization in a democratic context should lead to greater responsiveness to constituent demands. The level of local political influence on allocations decisions and the level of civic participation in the decision-making process are seen as two important aspects of the local government service provision process that relate to responsiveness. Where each is higher, one can expect a higher level of local government response to citizen demands. Apart from these process aspects, the authors also emphasize evaluating responsiveness in terms of the antipoverty perspective evident in budget allocations.

As with responsiveness, theory presents potential efficiency and accountability gains as a major reason why governments should decentralize. Consequently, the authors argue that efficiency and accountability concerns should also permeate an evaluation of local governments in developing countries. Specific evaluation criteria related to efficiency include the cost of production and the degree of competition in service production. Criteria related to accountability include several that require the ability to observe governance processes: the information citizens have regarding local governance (transparency), the access citizens have to the governance process and their ability to express their voice to officials, and the specific laws and processes governments adopt to either enhance or reduce their accountability to citizens.

Combining the discussion of the five factors yields an evaluation design in which a model local government would conform to legislation in process and structure, maintain its fiscal health (in outcomes and processes and in maintenance of a positive net worth), do the right things (be responsive) in the right way (with maximum efficiency), and be accountable to its constituents (in processes and for its outputs and outcomes).

Assessing Sectoral Performance

The remaining chapters are concerned with providing practical guidance on the service delivery performance of the government—on measurement issues commonly encountered in developing countries (chapter 4 by Hatry), local and municipal services (chapter 5 by Kitchen), health (chapter 6 by Soucat and others), and infrastructure (chapter 7 by Esfahani).

Results Focus in Basic Education, Welfare, and Solid Waste Collection and Disposal

Managers in any government and any government agency, whether at the national or the local level, need regular feedback on the quality and outcome of services. Harry Hatry, in chapter 4, presents practical guidance on outcome measurement procedures and basic steps in implementing them. He lists outcome indicators for elementary and secondary education, youth welfare, child development, and solid waste collection. He also provides guidance on the use of outcome data.

Hatry describes the difficulties involved in measuring results of public programs in developing countries. Despite these obstacles, the author argues that it is important to develop a results measurement program and provides tentative suggestions for developing such a system at an affordable cost.

Outcome (or results) measurement is the regular measurement and reporting of the results of public agency programs. It includes measurement of program results and the way in which the service is delivered (such as how long it takes to get service) and also sometimes the efficiency with which the service is provided (for example, output per unit of input).

Outcome measurement serves many purposes, including to identify problem areas, identify the extent to which service quality has changed after improvement actions have been taken, improve budgeting so that resources are allocated to produce the maximum benefit to citizens, make public agencies more accountable to the public, and increase the public's trust in their government.

Implementing outcome measurement is particularly difficult in developing countries due to limited data processing technology, lack of trained staff, lack of understanding by the government of the need for feedback, limited government experience obtaining feedback from citizens, and the different interests and degree of support for outcome measurement by donors. Measuring response times is particularly challenging.

The key issue for developing countries is discerning what can be done at low cost to undertake such measurement without compromising the ability to obtain at least roughly correct information. The first step is for agency personnel to identify the mission and objectives of each service, and from these mission statements the agency should identify the indicators to be used to measure outputs and outcomes. The remainder of the chapter discusses four basic data collection and measurement procedures that may be used:

■ *Indicators and proxies on service delivery performance from agency records:* These include measures such as incidence of disease, infant mortality, crimes, traffic accidents, educational achievement, and pollution in drinking water. Initially, the effort might be concentrated in major population areas because of difficulties in obtaining data from rural areas.

■ *Customer feedback surveys:* Customer surveys can provide various types of information for outcome measurement, including ratings from citizens of overall satisfaction with individual public services and timeliness of delivery; factual information about citizens' condition, attitudes, and behavior such as use of public services, extent of crime victimization, and corruption; problems with and suggestions for improvement of services; and demographic information. These surveys may be expensive and therefore it may not be possible to conduct them regularly without external financial support from donor agencies or NGOs. It is possible to reduce costs by requiring less precision in the results than a 95 percent confidence interval, while still conducting a representative survey.

■ *Focus groups:* If small representative sample surveys are infeasible, the government can fall back on a procedure that does not provide statistical credibility but can give some useful citizen feedback. The government could invite a small number of customers for a session during which they are asked about their experience with the service, how they would rate the service on various characteristics, and what their suggestions for improvement are.

■ *Trained observer assessment of key physical conditions:* In this case, public agencies themselves monitor and track the condition of key facilities under their responsibility, including such things as conditions of roads, sanitation facilities, hospitals, and school buildings. This should be a low-cost procedure, as long as staff members are available to do the ratings.

With regard to data quality control, the author suggests that an atmosphere be provided in which data findings are not threatening, that there to be adequate training, and that the government's audit office be made responsible for reviewing samples of the data and collection and tabulation procedures.

Overall the author takes a benevolent view of government and assumes that government agencies in developing countries are actively and vigorously attempting to improve their service delivery performance. To the extent that this view is contradicted in practice, much of what the author suggests may not yield reliable and useful information. This would be a particularly serious limitation for countries with a high incidence of corruption. In such countries, the data on the incidence of corruption and government performance are usually suspect. Further, the author's suggestions on indicators should be taken simply as illustrative examples and tailored to each country's individual circumstances. Many of his illustrative indicators may not be feasible to implement in low-income countries. Nevertheless, the merits of having meaningful objective measures of service delivery performance for the public sector in these countries cannot be overstressed.

Local and Municipal Services

Does the public manager face the right incentives for forging appropriate partnership or contractual relationships within and beyond government? What activities or programs should or could be transferred in whole or part to the private or voluntary sectors? Harry Kitchen addresses these questions in chapter 5 in the context of local and municipal services.

Kitchen argues that municipal services may be delivered in a variety of ways. Alternatives range from complete public provision to complete private provision to a mix of those forms, including public-private partnerships. For public sector provision, the economic and political arguments in support of independent and autonomous or semi-independent and semi-autonomous special purpose bodies instead of city hall are generally weak. Such special purpose bodies do not contribute anything unique. Their existence creates or has the potential for creating decision making problems and unnecessary costs both for local governments and for local residents. Eliminating special purpose bodies and transferring their responsibilities to municipal councils should improve the extent to which local public sector efficiency, accountability, and transparency can be improved. Certainly, it would remove the confusion over who is responsible for what and allow local councils to set priorities and to weigh and consider the trade-offs necessary in making decisions on the relative merits of ,say, spending on water and sewer systems versus spending on roads and public transit, police and fire agencies, local parks, or other services.

Although private sector provision of municipal services is generally interpreted as *contracting out* or entering into public-private partnerships, it also includes the use of franchises, grants for specific services or functions, vouchers, volunteers, and self-help and private nonprofit agencies. Privatization does not mean that governments should forgo ownership of municipal services. Indeed, they should retain the right to set standards and specify conditions and should generally retain overall responsibility through the use of contractual arrangements. The private sector's role is to deliver services according to the specifications and conditions laid out by government.

Kitchen states that there are a number of studies at the municipal level that compare the cost of delivering services in the public sector to the cost of delivering services in the private sector. In each study, the cost comparison is between local government provision and provision through contracting out to the private sector. In virtually all cases, significant per unit cost savings have been observed for private sector provision. Those savings, it is argued, are due to competitive forces that are present in private sector delivery but are generally absent in public sector delivery.

Kitchen argues that, overwhelming as the empirical evidence may be, it has not silenced some critics. Perhaps the strongest criticism has come from public sector unions, which feel particularly vulnerable because of possible job losses and reduced bargaining power. On the other hand, contracting out has the potential for increasing management's flexibility in managing manpower; for increasing productivity, especially if incentives are built into payment schemes; for increasing a manager's ability to hire specialized expertise when needed; and for lowering the public sector's payroll costs.

Although there has been relatively limited discussion and application of the role of franchises, grants, vouchers, volunteers, self-help programs, and private nonprofit agencies in delivering public services, those instruments or organizations may become important in the future, especially if governments reduce or discontinue some services. Similarly, there is increasing evidence that public-private partnerships will grow in importance.

Kitchen concludes that the debate about the future of private sector delivery of public services will continue. There will be advocates for greater privatization as well as critics. In reality, however, political pressure to reduce government expenditures and reduce or restrict increases of tax and user fee will force governments to resort to private sector delivery, in one form or another, for a variety of what are currently referred to as municipal services. In fact, this movement is even legislated or mandated in some countries.

Health

In chapter 6, Soucat and others provide various tools (including methodologies, sources of data, and indicators) to analyze the performance of the health sector. The sector's performance is assessed according to its capacity to (a) channel resources to the poor by funding pro-poor interventions; (b) reach the poor by providing outputs that influence the availability of quality health services to be used in the household production of health; and (c) minimize financial obstacles to the use of the interventions.

For an analysis of a health system's performance to be comprehensive, the authors argue that all suppliers of health care services in a country should be considered, including public, NGO, and private providers. In addition, a comprehensive assessment should be multidimensional and include various aspects of potential as well as actual coverage. A hierarchical model is described in order to carry out this analysis, corresponding to eight stages. The first five stages correspond to potential coverage and include accessibility, availability of human resources, availability of material resources, organizational quality and consumer responsiveness, and social accountability. The last three stages measure actual coverage and include relevance and utilization, continuity, and technical quality. Various possible measures or indicators for each of the eight stages are offered, as well as available data and suggestions for future data collection. The data suggested include hard data (for example, the percentage of children vaccinated against an illness as a measure for utilization) and survey data (such as asking the poor about their perceptions of care to measure consumer responsiveness).

The eight stages identified by the authors to provide effective health coverage for the poor include the following:

- *Physical accessibility:* One approach to measuring accessibility is to measure the service supply relative to the population served; for example, number of clinics per 1,000 population. However, this approach does not account for the distribution of services with respect to the poor. The data are more meaningful if they are broken down by district to compare rural versus urban or poor versus nonpoor, or if they take into account the physical size of the area served and the population in the area. Suggestions for data collection and analysis include linking health maps with poverty maps and household surveys.
- *Availability of human resources:* Shortages of qualified staff limits access, especially to the poor. Suggestions for data collection include collecting data on health personnel in the public, private, and NGO sectors.
- *Availability of material resources:* Shortages of drugs or equipment hamper the provision of health services. Suggestions for data collection and analysis include collecting data on the availability and distribution of equipment, drugs, and other inputs from central health information systems or by conducting surveys of a sample of facilities (for example, essential drugs surveys).
- *Organizational quality and consumer responsiveness:* A number of factors influence the user friendliness of services, including the attitude of health staff, hours of operation, waiting time, gender of the service provider, and modes of payment. Suggestions for data collection and analysis in this area include qualitative surveys, focus groups, exit interviews with patients, on-site assessment, and situation analysis. Situation analysis (which was developed for family planning but may be adapted for other services) combines various methodologies to collect information from a sample of facilities and communities on the availability of inputs, provider behavior, process quality indications, and perceptions of the community.

- *Social accountability:* Health staff members in government clinics are often unresponsive to the poor because they are not directly accountable to them. Data on the ability of the poor to exert influence on services may be collected through visits to a sample of communities and facilities, possibly by an NGO in collaboration with communities.
- *Relevance and utilization of services:* Utilization, which is defined as the first use of a service by a consumer in a given year, is a key indicator of the extent to which the poor come in contact with the health system. Data on utilization can be gathered from health information systems (numbers of visits, patients, vaccinations), and household surveys (for information on the percentage of a target population using a particular service), and by linking (with a poverty map) the quantity of services produced in a specific area to income levels by area.
- *Continuity and timing of interventions:* Timing and continuity examine whether consumers receive the requisite number of contacts for services that require repeated interventions, and whether time-sensitive services (such as prenatal, maternal, and emergency) are delivered in a timely manner. These can be assessed by looking at dropout rates and other indicators of follow-up, preferably using a combination of facility data and household surveys.
- *Technical quality:* The capacity of the sector to provide the appropriate combination of technology and empathy at a given level of utilization is key to ensuring that interventions are translated into effective outcomes. However, quality can be difficult to measure. Suggestions for data collection and analysis include compiling information on perinatal mortality rates, malaria fatality rates, tuberculosis cure rates, and maternal mortality. In addition, the WHO's Topical List of Priority Indicators for IMCI at the Health-Facility Level provides a useful instrument for assessing quality in the management of childhood illness.

The chapter also considers how health services can be better channeled to the poor. In order to do this, one must examine allocative efficiency (giving priority to health services that are public goods), equity of expenditures (whether interventions benefit the poor), and affordability of a health system for the poor. Allocative efficiency is the extent to which cost-effective and critical public good interventions are being funded, an example being a comparison of spending on more cost-effective preventive care versus spending on curative services. In terms of allocative efficiency, immunizations and management of communicable diseases deserve the highest priority, followed by basic clinical and acute care. Equity deals with the extent to which poor individuals benefit from public services in comparison to the rich, and affordability considers the extent to which out-of-pocket expenditures constitute a serious financial burden on the poor.

Infrastructure

Large parts of the population in many countries, especially the poor, bear substantial economic and human costs because of serious shortages in infrastructure services, in terms of both quantity and quality. To remove these shortages and improve the standard of living in these countries, governments need to create incentives for private and public service providers to invest and perform. Hadi Esfahani in chapter 7 argues that improving performance measurement is a crucial step in this endeavor. For this purpose, the problem that needs to be solved is efficient and systematic collection and processing of information about performance in infrastructure services. Since the nature of infrastructure services limits the relevance of simple productivity and profitability measures, one has to collect data on a variety of measures, both quantitative and qualitative. In this regard, involving communities to provide information about outputs and feedback on other performance measures can be very helpful. To put the collected data into effective use, one has to make a choice of which indicators are more important. Recent experience suggests that it may be better to focus on some key indicators and ensure that the others meet some minimum criteria. The chapter presents such indicators for power, telecommunications, road transport, water, and sanitation services.

Evaluating and using performance indicators poses problems of their own. One needs to have appropriate benchmarks and, as much as possible, to distinguish between the effects of exogenous factors and the consequences of actions taken by service providers. This cannot be achieved easily through quantitative analysis and, inevitably, one has to rely on judgment. Ensuring that the judgment is well informed and widely accepted requires appropriate institutional arrangements that can ensure that experts are involved in the process and act independently.

A key issue in the design of public policy on infrastructure is that the information needed for performance measurement is costly to obtain, mostly because both service providers and consumers have incentives to use the information under their control strategically. The literature on performance measurement has focused on this issue and has tried to understand how to reduce these costs.

Measuring performance may be difficult for various reasons. For instance, quality and cost have a variety of dimensions that may be hard to observe. Another reason is the monopoly feature of many public services: competition reduces the need to measure all the details of quality and cost because inefficient and low-quality firms are automatically disciplined by the market—that is, weak performers in efficiency and in quality will also have poor profits. However, when the service provider is a monopoly public enterprise, profit is no longer a sufficient performance measure. Nonetheless, competition can be part of the solution to the infrastructure performance problem in areas where technology allows for parts of infrastructure to be organized in a competitive fashion.

There is a wide range of both qualitative and quantitative indicators for measuring performance in infrastructure services. One common form of categorization is to distinguish among the measures of assets, inputs, process, outputs, and outcomes and then use them to define indicators of efficiency, effectiveness, and productivity. The author provides tables of example indicators for power infrastructure, telecommunications, transportation, water, and sanitation. Given that there are many variables to be selected that reflect both quality and cost, one approach has been to restrict the measures to a very limited but crucial set of indicators, so as to not lose sight of what really matters to the public. However, focusing on a few measures may distort the incentives of service providers and encourage them to concentrate only on what is monitored, to the detriment of everything else. These concerns have led to the "balanced scorecard" approach, which focuses on a few crucial indicators but minimum standards for a variety of other measures must also be met.

Another variable that the author considers important but that has not been paid much attention in the literature is flexibility—the assets and skills available in an organization that allow it to cope with change and take advantage of new knowledge and technology.

In selecting indicators, the following criteria should be met. The indicators should be valid, reliable, understandable, timely, resistant to perverse behavior, comprehensive, nonredundant, focused on controllable facets of performance, and sensitive to data collection cost.

Once indicators have been selected and data have been collected, the task of evaluating performance can begin. To assess whether a given level of a measure indicates good or bad performance requires a comparison with established benchmarks based on the history of an enterprise and the experience of others. Benchmarks can be best-practice standards defined by experts or the performance of actual enterprises that are comparable with the one under review. There is a large literature that discusses how benchmarks should be selected. Systematic analysis of the role of exogenous "noise" in each specific situation is a desirable approach, but it may be too costly. Three methods may be used to evaluate performance indicators: evaluation by peer enterprises, evaluation by boards that are responsible to customers and stakeholders, and evaluation by independent rating agencies.

1

Issues Associated with the Implementation of Governmentwide Performance Monitoring

ALASDAIR ROBERTS

In the past 10 years, many western democracies have dramatically restructured their public sectors. The forces that have driven this restructuring are now familiar. Government expenditure in many jurisdictions grew significantly throughout the late 1970s and 1980s, for a combination of reasons. At the time, however, there was little popular support for new tax measures to defray the cost of new spending. The taxing power of governments was also constrained by the increasing ease with which citizens and businesses could move from one jurisdiction to another. The result was a rapid expansion in governmental indebtedness. By the early 1990s, the cost of servicing this debt was itself a significant burden on government treasuries. Governments began substantial efforts at retrenchment that were aimed, as Vice President Al Gore of the United States put it in 1993, at making government "work better and cost less" (Gore 1993).

At the same time, citizen dissatisfaction with government appeared to be growing in many jurisdictions. The erosion of faith in government may have been driven more by broad social, economic, and cultural trends than by the behavior of governments during this period. However, dissatisfaction may also have been aggravated as a consequence of the difficult re-allocative decisions that governments were obliged to make in order to deal with the

1

problem of chronic indebtedness. Faith in government may also have been eroded as cutbacks led to an erosion of service quality in the public sector.

In the late 1980s, governments began responding to the twin problems of indebtedness and an erosion in citizen trust by placing more emphasis on the need to identify and report on performance measures for government programs. The idea of encouraging a results orientation within government became a key component of the new paradigm (OECD 1996) for restructuring public sectors that had become established in many nations. The idea itself was not new: it had precedents stretching back to the use of planning, programming, and budgeting systems (PPBSs) in the 1960s. But the attention given to this idea in the 1990s in terms of governments' communication with nongovernmental stakeholders was new. Governments not only encouraged more emphasis on results in internal administrative arrangements; they also went out of their way to show external audiences that governments were conscious of the need to measure their effectiveness, and often successful in ameliorating public problems.

A results orientation was expected to enhance governmental performance in a variety of ways. Internally, better data about the performance of programs would allow central agencies and political executives to make better decisions about the allocation of scarce resources. Performance measures could also be used as a new instrument for holding the managers of public programs accountable, replacing input-based controls that were thought to discourage efficiency and innovation within government. It was hoped that public reporting of performance data would also change the behavior of nongovernmental actors. Advocates of performance reporting hoped that public debate would focus more on the effectiveness of programs as instruments for achieving substantive policy goals, rather than administrative processes used within those programs. Advocates also believed that citizens would be impressed by the extent to which many government programs had succeeded in remedying important social ills.

Early attempts to encourage a results orientation within government typically focused on the identification of performance measures at the bureau or program level. The U.K. government's Next Steps Initiative (NSI), begun in 1988, is still one of the most advanced examples of a system of bureau-based performance reporting. Under NSI, 130 agencies are required to make annual public reports on their success in achieving performance targets. The U.S. Government Performance and Results Act, adopted in 1993, is mainly intended to establish a similar system of bureau-based performance reporting within the U.S. federal government. Canada's business planning reforms and its Improved Reporting to Parliament Project, begun in 1995, are other illustrations of an attempt to encourage bureau-based performance reporting within a national government. A large majority of subnational governments in the United States and Canada have undertaken similar initiatives (Melkers and Willoughby 1998).

A few governments have attempted to push the idea of performance reporting even further. Their aim is to complement bureau-level performance reports with a system of performance planning and reporting for government as a whole. The concrete result that is aimed for is a governmentwide performance plan that identifies specific measures of societal well-being that are regarded as important, and assesses the effectiveness of government as a whole in improving those measures. A legislative requirement to develop a governmentwide performance plan was included in the U.S. Government Performance and Results Act, and the Canadian government also committed to the development of a governmentwide performance plan in 1995. A handful of states and provinces are also experimenting with governmentwide performance plans.

Advocates of this ambitious attempt to extend a results orientation to government as a whole hope that it will produce several benefits. It is hoped that the process of drafting and refining a governmentwide plan will help build consensus inside and outside government about priorities, thus making it easier for governments to make re-allocative decisions in a period of retrenchment. Annual plans might also improve popular confidence in government, by showing the connection between governmental actions and aspects of community well-being that are regarded as important by the public. Such plans might also demonstrate the ineffectiveness of some government interventions, reducing popular pressure on governments to make irrational expenditure decisions.

Before governmentwide performance plans can realize these goals, governments must overcome four problems in implementation. Limited experience has already shown that care must be taken in designing processes for the selection of performance measures. The collection of credible data that measure progress toward important aspects of societal well-being may also prove difficult, as may attempts to draw causal links between the everyday activities of government bureaus and high-level social indicators. It may also prove difficult to ensure that governmentwide performance plans have a real influence on broader popular debate about governmental priorities.

Experience seems to suggest that governmentwide performance monitoring is more likely to prove effective when it is done in smaller, more homogeneous communities, in which agreement on appropriate outcome measures is easier to attain. Such schemes may also be more effective where the task of selecting outcomes is left to a body that is partly or wholly independent of government. At first, such an arrangement seems one of doubtful legitimacy, particularly if the outcome measures selected are expected to have a real influence on the shape of policy debate. However, an independent body is not constrained by some of the bureaucratic and political considerations that may make it difficult for governments to select a narrow group of outcome measures and report regularly on those measures. In the end, however, even a well-designed performance monitoring scheme may have only a limited impact on internal budgetary decision making or on popular opinion about government priorities.

Current Efforts at Governmentwide Performance Monitoring

Many students of reform within U.S. and Canadian governments have observed that institutional innovations tend to be diffused in a regular pattern. In the first phase, an innovation is tried, with some success, in one or two subnational governments. Several other subnational governments then replicate the innovation, which eventually becomes established in conventional wisdom as the appropriate way of organizing government affairs. In the last phase, the remaining jurisdictions adopt the form—if not the substance—of the innovation, in an attempt to rationalize their practices with generally accepted practice (Rogers 1983).

Governmentwide performance monitoring is an institutional innovation that may eventually be diffused across North America in this classic pattern. It has already had notable successes in a small number of jurisdictions, and several other jurisdictions have begun to emulate these early innovators. However, there have been notable variations in practice between jurisdictions. Two national governments have endorsed the idea of governmentwide performance planning but have had no real success in putting the idea into practice.

Efforts by Subnational Governments

Oregon

The first and most prominent effort at governmentwide performance planning was begun in the U.S. state of Oregon. In 1987, Democratic Governor Neil Goldschmidt began a series of public consultations aimed at building consensus on long-range priorities for the state. The consultations took place in a context of continuing economic distress and contention over several important issues, including the balancing of economic development and protection of Oregon's extensive natural resources. The consultations led to the publication of a 1989 report, *Oregon Shines,* which outlined a broad 20-year development plan for the state. The report also recommended the establishment of a new body, the Oregon Progress Board, to monitor implementation of the plan. The Board was established by the state legislature in 1989. The Board is chaired by the governor and consists of nine leading citizens (Oregon Progress Board 1998) appointed by the governor.

The legislation establishing the Board required it to develop an economic and social development strategy for the state that included concrete goals and "measurable indicators of attainment . . . that show the extent to which each goal is being achieved" (Oregon Laws, Section 285A.150). The Board was also directed to produce a biennial report that used these indicators to assess the state's progress in implementing the development strategy. The first report, titled *Oregon Benchmarks,* was completed in 1991, and included 158 measures of societal well-being. The Board described the report as "a report card on how well [Oregon] is achieving its dreams" (Oregon Progress Board 1998). Revised reports were published in 1993, 1995, and 1997. (The measures currently used by the Board are listed in annex 1.A.)

The Board claims that its *Benchmarks* reports have had a substantial impact on popular and legislative debates. The state legislature has maintained continued support for the Board. The exercise has also attracted extensive attention outside the state. The Corporation for Enterprise Development, a national nonprofit organization that promotes strategies for economic and social development, credited *Benchmarks* as a successful attempt to build methods of accountability that did not "simply count the number of program inputs" (Oregon Progress Board 1998). The Ford Foundation's Innovations in American Government program gave the exercise an award for innovation in 1994, and the National Governors' Association has encouraged other states to begin similar performance-monitoring exercises. *Benchmarks,* Vice President Gore said in 1996, was "the wave of the future" (*National Performance Review* 1996, 57).

Florida

Of the eight state governments that have followed Oregon's example, Florida is perhaps the most advanced.[1] A commission appointed by Republican Governor Lawton Chiles, Jr. to review the activities of the state government observed in 1991 that the state had "no systematic means for measuring how well the state is doing across broad areas of concern" (Florida Governor's Commission for Government by the People 1991). Governor Chiles responded to this finding by appointing the Commission for Government Accountability to the People—commonly known as the GAP Commission—in December 1992. The commission consists of 15 citizens nominated by the governor and approved by the state senate (Florida Commission on Government Accountability to the People 1996).

The GAP Commission's mandate, endorsed by the state legislature in its 1994 Government Performance and Accountability Act, is to "track the impact of state agency actions upon the well-being of Florida citizens" (F.S. 14.30, s. 10). Its first benchmarks report, modeled on the Oregon precedent, was released in February 1996. It included 268 indicators tracking Florida's progress in seven major areas: families and communities, safety, learning, health, economy, environment, and government. The GAP Commission later said,

> In a single document, . . . citizens received the comprehensive information needed to take an active role in steering government toward better results. A part of Florida's overall performance measurement framework, the Florida Benchmarks Report provides citizens with the ultimate test of effective government by addressing how citizens are faring. It allows Floridians to track whether the state is doing better or worse in areas where we invest state dollars. (Florida Commission on Government Accountability to the People 1996)

A second report, *Critical Benchmarks Goals,* was issued by the Commission in June 1997. The GAP Commission had narrowed its focus to 60 critical measures and suggested performance goals for each measure for the years 2000 and 2010, based on surveys of popular opinion (Florida Commission on Government Accountability to the People 1997). A 1998 report, *Florida Benchmarks,* provides updated performance data on the 60 critical measures (Florida Commission on Government Accountability to the People 1998). These critical measures are listed in annex 1.B.

The Commission's work has been widely endorsed by the popular press in Florida, but the state legislature has been more ambivalent in its support. The Commission's already small budget was cut substantially in 1995–96. In the spring of 1998, legislators eliminated funding for the Commission entirely. The statute authorizing the Commission has not been repealed, however, and commissioners are presently attempting to raise funds from the private sector to continue its work (K. Stanford, personal communication, December 1998).

Province of Alberta

Several Canadian provinces are engaged in serious efforts to introduce results-based reporting, although primarily at the agency or departmental level. Two Canadian provinces have extended their experiments to include efforts at governmentwide performance planning.[2] The first is Alberta, under the Conservative government of Premier Ralph Klein. Its 1995 Government Accountability Act obliges the provincial treasurer to publish a "consolidated business plan" that includes "measures to be used in assessing the performance of the government for each of its core businesses"; the treasurer is also required to publish an annual report that presents data for each of the measures included in the governmentwide business plan (Statutes of Alberta G-5.5, ss. 7 and 10). The Klein government has identified three core businesses for the government as a whole, and uses only 27 core measures to assess progress in these three areas. Four annual reports on these core measures— titled *Measuring Up*—have now been tabled in the provincial legislature (Alberta Treasury 1998). The core measures are listed in annex 1.C.

In Alberta, the process of developing a governmentwide performance report is integrated tightly with the preparation of the annual budget. Like the budget, the performance report is produced within the provincial bureaucracy. There is no independent commission which selects and reports on performance measures, as there is in Oregon or in Alberta. A small staff within the province's Office of Budget and Management assists the Klein Cabinet in the selection of priorities and the identification of measures.

Province of Nova Scotia

Nova Scotia, like Alberta, went through a period of severe retrenchment in the middle 1990s. It also adopted a governmentwide planning and reporting system that was in many respects comparable to Alberta's. The Nova Scotian exercise was begun as part of the provincial budget-making cycle and was led by officials within the province's Department of Finance. A tentative list of 80 governmentwide performance measures was published in 1995 (Nova Scotia Department of Finance 1995). A refined list, developed by officials after informal consultations with representatives of business and other nongovernmental organizations (NGOs), contains 55 measures. The government's first formal report on these measures, *Nova Scotia Counts,* was released in October 1998. As in other jurisdictions, the Nova Scotian government argues that agreement on key outcome measures will help to overcome "ad hoc planning" and the "weak link between government priorities and departmental goals" (Nova Scotia Priorities and Planning Secretariat 1998). It also suggests that its public report "is fundamental to accountability. . . . Knowing where we stand and how we are progressing tells us where we need to increase or redirect our efforts" (Nova Scotia Department of Finance 1998, 1). (The Nova Scotia measures are listed in annex 1.D.)

Efforts by National Governments

United States

The growing interest in governmentwide performance planning has also affected national governments. In the United States, the production of a governmentwide performance plan for the federal government was mandated by the U.S. Government Performance and Results Act, passed by Congress in 1993. In its report on the Act, the Senate Government Affairs Committee explained that the governmentwide plan was to provide "a single cohesive picture of the [government's] annual performance goals for the fiscal year" (U.S. Senate 1993, Section 4) The first plan was prepared by officials in the U.S. Office of Management and Budget as part of its preparation of the president's budget proposal for fiscal year 1998/99, and was released publicly in February 1998.

Although it has been described by U.S. officials as the "world's first" national governmentwide performance plan, the document is quite distinct from plans prepared by state and provincial governments. The report does not provide a succinct list of social indicators, as state and provincial plans do. In fact, the plan is a reproduction of three chapters from the president's 1998 budget: the first describing the nation's fiscal performance, the second describing the government's management reform initiatives, and a third recapitulating major performance commitments developed in departmental and agency performance plans (U.S. Office of Management and Budget 1998).

Canada

The Canadian government has also experimented, with very limited success, in the development of a governmentwide performance plan. The government's central budget office, the Treasury Board Secretariat, began an extensive renovation of its expenditure management system in 1995, with the aim of developing planning and budgeting procedures that were "fact-based and results-oriented" (Treasury Board Secretariat 1995). As in other jurisdictions, the main emphasis was on the encouragement of results-based management at the departmental and agency levels. In 1996, however, the Treasury Board Secretariat indicated its interest in developing a system of governmentwide performance reporting such as those introduced by some states and provinces, which emphasized "a few core indicators of government performance"; such a system, the Secretariat thought, might provide "a single comprehensive perspective on the most important information that shapes the government's priorities and decisions" (Treasury Board Secretariat 1996, 2–3). In early 1997, the Secretariat organized a series of internal discussions aimed at identifying a set of indicators that could serve as the basis for a governmentwide performance plan.[3]

In an October 1997 report, the Treasury Board Secretariat reaffirmed its interest in the concept, observing:

> Agreement of key societal indicators . . . would contribute significantly to more effective and integrated policy and planning. Many jurisdictions have also found that engaging citizens in determining what matters and what to count can be a way of building a more meaningful relationship between government and citizens. (Treasury Board Secretariat 1997, 16)

At the same time, however, the Secretariat observed that the development of key indicators would be "a multiyear undertaking." It seemed to suggest that the more effective method of developing indicators would be on a sector-by-sector basis. The Secretariat observed that several federal departments were engaged in negotiations with provinces regarding program delivery in which the development of jointly agreed-upon outcome measures was being actively discussed (Treasury Board Secretariat 1997). A 1998 report from the Secretariat once again confirms the government's interest in the identification of "broad indicators" but suggests that this project will take several years (Treasury Board Secretariat 1998a, 9). A list of possible indicators drafted by an internal working group (see annex 1.E) was not adopted in the 1998 report (Treasury Board Secretariat 1998b).

Relationship to Social Reporting Movement

The problem of selecting appropriate measures of societal well-being, while novel to many advocates of governmentwide performance planning, is familiar within another professional community, often known as the social indicator movement or the social reporting movement. This movement has its roots in attempts in the 1950s by agencies of the United Nations to define and measure what was then referred to as the "standard of living" (Rothenbacher 1993, 2). However, the movement truly gained momentum in the United States in the next decade, driven in large part by the frustration of many policy analysts over the neglect of serious social problems. Political leaders, these analysts thought, suffered from "economic philistinism" (Gross 1966, ix): a tendency to equate societal well-being with progress on a handful of macroeconomic indicators, such as growth in gross domestic product (GDP).

The remedy to this problem was thought to be the development of systems of social statistics, built on a broader set of indicators of societal welfare. Early advocates, such as Mancur Olson, hoped that performance on these neglected measures might be reported regularly in a social report comparable in form to the *Economic Report of the President* (U.S. Department of Health Education 1969). Social reports, it was thought, would reveal "the social costs of growth" (Noll 1998) and change the course of policy making. Olson later said,

> With better and more nearly balanced information, . . . the country could reasonably hope for more informed debate and wiser judgments about the options that society faced. A social report could present a better and wider array of information about how society was doing and about the choices it would have to make. (Olson 1988, 3)

Not only would social reporting encourage attention to a broader range of issues; it would also encourage better social planning. Social reports, Franz Rothenbacher observes, were expected to become "a tool for the measurement and evaluation of national goal attainment, advance warning, and forecasting of social events" (Rothenbacher 1993, 2).

The 1970s and early 1980s became a boom period for the social indicators movement (Noll 1998). The statistical agencies of many Western democracies began producing social reports, and international agencies maintained a continuing interest in the area (OECD 1976, 1982). However, enthusiasm for the concept cooled in the 1980s. Social reporting became an "incompletely diffused" innovation; there were "distinct signs of declining scientific interest, as well as diminished financial and institutional support" (Rothenbacher 1993, 3, 38).[4] One informed observer suggests that efforts at producing a single, comprehensive social report have been displaced by attempts to develop appropriate social indicators within policy sectors. This approach makes conceptual and technical problems more tractable, and also accommodates the reality that the policy communities that rely most heavily on these indicators are already segmented functionally (Felligi and Wolfson 1997).

There are clear parallels between the aims and methods of the social indicator movement and those of the benchmarking movement in Canada and the United States. Both aim at developing and reporting on a range of measures of societal well-being, with the expectation that the publication of this information will improve the quality of policy making. Despite the similarities, however, the benchmarking movement emerged without any apparent awareness of its predecessor, or any attempt to draw on lessons learned from earlier experiments in social reporting. This may be explained by the fact that benchmarking first became popular among subnational governments with weakly developed statistical services. These governments may have lacked the personnel who, by training or professional association, would have been familiar with earlier efforts.

Within the Canadian federal government, discussions about the development of governmentwide performance indicators have included representatives of the national statistical service, Statistics Canada, who are familiar with earlier attempts to develop social reports. This may partly account for the relative caution with which the Canadian government has approached the development of a governmentwide performance plan. It might also provide a partial explanation for Treasury Board Secretariat's apparent inclination toward a sector-based approach to the development of outcome measures—a path already taken by some advocates of social reporting (Treasury Board Secretariat 1998a).

Difficulties in Execution

Whether governmentwide performance planning will prove to be a widely adopted institutional innovation in U.S. and Canadian government remains to be seen. There is evidence from some early adopters that the innovation may produce significant social benefits. However, there are some serious obstacles to the successful implementation of this sort of planning. Four of these are discussed in this section.

Processes for Selecting Outcome Measures

If a government decides to produce a plan that includes a list of key societal indicators, a crucial question is then how those indicators should be selected. This had already proved to be one of the major stumbling blocks, as encountered by earlier proponents of social reporting. The job of producing a social report, Mancur Olson observed, "proved an awesomely difficult task" (Olson 1988, 3), in large part because of the inability of specialists to reach consensus about the aspects of societal well-being that ought to be given emphasis in a system of social statistics (Felligi and Wolfson 1997; Noll 1998).

The problem of selecting indicators may have proved intractable because it is a normative problem that cannot be resolved through scientific inquiry by a community of specialists. Some kind of mechanism for legitimating choices of indicators is required. The social reporting movement, consisting primarily of academics and professionals within national statistical services, does not appear to have developed any effective method of securing popular consent for the choice of indicators. The benchmarking movement, by contrast, has developed such mechanisms. In fact, subnational governments have developed two distinct approaches for the selection of social indicators. The approach taken by U.S. state governments relies on a quasi-independent commission, which undertakes wide public and legislative consultations. The approach taken by Canadian provincial governments relies on the authority of an elected executive, with limited informal consultation. In this section, some strengths and weaknesses of the two approaches will be noted. In both approaches, however, the selection of indicators is recognized as a political rather than strictly technical decision.

In Oregon and Florida, the task of identifying social indicators and performance targets for those indicators has been delegated to a board that is intended to operate independently of both the executive and legislative branches of government. The Oregon Progress Board consists of nine individuals appointed by the governor. The original legislation apparently required ratification of those appointments by the senate (Rarick 1989), but the current legislation does not. The law requires that appointments be "representative of the ethnic, cultural, social and economic diversity of the people of this state" (Oregon Laws, Section 285A). In practice, governors appear to have made an effort to enlist leading citizens representing business, labor, and other nongovernmental organizations. An effort has also been made to maintain an appearance of bipartisanship; for example, former Governor Barbara Roberts appointed to the Board the Republican whom she had defeated in the 1990 gubernatorial race (Peirce 1994). Florida's GAP Commission is similarly organized. State law requires that the commission include 15 members appointed by the governor and approved by the senate. Nine appointees must be selected from the private sector, and six from the public sector. A modest attempt at bipartisanship was also made in Florida: its Democratic governor appointed two Republicans to the commission (Barrett and Greene 1998).

To a large extent, the decision to establish an independent commission represents an attempt to deal with the challenges posed by a system of government characterized by a clear separation of powers between the executive and legislative branches. Reformers have said for many years that effective long-range budgeting is nearly impossible in such a system because of the relative weakness of the executive and the independence of a large number of legislators. Conventional reform proposals have centered on strengthening the executive's powers over the budget process,[5] but these have been rejected by legislators as an obvious erosion of their influence over spending. The reluctance of legislators to give up influence to the executive is particularly strong when, as in Florida until 1998, opposing political parties control each branch.

Proposals to give planning authority to an independent body, such as the Oregon Planning Board or the GAP Commission, represent an attempt to improve the rationality of budget making without arousing legislators' concern about the erosion of their authority. The success of the method clearly depends on the construction of a board that is regarded by the legislative branch as being largely autonomous of the executive branch. In Florida, for example, the ambivalence of the state legislature with regard to the GAP Commission may be largely attributable to its perception that the commission was not truly neutral (Barrett and Greene 1998). The success of this approach also depends on another historical particularity: the long tradition in American politics, especially at the state and local levels, of nonpartisan "good government" movements. The notion of giving policy influence to a group of leading citizens is therefore a familiar one.

The notion that these boards represent attempts to improve the orderliness of budget making is recognized by other observers. One commentator observes that the Oregon Benchmarks exercise "attempts to impose rationality on the political process of budgeting" (*Cincinnati Enquirer* 1994, A12). The National Conference of State Legislatures has compared the Oregon Board and others like it to "state versions of Japan's Ministry of International Trade and Industry," designed to lead state planning for economic development (Knickerbocker 1991, 8).

At the same time, the idea of transferring policy influence to an unelected body clearly creates significant questions of political legitimacy. Although both the Oregon and Florida statutes create an obligation to appoint a representative board, there is clearly no way in which such small boards could represent all significant dimensions of society. Problems of representation would be aggravated in polities that are larger and more socially heterogeneous than Oregon or Florida.[6] The method of selection—that is, appointment, rather than election—aggravates legitimacy problems.

The two boards appear to have dealt with potential legitimacy problems in two ways. First, both planning exercises have been built on widespread public consultations. The Oregon Planning Board has relied heavily on advisory committees, advice from other organizations, and regional meetings, when choosing and refining its benchmarks. The Board also relies on broad biennial surveys of public opinion and smaller, more specialized opinion surveys. Second, the planning process incorporates legislative review of proposed outcome measures. The Oregon benchmarks were reviewed by 18 legislative committees and ultimately given approval by the state legislature as a whole (Peirce 1994).[7]

There is another risk with the use of a quasi-autonomous board: that its work will be ignored by both the executive and the legislative branches and have no real effect on budgetary decisions. A recent commentary on the Oregon experiment observes:

> This is Oregon's Achilles heel. While the benchmarks have had a remarkable impact on the private and nonprofit sectors—and many counties have imitated the effort and developed their own benchmarks—state government has not significantly reoriented its spending priorities to pursue the new goals. (Osborne and Plastrik 1997a, 104)

The Floridian experiment—which the state legislature ultimately stopped funding—may illustrate this point even more dramatically.

Canadian governments are based on the parliamentary rather than the congressional model and consequently do not suffer the same difficulties in budget making. The legislature is controlled by the executive and rarely upsets expenditure proposals put forward by the executive. There is consequently no need for a device to build consensus between the two branches on long-run goals. In both provincial experiments with governmentwide performance planning, the selection of social indicators and performance targets has been conducted inside the executive branch.

At first glance, this approach seems to resolve two of the problems associated with experiments by state governments. The risk that planning will be detached from budgeting would seem to be reduced, since the same group of actors within the executive is presumably making both planning and budgeting decisions. Furthermore, an elected executive might seem to have a better-established right to make decisions about the selection of social indicators than an unelected board or commission. However, this approach may also have its own significant weaknesses.

The first may be a difficulty in defining a narrow set of key performance measures. The two state governments have gradually winnowed their list of social indicators to a small number that are thought to be most central to community well-being. The Oregon Benchmarks exercise began with more than 250 measures; this list was eventually narrowed to 92 indicators, of which 20 are given special attention as key benchmarks (Oregon Progress Board 1997). Similarly, the GAP Commission began with a list of 270 benchmarks, but its focus later narrowed to 57 critical benchmarks (Florida Commission on Government Accountability to the People 1998). In both cases, shortening the list has necessarily required some important judgments about the relative importance of different policy areas.

Independent commissions may have an easier time in making public statements about priority areas than the central agencies within governments. This may be so for two reasons. First, unelected officials within central agencies may not have the authority to make deeply political decisions about which of the many indicators proposed by other departments and agencies ought to be regarded as key measures. The inclination may be to maintain an expansive list and allow political executives to make decisions about key priorities. But political executives may also face few incentives to produce a narrow list of indicators. A neat list of indicators may please a few stakeholders whose interests have been attended to, but displease a larger number of stakeholders whose interests appear to have been neglected.

There is precedent to suggest that this may be a serious problem. In 1974–75 the Canadian government undertook a planning exercise that was in many respects comparable to the sort of effort required to produce a governmentwide performance plan. Central agencies consulted with ministers and departmental officials in an attempt to settle on priorities for the government elected in 1974. A brief list of priorities was thought to be essential if senior decision makers were to make effective use of newly introduced PPBS procedures. There was strong ministerial and departmental pressure to expand the list of priorities, and neither central agencies nor the Cabinet seemed able to resist this pressure. The effort to articulate a few top priorities was eventually abandoned (French 1984). Difficulties in reaching internal agreement about top priorities may have been encountered during the development of the U.S. government's governmentwide performance plan. A recent U.S. General Accounting Office (GAO) study notes that the process for developing the plan had been "decentralized," with the result that it lacked an "integrated, consistent" perspective on government priorities (GAO 1998b, 2, 6).

One of the reasons that governments may prove reluctant to give attention to a few key social indicators is the fear that in so doing they will have made explicit the criteria by which their performance should be judged in the future. The concern is a reasonable one: in fact, one of the primary purposes of governmentwide performance plans is to promote accountability in this way. But governments may have legitimate concerns that a range of considerations beyond their control could influence those indicators. Actually stipulating performance targets—that is, the desired value of a social indicator at some point in the future—raises the political stakes even further.

This may explain why governments that have produced their own performance plans—rather than having one produced for them by an independent commission—have been reluctant to make commitments about progress on social indicators except in rough terms. The performance plan for the U.S. government, for example, includes many commitments to "strive toward," "promote," or "help achieve" outcomes. It may be understandable for a government to avoid specificity on performance targets, particularly when success depends so heavily on the cooperation of state, local, or foreign governments, private contractors, or a healthy economy. Nevertheless, there is a marked difference in tone in plans produced by independent bodies, which make much more specific commitments about progress on indicators—including, for example, precise targets for per capita income and unemployment in 2000 and 2010 (Oregon Progress Board 1998).

Other difficulties may arise when governments attempt to produce their own performance plans. One is the danger that the performance plan may become an object of political contention rather than an instrument for building social consensus. A plan that is closely associated with a current government will, if it is taken seriously at all, be criticized by opposing parties, for its inattention to certain indicators, the timidity of its targets, or the unreliability of data used to assess progress.[8] The Alberta plan anticipates this difficulty and includes an attestation by the provincial Auditor General about the methods used to collect and report data (Alberta Treasury 1998). However, this is only a partial solution to the danger of politicization. Plans produced by apparently nonpolitical commissions may not attract such attacks. Furthermore, the consultations that commissions may undertake in an effort to legitimize their plans may prove to be more effective in building agreement on priorities and indicators.

Within the Canadian government, the task of selecting social indicators is also complicated by continuing tensions in federal-provincial relations. A decision by the federal government to set benchmarks in certain policy areas might be construed as a more vigorous assertion of federal authority in those areas. In some fields, the federal government is also negotiating with provinces about the devolution of program responsibilities. These negotiations have been partly premised on the notion that rules about the use of federally provided funds might be loosened if provincial governments succeed in achieving stipulated outcomes. A decision by the federal government to select social indicators and specify targets as part of a government-wide performance plan might affect these negotiations. The result may be to encourage a more incremental, sectorally based approach to the selection of governmentwide performance measures.

Availability of Credible Information about Outcomes

A second difficulty that will need to be confronted if governments are to track performance on key indicators of societal well-being is the lack of good data for many of these indicators. This may be a particular difficulty for smaller subnational governments whose statistical capabilities are limited. Larger subnational governments, and even national governments, may also need to grapple with deficiencies in their statistical systems.

A review of Oregon's key benchmarks (annex 1.A) may illustrate the difficulty confronting smaller subnational governments. The benchmarks appear to rely significantly on data collected during the normal administrative activities of state agencies. The measures relate to activities that are thought to be causally related to improvements in well-being; but direct measures of well-being—evidenced, for example, by popular opinion about personal economic circumstances, personal safety, or environmental quality—are not included. Oregon's Planning Board has attempted to remedy data shortages by commissioning its own population surveys,[9] but these may be too broad or irregular to serve as good foundations for benchmarks. By contrast, Florida's benchmarks (annex 1.B) include more indicators that are based on citizen assessments of their personal circumstances. It may be that Florida—with a larger population and more expansive state government—also has more expansive statistical capacities than does Oregon.

All subnational governments also include measures that can only be tracked using data that are collected by statistical agencies within national governments (MacRae 1985, 301). (To a lesser degree, these governments also rely on data collected in the course of the administrative activities of other parts of the national government.) Of course, the benchmarking efforts of national governments also depend directly on the range and quality of data available from national statistical agencies. However, national statistical agencies vary in quality, and they may prove unable to generate the data needed if either level of government is to measure relevant dimensions of societal health. Concerns about the limitations of national statistical systems have been expressed for many years. Even within the domain of economic activity—traditionally regarded as one in which data collection is relatively good—important gaps have been noted (Prewitt 1987, 266). Larger gaps can be found in other domains (Brink and Zeesman 1997).

It has been suggested that the past 15 years of governmental restructuring has significantly eroded the capabilities of national statistical agencies. In Canada, cutbacks within the public service are said to have eliminated the "critical mass of analytic capacity" that is necessary to do effective social reporting (Deputy Minister Task Forces on Policy Capacity 1996; Felligi and Wolfson 1997, 19). In the United States, a combination of trends are said to have weakened statistical capabilities: cutbacks, reductions in data collection activities as part of attempts to reduce the burden of paperwork requirements on NGOs, and increasing difficulties in collecting data from state and local agencies (Bonnen 1983; Triplett 1990; Weiss and Gruber 1987; Morin 1994). One critic suggests that these trends have contributed to a string of "major gaffes in statistical provision" (Mitchell 1995). Cutbacks and efforts at deregulation are also said to have undermined statistical capabilities in the U.K. statistical agency (Tant 1995, 261).

Governments that are committed to the idea of governmentwide performance monitoring may need to consider closely whether their statistical capabilities are adequate. A related danger is the politicization of statistics produced by national statistical agencies and of the agencies themselves. If, as advocates hope, performance plans become a focus for public debate about governmental priorities, there will be a natural tendency for some social actors to question the manner in which statistics have been defined and the accuracy of the data presented in the plans. Political executives, sensitive to the fact that popular judgments about their performance will be influenced by statistics in their plans, may also look for opportunities to define statistics or present results in favorable ways. The risk is that the credibility of statistical agencies will be undermined, as well as the credibility of the statistics that they produce. Such an erosion of credibility might make performance plans useless as instruments for shaping public debate or holding governments accountable.

The risk is not a hypothetical one. Economic indicators are now widely used to assess governmental performance, and they have sometimes become politicized in this way. Debates have arisen about the manner in which statistics measuring unemployment, poverty, and inflation have been defined, with inferences that government agencies have redefined those statistics in ways that favor political executives (Tant 1995). Similar debates may arise about the broader range of social indicators that are likely to be included in governmentwide performance plans, particularly if the indicators are unfamiliar. The usual recommendation is that "strong institutional safeguards" (Bonnen 1983, 188) should be established to reassure the public about the integrity of data produced by national statistical agencies. But this proposal may induce other problems. Political executives may complain that statistical agencies are preoccupied with narrow professional concerns—such as the need to maintain consistency in statistical concepts and data collection methods over time—and insensitive to the need to adapt their procedures to suit contemporary priorities (MacRae 1985).

Linking Governmental Activities to Performance Outcomes

Advocates of governmentwide performance planning hope that it will improve the rationality of governmental budgeting. It is expected to do this in two ways. First, the obligation to select concrete outcome measures will oblige decision makers to clarify our expectations about the results desired from government action. Second, the availability of information about the effects of different types of government action on outcome measures will enable decision makers to allocate resources where they are most likely to be effective. Programs that affect outcome measures favorably will be expanded, and programs that do not will be eliminated.

Some governmentwide performance plans have taken a first step toward improved rationality by attempting to identify activities that are broadly related to key outcome measures. (The Florida government uses an innovative web page to identify programs that are related to each of the GAP Commission's key benchmarks.[10]) But substantial improvements in the quality of budgetary decision making will be attained only if officials within departments and agencies are able to develop performance management systems that can link their activities to higher-level societal outcomes. To do this, officials must be able to specify the logic underlying the program design (Rossi and Freeman 1993)—that is, the causal chain that links their work to changes in social indicators. They must also have the data needed to test whether the causal chain is working as expected, and they must be able to discount the effect of exogenous factors appropriately.

Experience shows that it is extremely difficult for officials to make clear links between their activities and higher-level outcomes. But it is not for lack of trying. The attempt to make such links was central to several earlier budget reform efforts, including most notably the attempt to introduce the PPBS in the late 1960s and early 1970s (Carter, Day, and Klein 1994). The PPBS was also introduced as "a revolutionary development in the history of government management" (Schick 1966, 243), but its limitations soon became evident. Departments and agencies often had difficulty in defining the logic underlying their programs, collecting appropriate information, and accounting for exogenous influences (GAO 1997a, 3). Overall, the effort to link activities and outcomes proved "far more difficult than expected" (GAO 1997b, 16).

The difficulties that confounded earlier efforts to rationalize budgeting are evident in current reform initiatives as well. The GAO, reviewing the first set of performance plans submitted by federal departments and agencies under the U.S. Government Performance and Results Act, concluded that most "did not relate strategies and resources to performance" (GAO 1998a, 3). A similar complaint has been made about many of the performance plans recently produced by Canadian government departments (Auditor General of Canada 1997, s. 5.85). Even in the United Kingdom, which is sometimes regarded as a leader in this field, executive agencies rarely make clear connections between their work and changes in social outcomes. Their performance is defined for accountability purposes with a mix of input, activity, and output measures (Talbot 1996).

It has also been suggested that the challenges of linking departmental activities with outcome measures may have increased substantially because of important structural changes within the public service over the past 20 years. Contemporary U.S. government has been described as a "hollow state" (Milward, Provan, and Else 1993), that relies more extensively on the cooperation of third parties—subnational governments, NGOs, and contractors—in the execution of its responsibilities. Under such conditions, the GAO has suggested, the task of tracing the effects of federal policies might be even more difficult (GAO 1997b, 17).

The GAO suggests that one of the barriers to the implementation of performance reporting within departments and agencies may be a shortage of staff members who are skilled in performance measurement or program evaluation (GAO 1997a, 1998a). This trend may be aggravated as departments attempt to meet downsizing requirements by cutting staff members not directly involved in program delivery. The GAO's observation suggests a potential remedy: a strengthening of analytic capacity within departments and agencies. This might improve performance reporting, but not radically. It must be recognized that this is a road that governments have traveled before. The failure of earlier efforts to rationalize budgeting also led to an expansion of program evaluation capabilities throughout the 1970s (McQueen 1992; Henry 1995). This improved, but did not revolutionize, the quality of decision making within governments.

The usefulness of a governmentwide performance plan is contingent on the success of bureau-level efforts to make connections between their activities and larger social outcomes. Otherwise the public may find itself agreed on the need to improve a particular social indicator, but uncertain about what changes should then be made to government's spending decisions. The problem is anticipated by the GAO, which observed that

> The difficulties associated with selecting appropriate measures and establishing relationships between activities and results will make it difficult in many cases to judge whether changes in funding levels will affect the outcomes of federal programs. (GAO 1997b, 3)

Shaping Public Debate

Advocates of governmentwide performance planning suggest that the availability of such plans will shape public opinion in a variety of ways. The publication of targets, it is suggested, will focus public opinion and encourage consensus on social priorities. It might encourage tolerance of alternative methods of delivering public services that, though unconventional in design, are seen to be effective in ameliorating social problems. Confidence in government might also be restored, as citizens see that government is attentive to results and effective in dealing with problems. These are ambitious goals, and it is unclear to what degree governmentwide performance planning can contribute to their attainment.

The experience in some U.S. states is encouraging. Oregon Governor Goldschmidt's original initiative to craft a statewide strategic plan, and continuing efforts by the Oregon Progress Board to define and track benchmarks that relate to the goals included in that plan, are said to have had a substantial impact on public opinion. Goldschmidt's successor, Barbara Roberts, found that the benchmarks helped moderate popular reaction to spending cuts during a 1991–92 fiscal crisis (Peirce 1994). Roberts' successor, John Kitzhaber, repeated the planning exercise in 1996. Since 1990, many county and local governments have undertaken similar benchmarking exercises (Osborne and Plastrik 1997b). The most significant of these may be the exercise undertaken in the Portland area. Local and regional governments established a Portland-Multnomah County Progress Board, modeled on the state board, and began a consultative exercise that resulted in the selection of 85 benchmarks. A smaller number of "urgent benchmarks" are said to have proved useful in guiding budget making by local authorities (Portland-Multnomah Progress Board 1998).

Florida's GAP Commission has had less resounding success but appears to have built up significant public support. When legislators in the state's house of representatives threatened to stop funding the Commission in the spring of 1998, many leading state newspapers editorialized in favor of the Commission's work. The benchmarks report, one said, "is extremely useful to citizens and politicians" (*Tampa Tribune* 1998, 14). However, there did not appear to be sufficient popular support to block the proposal.

Other experiences with performance-reporting exercises have not proved so promising. In Canada, for example, observers have noted the lukewarm response of legislators to the increased volume of performance information now being produced by federal and provincial agencies. One commentator suggests there is a "utilization gap" within the federal parliament: many legislators do not evince an interest in performance plans and reports produced by federal departments under the government's Improved Reporting to Parliament Project (Lindquist 1998). The same problem has been noted in a recent report by Canada's Auditor General (Auditor General of Canada 1997, Ch. 5).

There is evidence that this is a pattern common to many jurisdictions. A recent study of legislative use of performance information in Australia, New Zealand, and the United Kingdom found that the "greatest disappointment . . . is the unwillingness or inability of Parliament to use better information when it is provided" (Thomas 1996, 3). This may even be a difficulty in the United States, notwithstanding its tradition of legislative independence and the strong interest of some congressional committees in the implementation of the 1993 U.S. Government Performance and Results Act. In a 1997 study, the GAO found that legislative staff members "questioned the validity and usefulness of outcome data in decision making and perceived a potential for loss of needed detail" (GAO 1997b, 15).

The reaction of legislators to the publication of performance information is important because they play an important role as intermediaries in the communication of government information to the broader public (MacRae 1985, 320–23). So, too, do journalists. But the media seem to share legislators' indifference to results-based reporting. "The introduction of performance reports has been a journalistic nonevent in Ottawa," says one observer:

> There has been virtually no reporting on the initiative nor on the progress on the results commitments identified in the reports . . . Journalists are cynical about the information contained in the performance reports, seeing them as communication documents that leave considerable "wiggle room" for governments. (Lindquist 1998)

Another report suggests that the inattentiveness of legislators and journalists represents the main barrier to achievement of a results-based management culture in Canadian governments (English and Lindquist 1998).

To some extent, the muted enthusiasm of legislators toward performance reporting is understandable. The organization of government work has implications for the redistribution of social resources that are often more important than the achievement of formally articulated program objectives. There are also other explanations of legislative and media indifference. One is skepticism about the credibility of information about outcomes provided directly by government departments. In this respect there is a clear difference between the structure of the Canadian and U.S. federal performance reporting exercises, and several state exercises. Data provided by groups such as the Oregon Progress Board or GAP Commission may be given more credence because these organizations are not believed to have incentives to engage in misrepresentation.

Other studies have suggested that widespread public participation in the formulation of plans and selection of benchmarks is necessary to ensure that the public, legislators, and media are receptive to performance information. The GAO suggests this explains the continued public interest in the Oregon benchmarks (GAO 1993). A Canadian study agrees, and contrasts experience in the province of Alberta. Alberta, it says, "has received less public commentary on its results because there was no extensive public consultation process prior to implementation" (Public Policy Forum 1998, 6).

Mancur Olson observes that early efforts at social reporting also met with limited public interest and did not prove to be "a starting point for the nation's debates and choices" (Olson 1988, 3). In part, this may be the result of an overestimation of what the revelation of information about social conditions was likely to accomplish, without a rebalancing of forces within civil society. Statistics that show clear deficiencies in some aspect of societal well-being may be newsworthy for a brief time (Kingdon 1984, 95–121). But the willingness of governments to take the actions needed to address those deficiencies depends largely on the ability of the constituencies who feel those deficiencies most directly to exert political influence. We imagine that the failure of governments to remedy certain social ills is the result of poor information about those problems; but it may be that the lack of information about those problems is a result of the political weakness of certain sectors of society.

Prospects for Governmentwide Performance Planning

Some U.S. and Canadian governments, like those in other jurisdictions, have recently confronted many serious threats to governability, including debt-induced constraints on spending authority and a substantial erosion in popular respect for public institutions. A range of institutional innovations—including governmentwide performance planning—are now being tested as devices for responding to these threats. Advocates suggest that these innovations might dramatically improve governmental capabilities and restore public trust. But there are respects in which current reforms are not "innovations" at all: sometimes, they are reworkings of ideas that have already been tested. The problems that limited the usefulness of similar efforts in budgetary reform and social reporting are likely to hamper current efforts at governmentwide performance planning.

There is some evidence that planning exercises are effective in building popular consensus on governmentwide performance planning in subnational governments. But effectiveness appears to depend on a planning process that is regarded by nongovernmental actors as independent of the political executive, and which allows for extensive consultation with all sectors of society. In fact, it is not clear whether the use of quantifiable indicators of societal well-being is the most important characteristic of these planning exercises. Oregon's benchmarks have attracted wide attention, but it may be the process that led to the selection of policy priorities—and not the benchmarks themselves—that is the most important feature of Oregon's innovation. Furthermore, it may be difficult to replicate this process with equal effectiveness in jurisdictions that are more populous, geographically larger, and more demographically heterogeneous. National-level consultative exercises have had a much less impressive record in building consensus on policy priorities.

We may also need to temper our expectations about the capacity of governmentwide performance planning to improve the rationality of the budgeting processes within government. Such planning may help polities to make a rough ordering of priorities, but the capacity to make precise calculations about the merits of alternative programs may not be dramatically improved. The task of linking governmental activities to high-level societal outcomes may prove too analytically complex. A veteran of the social reporting movement recently observed that

> The ambitious ideas of using social indicators to contribute to a rationalization of the political process, to establish goals and priorities, to evaluate political programs, and develop an early warning system have proven to be too far from reality. In this regard, social indicators have suffered a similar fate as other scientific instruments of political decision making, such as cost-benefit analysis or the [PPBS]. (Noll 1998)

A related question is whether polities will be prepared to make substantial re-allocative decisions even when there is good evidence that current programs are ineffective in influencing outcome measures, or that alternative programs are likely to be more effective. As noted earlier, advocates of planning may underestimate the politics of budget making, and in particular the ease with which expenditure decisions can be changed in the absence of well-organized constituencies who care about the societal outcome in question. There is also doubt about whether polities will be open to substantial budgetary changes in the absence of a popularly recognized fiscal crisis. The willingness to tolerate hard decisions about budgetary reallocations that was evident in Canada and the United States three years ago is now dissipating, as governments move into a new era of budget surpluses. Better information about program effectiveness may be overlooked by a public that is reluctant to bear the pain of further budgetary reallocations.[11]

A prudent strategy for governments in larger jurisdictions may be to develop mechanisms for establishing and publicizing priorities that do not require the identification of quantifiable outcome measures or the specification of specific targets for those measures. A model may be the approach developed by the New Zealand government, in which ministers define and publish a set of medium-term policy goals that are referred to as *strategic result areas*. A set of more detailed departmental objectives, known as *key results areas,* are then developed for each strategic result area. It is noteworthy that New Zealand—a jurisdiction that is widely regarded as a leader in efforts to encourage results-based management—does not attempt to select quantifiable indicators or specific performance targets in either its strategic result areas or its key results areas (Boston and Pallot 1997; New Zealand 1997). Such an approach has at least three advantages. It avoids the difficult technical problems of defining appropriate outcome measures, as well as the political risks of stipulating performance targets for indicators that may be only loosely influenced by government action. The danger of politicization of key statistics or statistical agencies is also reduced.

At the same time, a government could encourage the development and publication of outcome measures on a sectoral basis. Such an approach may have the advantage of making methodological problems more tractable and of reducing the political sensitivity of the work of selecting targets. The approach might be one that includes wide consultation with the nongovernmental stakeholders who have a direct interest in a specific policy area and who are most likely to use social indicators in public deliberations over policy. To be effective, such an approach still requires adequate capacity for data collection and interpretation within central statistical agencies, and adequate analytic capacity within line departments. The extent to which the capacity and independence of statistical services has been weakened as a result of recent efforts at retrenchment may deserve further consideration.

Notes

1. Other states that have begun similar initiatives include Connecticut, Hawaii, Maine, Minnesota, North Carolina, Texas, and Utah. Of these, Minnesota's initiative—known as Minnesota Milestones—appears to be the most advanced.
2. Two other provinces—Ontario and Quebec—are reported to be considering similar initiatives (Thomas 1997).
3. The Secretariat has begun an internal exercise known as the Societal Indicators Project. An NGO, the Canadian Policy Research Network, has also been commissioned by the government to begin a project on societal indicators that might serve as the basis for selection of government performance measures (Canadian Policy Research Network 1998).
4. It has been suggested, however, that the movement is enjoying a resurgence, fueled by the same frustration about "economic philistinism" among policy makers that motivated its early adherents (Brink and Zeesman 1997).

5. There is a long list of such proposals, including the recommendations of the 1937 Brownlow Committee and the two Hoover Commissions. The budget reform proposals made in 1993 by the National Performance Review are comparable. Historically, reformers who have pushed for stronger executive authority were known as the "executive budget movement" (Wildavsky 1987, 53–64).

6. Oregon has a population of 3 million; Florida, 13 million.

7. To some extent, the use of social indicators may also serve to legitimize policy making by an autonomous and unelected body. The real point may be to forge common ground between the executive and the legislative branches and thus to improve the rationality of budget making. The use of quantitatively defined benchmarks may serve to give this function a technical, rather than overtly political, appearance.

8. There was apparently a long debate within the Canadian government about the political risks of specifying measurable performance goals for a major new federal program, the National Child Benefit (Greenspon 1997).

9. The Oregon Progress Board has conducted a biennial population survey since 1990. It also undertakes smaller, more specialized surveys, such as a 1991 survey on literacy (Times Wire Services 1990).

10. http://www.oppaga.state.fl.us/government/s_gap.asp.

11. *Governing* magazine, commenting on the defunding of Florida's GAP Commission, observes: "Then there's the fact that Florida, like many states, is running a significant surplus right now, and the pressure to keep a tight watch on state programs is diminished. Efficiency and effectiveness are far more popular in hard times. When there's money to be brought back to home districts—for boat basins, say, or exit ramps—people who question whether those projects genuinely contribute to the overall good of the state are not likely to be popular" (Barrett and Greene 1998, 68).

References

Alberta Treasury. 1998. *Measuring Up: Fourth Annual Report on the Performance of the Government of Alberta.* Edmonton, AB: Alberta Treasury.

Auditor General of Canada. 1997. *1997 Report of the Auditor General.* Ottawa: Office of the Auditor General. http://www.oag-vg.gc.ca/domino/reports.nsf/html/97menu_e.html.

Barrett, K., and R. Greene. 1998. "Why Good Programs Die." *Governing* (July): 68.

Bonnen, James T. 1983. "Federal Statistical Coordination Today: A Disaster or a Disgrace?" *American Statistician* 37 (August): 177–202.

Boston, Jonathan, and June Pallot. 1997. "Linking Strategy and Performance: Developments in the New Zealand Public Sector." *Journal of Policy Analysis and Management* 16 (3): 382–404.

Brink, Satya, and Allen Zeesman. 1997. *Measuring Social Well-Being: An Index of Social Health for Canada.* R-97-9E. Ottawa: Human Resources Development Canada.

Canadian Policy Research Network. 1998. "Societal Indicators: Synthesis of Discussions to Date." Canadian Policy Research Network. http://www.cprn.com/cprn.html.

Carter, Neil, Patricia Day, and Rudolf Klein. 1994. *How Organisations Measure Success: The Use of Performance Indicators in Government.* London and New York: Routledge.

Cincinnati Enquirer. 1994. "Bright Ideas: States Have Inventive Solutions to Shared Government Problems." November 21, A12.

Deputy Minister Task Forces on Policy Capacity. 1996. *Strengthening Our Policy Capacity.* Ottawa. http://www.ccmd-ccg.gc.ca/documents/dmtf/policye.pdf.

English, John, and Evert Lindquist. 1998. *Performance Management: Linking Results to Public Debate.* Ottawa: Institute of Public Administration of Canada. http://www.ipac.ca/files/newdirect2.pdf.

Felligi, Ivan, and Michael Wolfson. 1997. "Toward Systems of Social Statistics." Paper presented at the 51st session of the International Statistical Institute, Istanbul.

Florida Commission on Government Accountability to the People. 1996. *Annual Report, 1995–96.* Tallahassee: Florida Commission on Government Accountability to the People. http://fcn.state.fl.us/eog/govdocs/gapcomm/annual.html.

———. 1997. *Critical Benchmark Goals.* Tallahassee: Florida Commission on Government Accountability to the People. http://www.fcn.state.fl.us/eog/govdocs/gapcomm/critical/critical_bnchmrks_index.html.

———. 1998. *Florida Benchmarks 1998.* Tallahassee: Florida Commission on Government Accountability to the People. http://www.fcn.state.fl.us/eog/govdocs/gapcomm/bench98/flbench_report.html.

Florida Governor's Commission for Government by the People. 1991. *Final Report.* Tallahassee: Florida Governor's Commission for Government by the People.

French, Richard. 1984. *How Ottawa Decides.* Toronto, ON: J. Lorimer.

GAO (General Accounting Office). 1993. *Performance Budgeting: State Experiences and Implications for the Federal Government.* Washington, DC: GAO.

———. 1997a. *Managing For Results: Analytic Challenges in Measuring Performance.* GAO/HEHS/GGD-97-138. Washington, DC: GAO.

———. 1997b. *Performance Budgeting: Past Initiatives Offer Insights for GPRA Compliance.* GAO/AIMD-97-46. Washington, DC: GAO.

———. 1998a. *Managing for Results: An Agenda to Improve the Usefulness of Agencies' Annual Performance Plans.* GAO/GGD/AIMD-98-228. Washington, DC: GAO.

———. 1998b. *The Results Act: Assessment of the Governmentwide Performance Plan for Fiscal Year 1999.* GAO/AIMD/GGD-98-159. Washington, DC: GAO.

Gore, Al. 1993. *Creating a Government That Works Better and Costs Less.* New York: Times Books.

Greenspon, E. 1997. "Child Benefit to Face Public Eye." *Globe and Mail,* September 23.

Gross, Bertram. 1966. "A Historical Note on Social Indicators." In *Social Indicators,* ed. Raymond Bauer, ix–xviii. Cambridge, MA: MIT Press.

Henry, Nicholas. 1995. *Public Administration and Public Affairs.* Englewood Cliffs, NJ: Prentice Hall.

Kingdon, John W. 1984. *Agendas, Alternatives, and Public Policies.* Boston: Little, Brown and Company.

Knickerbocker, B. 1991. "States, Business Build New Alliances." *Christian Science Monitor* May 20, 8.

Lindquist, Evert. 1998. "Getting Results Right: Reforming Ottawa's Estimates." In *How Ottawa Spends, 1998,* ed. L. Pal, 153–90. Ottawa: Oxford University Press.

MacRae, J. Duncan. 1985. *Policy Indicators.* Chapel Hill, NC: University of North Carolina Press.

McQueen, Cameron. 1992. "Program Evaluation in the Canadian Federal Government." In *Action-Oriented Evaluation in Organizations,* ed. Joe Hudson, John Mayne, and Ray Thomlison, 28–47. Toronto, ON: Wall and Emerson.

Melkers, Julia, and Katherine Willoughby. 1998. "The State of the States: Performance-Based Budgeting Requirements in 47 out of 50." *Public Administration Review* 58 (1): 66–73.

Milward, H. Brinton, Keith G. Provan, and Barbara A. Else. 1993. "What Does the 'Hollow State' Look Like?" In *Public Management: The State of the Art,* ed. Barry Bozeman, 309–22. San Francisco: Jossey-Bass.

Mitchell, Daniel J. 1995. "Statistical Discrepancies in Our Federal Data Programs." *Challenge* 38 (July–August): 38–45.

Morin, Arthur. 1994. "Regulating the Flow of Data: OMB and the Control of Government Information." *Public Administration Review* 54 (5): 434–43.

National Performance Review. 1996. "The Best Kept Secrets in Government." *National Performance Review.* http://www.npr.gov/.

New Zealand. 1997. *Strategic Result Areas for the Public Sector.* Wellington: New Zealand Government.

Noll, Heinz-Herbert. 1998. *Social Indicators and Social Reporting: The International Experience.* Canadian Council for Social Development. http://www.ccsd.ca/noll1.html.

Nova Scotia Department of Finance. 1995. *Government by Design: Progress and Challenge.* Halifax, NS: Nova Scotia Department of Finance. http://www.gov.ns.ca/fina/financial/budget95/b95desn1.htm#toc.

———. 1998. *Nova Scotia Counts.* Halifax, NS: Nova Scotia Department of Finance. http://www.gov.ns.ca/finance/minister/counts/nscounts.htm.

Nova Scotia Priorities and Planning Secretariat. 1998. *Nova Scotia's Planning and Accountability Framework.* Halifax, NS: Nova Scotia Priorities and Planning Secretariat.

OECD (Organisation for Economic Co-operation and Development). 1976. *Measuring Social Well-Being: A Progress Report on the Development of Social Indicators.* Paris: OECD.

———. 1982. *The OECD List of Social Indicators.* Paris: OECD.

———. 1996. *Ageing in OECD Countries: A Critical Policy Challenge.* Paris: OECD.

Olson, Mancur. 1988. "Toward a New Social Report." *Public Opinion* 11 (November–December): 2–4.

Oregon Progress Board. 1997. *Oregon Shines II.* Salem, OR: Oregon Progress Board.

———. 1998. *The New Oregon Trail.* Salem, OR: Oregon Progress Board. http://www.econ.state.or.us/opb/what_is.htm.

Osborne, David, and Peter Plastrik. 1997a. *Banishing Bureaucracy: The Five Strategies for Reinventing Government.* Reading, MA: Addison Wesley.

———. 1997b. "Grading Governments." *Washington Post,* April 13.

Peirce, N. 1994. "Benchmarks of Government Effectiveness." *Baltimore Sun,* April 11.

Portland-Multnomah Progress Board. 1998. *History of the Benchmarks.* Portland, OR: Portland-Multnomah Progress Board. http://www.multnomah.lib.or.us/cc/bev/bmhist.html.

Prewitt, Kenneth. 1987. "Public Statistics and Democratic Politics." In *The Politics of Numbers,* ed. William Alonso and Paul Starr, 261–74. New York: Russell Sage.

Public Policy Forum. 1998. *Performance Management: Linking Results to Public Debate.* Ottawa: Public Policy Forum.

Rarick, E. 1989. "Goldschmidt Appointments Defeated." United Press International, Salem, OR, October 26.

Rogers, Everett. 1983. *Diffusion of Innovations.* New York: Free Press.

Rossi, Peter H., and Howard E. Freeman. 1993. *Evaluation: A Systematic Approach.* Newberry Park, CA: Sage Publications.

Rothenbacher, Franz. 1993. "National and International Approaches in Social Reporting." *Social Indicators Research* 29: 1–62.

Schick, Allen. 1966. "The Road to PPB: The Stages of Budget Reform." *Public Administration Review* 26 (4): 243–58.

Talbot, Colin. 1996. *Ministers and Agencies: Control, Performance and Accountability.* London: Chartered Institute of Public Finance and Accountability.

Tampa Tribune. 1998. "The Importance of State Benchmarks." March 13.

Tant, A. P. 1995. "The Politics of Official Statistics." *Government and Opposition* 30 (Spring): 254–66.

Thomas, P. 1997. "The Politics of Performance Measurement." *Public Sector Management* 8 (2): 17–19.

Thomas, P. G. 1996. *Evaluation of Information Disclosure Standards for the Improved Reporting to Parliament Project.* Winnipeg, MB: University of Manitoba.

Times Wire Services. 1990. "Test Gauges Skills of Oregon's Work Force." *Los Angeles Times,* May 15.

Treasury Board Secretariat. 1995. *Strengthening Government Review.* Ottawa: Treasury Board Secretariat.

———. 1996. *Getting Government Right: A Progress Report.* Ottawa: Treasury Board Secretariat.

———. 1997. *Accounting for Results.* Ottawa: Treasury Board Secretariat.

———. 1998a. *Managing for Results.* Ottawa: Treasury Board Secretariat. http://www.tbs-sct.gc.ca/rma/communic/prr98/mfr98e.html.

———. 1998b. *Societal Indicators Project: Survey of Results Frameworks.* Ottawa: Treasury Board Secretariat. http://ww.tbs-sct.gc.ca/rma/account/socinde.doc.

Triplett, Jack E. 1990. "Reviving the Federal Statistical System: A View from Within." *American Economic Review* 80 (May): 341–44.

U.S. Department of Health Education. 1969. *Toward a Social Report.* Washington, DC: U.S. Government Printing Office.

U.S. Office of Management and Budget. 1998. *Government-Wide Performance Plan, Fiscal Year 1999.* Washington, DC: OMB. http://www.whitehouse.gov/WH/EOP/OMB/html/gpptoc.htm.

U.S. Senate. 1993. *Report on the Government Performance and Results Act.* S. Rep. 103–58. Committee on Governmental Affairs, Washington, DC.

Weiss, Janet, and Judith Gruber. 1987. "The Managed Irrelevance of Federal Education Statistics." In *The Politics of Numbers,* ed. William Alonso and Paul Starr, 363–91. New York: Russell Sage.

Wildavsky, Aaron. 1987. *The New Politics of the Budgetary Process.* Glenview, IL: Scott, Foresman.

Annex 1.A: Outcome Measures in the Oregon Plan

Quality of Jobs

- Eighth grade reading/math skills
- Oregonians with bachelor's degrees
- Adults with intermediate literacy skills
- Industry research and development spending
- Employment outside Portland and Willamette Valley
- Manufacturing exports
- Professional services exported (imported)
- Oregon's national rank in new companies
- Per capita personal income relative to the United States

Safe, Caring, and Engaged Communities

- High school dropout rate
- Eighth grade use of alcohol, illicit drugs, and cigarettes
- Incomes below 100 percent of federal poverty level
- Overall reported crime
- Reported child abuse
- Oregonians without health insurance
- Volunteerism

Healthy, Sustainable Surroundings

- Urban highway congestion
- Forest, agricultural, and wetlands preservation
- Air quality
- Salmon/steelhead populations

Source: Oregon Progress Board 1998.

Annex 1.B: Outcome Measures in the Florida Plan

Families and Communities

- Percentage of Floridians who said that Florida was a good place to live
- Percentage of Florida children living in poverty
- Number of teenage mothers ages 15–19 who gave birth per 1,000 teenage girls ages 15–19 in Florida
- Percentage of Floridians age 65 and older living in poverty
- Percentage of low-income households in Florida spending more than 30 percent of their income on housing
- Percentage of Floridians who believed that race relations in their communities were good or excellent

Safety

- Number of violent crimes reported per 100,000 Florida residents
- Number of nonviolent crimes reported per 100,000 Florida residents
- Percentage of Floridians who said that they were afraid to walk alone at night in an area near where they lived
- Number of child abuse and neglect victims whose maltreatment was verified or found to have some evidence of occurrence (per 100,000 Florida children)
- Number of people murdered by a family or household member per 100,000 Florida residents
- Number of people who died in alcohol-related traffic crashes per 100,000 Florida residents
- Number of children (per 100,000 Florida children) who were referred to the Florida Department of Juvenile Justice for (a) violent crimes, and (b) property felonies
- Number of children who were judged guilty of a criminal offense children (per 100,000 Florida children)

Learning

- Percentage of public school students in grade 8 who scored 4.0 or above on the Florida Writes! test
- Percentage of public school students in grade 10 who scored 4.0 or above on the Florida Writes! test

- Percentage of Florida public high school graduates who were referred for remediation in one or more subject areas after entering (a) community colleges, and (b) state universities
- Percentage of Floridians who rated the job their local public schools were doing as good or excellent
- Percentage of Floridians who believed the availability of high quality, affordable college education was about the same or better in Florida compared with other states
- Percentage of Floridians age 25 or older who had at least a high school diploma or GED
- Percentage of Floridians age 25 or older who had at least a bachelor's degree
- Percentage of Floridians ages 19–34 who had a middle or high level of literacy: (a) prose literacy; (b) quantitative literacy; (c) document literacy

Health

- Number of infants who died before their first birthday per 1,000 live births in Florida
- Percentage of babies in Florida who weighed less than 5 pounds, 9 ounces at birth
- Percentage of two-year-olds in Florida who were immunized
- Average lifespan in Florida (in years)
- Number of deaths from cancer per 100,000 Florida residents
- Number of new cases of sexually transmitted diseases reported per 100,000 Florida residents
- Number of new cases of AIDS reported per 100,000 Florida residents
- Percentage of Floridians who did not have health insurance: (a) under age 18; (b) ages 18–34; (c) ages 35–64; (d) age 65 and older
- Florida's total personal health care expenditure as a percentage of total personal income.

Economy

- Percentage change in the number of full- and part-time jobs in Florida
- Florida's unemployment rate as a percentage of the U.S. unemployment rate
- Florida's average personal income as a percentage of the U.S. average personal income
- Florida's average wage as a percentage of the U.S. average wage
- Percentage of Florida households that believed they were better off financially than a year ago
- Percentage of Floridians living in poverty

Environment

- Millions of gallons of fresh water used per day in Florida for agricultural use
- Gallons of water used per Florida resident served by Florida's public water suppliers, such as city and county water departments
- Percentage of domestic wastewater that was reclaimed and reused for agriculture, landscaping, or other beneficial purposes
- Number of plant and animal species in Florida that were showing a decline in population or living in a habitat prone to development or subject to other disturbances: (a) plants, and (b) animals
- Percentage of high-quality natural areas in Florida that were protected from development
- Percentage of surface-water bodies in Florida where the water quality was rated good: (a) lakes, (b) streams, and (c) estuaries
- Percentage of Floridians living in areas where the outdoor air meets or exceeds air quality standards
- Pounds of municipal solid waste collected per Florida resident
- Percentage of municipal solid waste collected that was recycled

Government

- Percentage of Floridians who trusted state government to do what was right almost always or most of the time
- Percentage of Floridians who trusted the federal government to do what was right almost always or most of the time
- Percentage of Floridians who rated the job their local government was doing as good or excellent
- Percentage of Floridians who rated the local law enforcement services where they lived as good or excellent
- Percentage of Floridians who rated highways and roads where they lived as good or excellent
- Percentage of Floridians who rated the freshwater quality (lakes, streams, and rivers) where they lived as good or excellent
- Percentage of Floridians who rated the social services where they lived as good or excellent
- Percentage of Floridians who voted in presidential elections
- Percentage of Floridians who voted in nonpresidential elections

Source: Florida Commission on Government Accountability to the People 1998.

Annex 1.C: Outcome Measures in the Alberta Plan

Helping Albertans to Be Self-Reliant, Capable, and Caring

- Life expectancy at birth
- Health status
- Births to mothers under age 18
- Educational attainment
- Literacy and numeracy
- Family income distribution

Promoting Prosperity of Albertans

- Gross domestic product
- Job creation
- Resource wealth
- Skill development
- Adoption of new technologies
- Cost of government
- Infrastructure capacity
- Taxation load
- Provincial credit rating
- Net debt
- Workplace climate
- Export trade

Preserving the Alberta Tradition

- Crime rate
- Serious youth crime
- Resource sustainability
- Air quality
- Water quality
- Land quality
- Heritage appreciation
- Intergovernmental relations

Source: Alberta Treasury 1998.

Annex 1.D: Outcome Measures in the Nova Scotia Plan

Social Responsibility

- Education profile of population
- High school graduation rate
- Self-reported health status
- Perinatal mortality rate
- Healthy weight
- Crime rate
- Safety at night
- Life lost due to accidental causes
- Workplace accident rate
- Disposable income
- Labor force composition
- Participation in events and activities
- Civic and voluntary activities
- Charitable donations
- Cooperatives' equity
- Geographic distribution of board membership
- Municipal voter turnout
- Number of school advisory councils
- Child poverty rate
- Participation in leisure activities
- Optimism about the future
- Waterways stewardship
- Safe municipal water supplies
- Involvement in recycling programs
- Seniors living independently
- Prevention of family violence

Economic Growth

- New public and private capital investment
- Employment and participation rates
- Net number of new jobs created
- Net number of new full- and part-time jobs created
- Regulatory burden
- Corporate tax burden
- Strikes and lockouts

- Worker absenteeism
- Weekly hours of work
- Education of the labor force
- Participation in company-sponsored training
- Participation rate in adult education and training
- Gross domestic product
- Company registrations
- Value added in manufacturing

Responsive Government

- Provincial government employment, wages, and salaries
- Review of departmental programs
- Public satisfaction with services received
- Departmental outcome measures meeting or exceeding targets
- Service satisfaction surveys
- Government services meeting quality standards

Fiscal Stability

- Net direct debt
- Net direct debt and GDP
- Net direct debt per capita
- Debt-carrying charges
- Credit rating
- Balanced budget
- Effective personal tax rate

Source: Nova Scotia Department of Finance 1998.

Annex 1.E: Draft Outcome Measures for the Canadian Government

A Secure and Confident Society

- Life expectancy at birth
- Incidence of low income among children and seniors
- Knowledge workers as a percentage of total employment
- Distribution of the population by literacy level
- Crime rates in Canada
- Canada's trade in cultural goods and services

A Sound and Prosperous Economy

- Net employment growth in Canada since 1989
- Real disposable family income
- Real gross domestic product percentage change
- Total factor productivity in G-7
- Population by educational attainment
- Business investment in plants and equipment
- Canada's infrastructure—international ranking
- Use of technology
- Canada's competitiveness—international ranking
- Trade
- Tort costs as a percentage of GDP, 1994
- Projected CPI inflation, 1997

A Safe and Healthy Environment

- New Canadian supplies of ozone-depleting substances (ODS)
- Carbon dioxide emission from fossil fuel use (1958–94)
- Sulfur dioxide emissions in Canada and the United States (1980–94)
- Changes in species conservation status from 1978 to 1997
- Number of hours that ground-level ozone levels exceed guidelines
- Discharge of dioxins and furans from Canadian pulp mills using chlorine bleaching (presented as toxic equivalents) (TEQs)
- Level of municipal water use by sector, 1983–94
- Erosion control practices
- Percentage of distribution of households by household environmental practices, goods or services, 1991 and 1994

Responsive and Accountable Governance

■ Government efficiency and transparency—Canada's 1996 ranking among G-7 countries
■ Federal deficit to GDP
■ Federal debt rating as of June 1997
■ Federal taxes and debt as percentage of GDP
■ Foreign held debt to federal government debt
■ Level of education of federal government employees
■ Representation of designated groups in the public service

Source: Treasury Board Secretariat 1998b.

2

A Simple Measure of
Good Governance

JEFF HUTHER AND ANWAR SHAH

Debates on the appropriate role of the state and appropriate policies and institutions to further this role are typically carried out by relying upon anecdotal evidence in the absence of a quantifiable definition of *good government*. This chapter attempts to fill this void by developing a gauge of the quality of government through the construction of an index of governance quality for a sample of 80 countries.[1] This index is offered as a starting point for an objective assessment of various economic policies to further the quality of governance, rather than as a precise and definitive indicator of governance quality. After describing the construction of the index and the results, we provide an application to the debate on the appropriate level of decentralization of fiscal powers.

This application provides empirical support for the theoretical underpinnings of the fiscal federalism literature. Governance quality is enhanced, according to this theory; more closely matching services with citizen preferences, and moving governments closer to the people they are intended to serve, ensures greater accountability of the public sector. The chapter is organized as follows. The first section presents an approach to the measurement of governance quality. The next section applies this measurement to the decentralization debate. The following section notes limitations of the approach, and the last section highlights main conclusions.

Measuring Governance Quality

Governance is a multifaceted concept encompassing all aspects of the exercise of authority through formal and informal institutions in the management of the resource endowment of a state. The quality of governance is thus determined by the impact of this exercise of power on the quality of life enjoyed by its citizens. There is growing awareness in the development community that a comprehensive look at the enabling environment of institutions (World Bank 1992, 1994; Picciotto 1995; Hansen 1996; Huther, Roberts, and Shah 1997; Shah 1994, 1995, 1998a, 1998b); interests; and policies is needed in determining the net impact of the state on the well-being of its citizens.

Although no single index can conceptually capture all aspects of this enabling environment, a focus on key observable aspects of the governance dimensions can be helpful in providing a comparative perspective on differentials in the quality of governance among different nations. The key observable aspects of the governance dimension considered in this chapter are citizen voice and exit, government orientation, social development, and economic management. Accordingly, the governance index we have composed has four composite indexes, chosen to provide an indication of a government's ability to (a) ensure political transparency and voice for all citizens, (b) provide efficient and effective public services, (c) promote the health and well-being of its citizens, and (d) create a favorable climate for stable economic growth. These factors are among those cited in the World Bank (1992) booklet, *Governance and Development,* as representing the most important goals that should be faced by governments. It is important to note that these are goals that all governments can be expected to pursue regardless of their country's wealth. In developing these indexes, we have relied on existing indicators that measure salient characteristics of each of these indexes (see table 2.1).

The ability to create an index of governance quality has been enhanced by the creation of several quality-of-life indexes in recent years. For example, we make use of previously published indexes measuring health, education, political freedom, and government corruption. The increasing interest in developing countries as potential borrowers has led to increased data, largely through surveys, on a wide variety of institutional issues. The index developed in this chapter takes advantage of this increase in data availability, as well as more traditional sources of information on developing countries such as the World Bank and International Monetary Fund (IMF).

TABLE 2.1   Components of Governance Index

Index name		Component indices	
CP	Citizen Participation Index		
		PF	Political Freedom
		PS	Political Stability
GO	Government Orientation Index		
		JE	Judicial Efficiency
		RT	Bureaucratic Efficiency
		CO	Lack of Corruption
SD	Social Development Index		
		HD	Human Development
		GI	Egalitarian Income Distribution
EM	Economic Management Index		
		OO	Outward Orientation
		CB	Central Bank Independence
		DB	Inverted Debt-to-GDP Ratio

Using the objectives described above, the resulting index of governance quality (GQI) is

$$GQI = CP^{\alpha_1} * GO^{\alpha_2} * SD^{\alpha_3} * EM^{1-\alpha_1-\alpha_2-\alpha_3},$$

where

$$CP = PF^{\vartheta} * PS^{1-\vartheta},$$
$$GO = RT^{K_1} * CO^{K_2} * JE^{1-K_1-K_2},$$
$$SD = HD^{\Lambda} * GI^{1-\Lambda},$$
$$EM = OO^{M_1} * CB^{M_2} * DB^{1-M_1-M_2}.$$

α, ϑ, K, Λ, and M are weights indicating the relative importance of components to overall governance assessment.

The citizens' participation index is composed of two indexes—one that assesses the degree of political freedom within a country and one that assesses the level of political stability of a country. Political freedom assesses the ability of citizens to influence the quality of governance they receive. The political stability index was composed by a commercial group with the perspective of an investor in mind. This perspective may understate the ability of citizens to participate in governance decisions in some countries, but it is a reasonable indicator of the continuity of citizen participation.

The orientation of governments toward the provision of public goods and services is assessed through three indexes: judicial efficiency, bureaucratic efficiency, and lack of corruption. Improving judicial efficiency has been recognized as a prerequisite for a country's development at least since the 1960s (Blair and Hansen 1994), and the costs of bureaucratic inefficiency and corruption have been well documented (de Soto 1989). All three of these indexes are based on surveys that attempt to gauge the degree to which public sector employees are focused on serving the populace rather than enriching themselves or their political parties.

Social development within a country is assessed through two widely known components, the United Nations' Human Development Index (HDI) and Gini coefficients (which quantify the degree of income inequality). The HDI combines estimates of life expectancy, average education levels, and per capita income. The Gini coefficients are based on recent surveys of income distribution.

The quality of a government's economic management is assessed through performance indicators of fiscal policy (ratio of debt to gross domestic product [GDP]), monetary policy (central bank independence), and trade policy (outward orientation). For monetary and trade policy, we were able to use indexes that capture, to some degree, the institutional orientation of government. The central bank independence index is based on the legally stated independence of the central bank. The outward orientation index includes a component of investors' perceptions of the receptivity of a government to trade. Unfortunately, the fiscal policy index, the debt-to-GDP ratio, is a particularly imperfect measure of institutional orientation. This limitation is offset to some degree by the historical perspective it provides, since debt is a cumulative measure of a country's fiscal policies. The indexes of fiscal and monetary policy may be subject to a bias against poor countries. It is possible, for example, that the debt-to-GDP ratio may be biased against countries that are growing rapidly, regardless of the quality of their economic management, since public investment typically has very long term payoffs. Or, conceivably, a country with a poorly developed revenue collection system may find monetization of debt to be the most efficient form of financing. However, neither of these indexes is strongly correlated with income, suggesting that bias, if it exists, is not strong.

A more general question regarding bias is whether aggregating these indexes introduces a systematic bias toward or against any country or group of countries. For example, does the better availability of data from developed countries mean that these countries, as a group, are rated higher or lower than least-developed countries? Or, does the composition of these indexes by Western-oriented academicians, businessmen, and economists lead to a bias against governments that are pursuing alternative goals? The answer to the first question is that it seems unlikely. The answer to the second question is yes, although ideological differences are more likely to develop over the weights applied to each objective rather than over which objectives should be included. The index is flexible enough that adjustments could easily be made if one wishes to argue, say, that citizen participation is not a relevant component of governance quality.

The issue of the appropriate weight of each category is clearly a sensitive one. For example, should a government that creates a favorable economic climate but lacks political freedoms be judged a higher- or lower-quality government than one that provides political freedom but hinders economic growth? Where possible, our answer has been to give each of these categories equal weight. This was done, in part, to convey a sense of impartiality to the process. More important, this approach places no excessive emphasis to any single index. This is important given the nature of the indexes used—some of them are, by necessity, subjective and others may reflect assessments that may change quickly. Equal weighting means that potential biases or errors do not unduly influence the composite index.

With the exception of the social development index, all component indexes were given equal weight. For social development, the HDI coefficient, Λ, was given a weight of 0.80 because of the broad, encompassing nature of the HDI (see annex 2.A for compilation techniques, sources, and limitations of these indexes). The results are presented for 80 countries in table 2.2. The indexes used to create this index were modified in two ways. First, indexes for which higher numbers represented worse governance (Gini and debt-to-GDP) were inverted. Second, all indexes were rescaled so that each has a mean of 50. The outward orientation index required additional modification to combine the initial 1980–83 index with the speed of integration index for 1980–83 to 1990–93. In cases where the underlying index did not provide an assessment of countries in our sample, we have extrapolated index numbers based on the performance of comparable countries (see annex 2.B for component indexes).

There is a high correlation between governance quality and per capita income—countries of the Organisation for Economic Co-operation and Development (OECD) dominate the top governance category and none are in the two categories with the poorest governance. Conversely, there are no African countries in the top governance category. The correlation between the index of governance quality and per capita GDP appears to be much stronger than its weight of 6.7 percent (through the HDI) would suggest. This high correlation between governance quality and per capita GDP raises

TABLE 2.2 Ranking of Countries on Governance Quality

Country	Governance quality index	Country	Governance quality index
(a) Good Governance			
Switzerland	75	France	60
Canada	71	Czech Republic	60
Netherlands	71	Belgium	58
Germany	71	Malaysia	58
United States	70	Israel	57
Austria	70	Trinidad and Tobago	57
Finland	68	Korea, Rep. of	57
Sweden	67	Greece	55
Australia	67	Spain	55
Denmark	67	Hungary	54
Norway	67	Costa Rica	54
United Kingdom	66	Uruguay	54
Ireland	66	Italy	53
Singapore	65	Chile	53
New Zealand	64	Argentina	52
Japan	63	Jamaica	52
(b) Fair Governance		*(c) Poor Governance*	
Romania	50	Egypt, Arab Rep. of	40
Panama	50	Morocco	40
Venezuela, R. B. de	50	China	39
South Africa	50	Kenya	39
Poland	49	Honduras	38
Mexico	48	Indonesia	38
Saudi Arabia	48	Cameroon	38
Jordan	48	Nicaragua	37
Peru	48	Nepal	36
Oman	48	Pakistan	34
Ecuador	48	Nigeria	33
Colombia	47	Ghana	32
Tunisia	47	Zambia	29
Russian Federation	46	Togo	29
Brazil	46	Uganda	28
Turkey	46	Yemen, Rep. of	28
Sri Lanka	45	Senegal	28
Paraguay	45	Sierra Leone	26
Philippines	44	Malawi	26
Zimbabwe	44	Iran, Islamic Rep. of	26
Thailand	43	Zaire	25
India	43	Rwanda	22
Côte d'Ivoire	42	Sudan	20
Papua New Guinea	41	Liberia	20

Source: Authors' calculations.

the question of causality. If demand for high governance quality is driven by high per capita income, then an index of governance quality will simply reflect per capita income. Or, if there are necessary preconditions for high per capita income, such as outward economic orientation and workforce education, then high per capita income will reflect high governance quality.

It seems likely to us that causality runs both ways—some components of governance do enhance the likelihood of higher per capita income, and higher per capita income does increase the demand for higher-quality governance. The challenges for those postulating a relationship between governance quality and income that runs in only one direction are the outliers—why, for example, is Ireland's per capita income so low given its high governance quality or, if causality runs the other way, why does the Czech Republic have such good governance, given its per capita income?

The good performance of European countries is not limited to Western Europe. The Central and East European countries (as well as Latin American countries) have combined improvements in citizen participation and economic management with relatively high marks for social development. Strong geographical patterns appear in all parts of the world—European countries govern well, African and South Asian countries govern poorly, Latin American and East Asian countries are somewhere in the middle. One possibility these patterns raise is that those countries' standards for governance quality may be influenced by the performance of their neighbors.

In table 2.3 we have shown correlation coefficients for several factors that may influence, or may be influenced by, governance quality: per capita purchasing power parity (PPP) income, GDP growth, and military spending.

TABLE 2.3   Governance Index Correlation Coefficients

	Governance Index	Income	Military (as % govt spending)	Annual Growth (85–94)
Governance	1.00	0.89 (0.00)	−0.16 (0.22)	0.25 (0.03)
Income		1.00	−0.11 (0.42)	0.26 (0.03)
Military			1.00	0.10 (0.47)
Annual growth				1.00

Sources: Income and Growth from World Bank (1996b), Military and Subnational Expenditures from International Monetary Fund (1995).

The strong positive correlation between income and governance quality supports the casual observations drawn above. The negative correlation of military spending with governance quality is not statistically strong, but it does suggest that it may be governments that are being defended rather than countries. The positive correlation between the 10-year economic growth rate and governance quality supports the argument that the institutional focus of government is an important determinant in economic development. Also, since the highest-income countries have generally not had the highest growth rates over the last decade, the positive correlation between higher growth and better governance suggests that good governance improves economic performance rather than vice-versa.

Impact of Fiscal Decentralization on Governance Quality

During the past half century, developing countries have, in general, followed a path of centralization. As a result, these countries are more centralized today than industrial countries were in their early stages of development (Boadway, Roberts, and Shah 1994). The economic framework developed in the fiscal federalism literature addresses the question of the appropriate level of centralization by assigning taxing, spending, and regulatory responsibility to various levels of government and their interface with the private sector and the civil society at large. This framework argues for the assignment of a responsibility to the lowest level of government that can internalize benefits and costs of decision making for the specific service (Shah 1994). The subsidiary principle adopted by the European Union conforms to this view by requiring that the assignment of responsibility should be to the lowest level of government unless a convincing case can be made for a higher-level assignment. A number of recent developments, discussed below, are prompting these countries to have a second look at this issue, and almost all developing countries with populations greater than 20 million are rethinking their fiscal arrangements.

Major catalysts for change include the demise of capitalism, national government failures, subnational government failures, assertion of basic rights by the courts, globalization of economic activities, and the demonstration effects of the European Union (Shah 1995). The demise of communism prompted a major change in government organization and the geographical boundaries of some countries. In other countries, national governments have failed to ensure regional equity, economic union, central bank independence, a stable macroeconomic environment, or local autonomy. The record of subnational governments is also not very commendable. Subnational governments have often followed "beggar thy neighbor" policies, sought to "free-ride" with no accountability and, in pursuit of narrow self-interest, often undermined national unity.

The judicial systems in some countries are also providing stimuli for change by providing a broader interpretation of basic rights and requiring that national and subnational legislation conform to the basic rights of citizens. The emergence of a new, essentially borderless world economy complicates this picture by bringing new challenges to constitutional federalism. These challenges arise from the decline of nation states in carrying out regulation of certain economic activities as borders have become more porous and information technology has weakened their ability to control information flows. The European Union's policies and principles regarding subsidiarity, fiscal harmonization and stabilization checks are also having demonstrable effects on country policies.

The overall impact of these influences is to force a rethinking on assignment issues and to force a jurisdictional realignment in many countries around the globe. In developing countries, rethinking these arrangements has led to gradual decentralization of responsibilities to lower levels in a small but growing number of countries. Some writers have cautioned against such a shift in division of powers in a developing country environment and have highlighted the "dangers of decentralization" (Prud'homme 1995; see also Tanzi 1996). These authors have expressed concerns ranging from macro mismanagement, to corruption, increased red tape, and the widening gulf between rich and poor regions under decentralized fiscal systems. Sewell (1996) and McLure (1995) provide rejoinders to these concerns by marshaling conceptual arguments and anecdotal evidence in support of their viewpoints.

In the following section, we reflect on various elements of the dangers of decentralization, on the basis of available empirical evidence. In relating decentralization to quality of governance, four aspects of governance quality are stressed: citizen participation, government orientation, social development, and macroeconomic management.

Citizen Participation

Citizen participation ensures that public goods are consistent with voter preferences and public sector accountability. Such participation is possible only if political freedom (voice and exit) is permitted and political stability prevails. We combined individual rankings of countries on these indicators to develop a composite index of citizen participation. We find that both subindexes are positively correlated with fiscal decentralization. The correlation coefficients in table 2.4 indicate that this relationship is statistically significant, which suggests that citizen participation and public sector accountability go hand in hand with decentralized public sector decision making.

Government Orientation

Public sector orientation plays an important role in public sector performance. If the public service is oriented toward serving its citizens, bureaucratic red tape and corruption will be minimal and the judiciary will further enforce accountability through timely and fair decisions in the administration of justice. Such an orientation is typically lacking in some developing countries, where the civil service pursues rent seeking and power and influence through command and control and bureaucratic red tape and graft.

A composite ranking of countries on three indicators of government orientation—judicial efficiency, bureaucratic efficiency, and lack of corruption—provides a good indicator of public sector orientation and performance. We relate the degree of expenditure decentralization to the ranking of countries

TABLE 2.4   Correlation of Subnational Expenditures with Governance Quality Indicators

	Pearson correlation coefficients
Citizen Participation	
Political Freedom	0.599**
Political Stability	0.604**
Government Orientation	
Judicial Efficiency	0.544**
Bureaucratic Efficiency	0.540**
Absence of Corruption	0.532**
Social Development	
Human Development Index	0.369*
Income Distribution (inverse of Gini coefficient)	0.373*
Economic Management	
Central Bank Independence	0.327*
Inverse of Debt to GDP Ratio	0.263
Outward Orientation	0.523**
Governance Quality Index	0.617**

*Pearson correlation coefficient is significant at the 0.05% level (2-tailed test).
**Pearson correlation coefficient is significant at the 0.01% level (2-tailed test).

on individual indicators as well as to the composite rank on government orientation and find that all these correlations show a positive, and statistically significant, association (see table 2.4). This suggests that typically decentralized countries are more responsive to citizen preferences in service delivery and strive harder to serve their people than centralized countries. Several case studies corroborate these findings. Crook and Manor (1994), Meenakshisundaram (1996), based on a review of experience of the Indian state of Karnataka, and Blair (1996), based on the Philippines' more recent experience with decentralization, conclude that decentralized democratic governance had a positive impact on the quality of governance especially in reorienting government from a command and control to a service provider role (see also Blair and Hansen 1994). Landon (1996) carried out a study of education costs in Canada and concluded that local control regimes were more successful in controlling overhead costs than were provincial control regimes. Humplick and Moini-Araghi (1996) report that for a large sample of countries decentralization leads to lower unit administration costs for road services. Gurgur and Shah (2002) find that centralization of authority is an important determinant of the incidence of corruption for a sample of 30 countries. A synthesis of recent literature presented on this subject by Shah, Thompson, and Zou (2004) also supports this conclusion (see also Huther and Shah 2000; Shah and Schacter 2004).

Social Development

Two aspects of social development are considered: human development and income inequality. For ranking countries in terms of their achievements on human development, we rely solely on the United Nations' index on human development. This index incorporates life expectancy, adult literacy, educational enrollments, and per capita GDP in PPP terms. The egalitarian nature of the society is captured by an inverse rank on the Gini coefficients estimated by Deininger and Squire (1996). Table 2.4 shows that fiscal decentralization is positively correlated and statistically significant with both indexes.

Macroeconomic Management

It is frequently argued that a decentralized public policy environment of the type found in developing countries contributes "to the aggravation of macroeconomic problems" (Tanzi 1996, 305). In the following, we reflect on the available empirical evidence on aspects of monetary and fiscal policies to form a perspective on this issue.

Monetary Policy

Monetary policy is clearly a central function and best entrusted to an independent central bank (Shah 1994). The critical question then is whether or not independence of the central bank is compromised under a decentralized fiscal system. One would expect, a priori, that the central bank would have greater independence under a decentralized system since such a system would require clarification of the rules under which a central bank operates, its functions, and its relationships with various governments. For example, when Brazil in 1988 introduced a decentralized federal constitution, it significantly enhanced the independence of the central bank (Bomfim and Shah 1994). However, in centralized countries the role of the central bank is typically shaped and influenced by the ministry of finance. In an extreme case, the functions of the central bank of the United Kingdom, the Bank of England, are not defined by law but have developed over time by a tradition fostered by the U.K. Treasury.

For a systematic examination of this question, we relate the evidence presented in Cukierman, Webb, and Neyapti (1992) on central bank independence to a share of subnational expenditures in total spending. The correlation coefficient in table 2.4 shows a weak but positive association, confirming our a priori judgment that central bank independence is strengthened under decentralized systems. Increases in the monetary base caused by the central bank's bailout of failing state and nonstate banks represents an important source of monetary stability and a significant obstacle to macroeconomic management. In Pakistan, which is a centralized federation, both the central and provincial governments have in the past raided nationalized banks. In Brazil, which is a decentralized federation, state banks have made loans to their own governments without due regard for their profitability and risks. A central bank role in ensuring arm's length transactions between governments and the banking sector would enhance monetary stability regardless of the degree of centralization.

The empirical evidence presented suggests that such arm's length transactions are more difficult to achieve in countries with a centralized structure of governance than under a decentralized structure with a larger set of players. This is because a decentralized structure requires greater clarity on the roles of various public players, including the central bank.

Fiscal Policy

In a centralized country, central government assumes the exclusive responsibility for fiscal policy. In decentralized countries, fiscal policy becomes a responsibility shared by all levels of government, and the federal (central) governments in these countries use their powers of the purse (transfers) and moral suasion through joint meetings to induce a coordinated approach. Several writers (Tanzi 1996; Wonnacott 1972) have argued, without empirical corroboration, that the financing of subnational governments is likely to be a source of concern within open federal systems because subnational governments may circumvent federal fiscal policy objectives. Tanzi (1996) is also concerned with deficit creation and the debt management policies of junior governments. Available theoretical and empirical work does not provide support for the validity of these concerns. On the first point, at a theoretical level, Sheikh and Winer (1977) demonstrate that relatively extreme and unrealistic assumptions about discretionary noncooperation by junior jurisdictions are needed to conclude that stabilization by the central authorities would not work at all simply because of this lack of cooperation. Their empirical simulations for Canada further suggest that failure of a federal fiscal policy in most instances cannot be attributed to uncooperative junior governments' behavior. Saknini, James, and Sheikh (1996) further demonstrate that, in a decentralized federation with markedly differentiated subnational economies with incomplete markets and nontraded goods, federal fiscal policy acts as an insurance against region-specific risks. Therefore decentralized fiscal structures do not compromise any of the goals sought under centralized fiscal policies.

On the second point noted by Tanzi, empirical evidence from a number of countries suggests that, while federal fiscal policies typically do not adhere to the European Union's guidelines that deficits should not exceed 3 percent of GDP and debt should not exceed 60 percent of GDP, junior governments policies typically do. This is true both in decentralized federal countries such as Canada and in centralized federal countries such as India and Pakistan. Centralized countries do even worse on these indicators. For example, Greece, Turkey, and Portugal do not satisfy the European Union guidelines. The results in table 2.4 provide weak confirmation of our empirical observations—the coefficient, while positive, is not statistically significant at the 95 percent confidence level.

Outward Orientation

Economic liberalization is now commonly accepted as a cornerstone of good economic management. The World Bank has recently ranked countries on the openness of their economies, taking into account factors such as gross national product (GNP) originating from trade, manufacturing exports, foreign direct investment as a share of GDP, credit rating, and manufacturing content of exports. This index is related to the degree of expenditure decentralization and finds a positive relationship between these two indicators.

Economic Management

When we combine the three aspects of economic management considered above in an index of the quality of economic management, the result shows a positive association with the degree of fiscal decentralization. This is to be expected, because the decentralized systems are more transparent in defining the role of various public agents and place a greater premium on accountability for results.

Quality of Governance and Decentralization

Finally, we combine indexes on economic management, social development, government orientation, and citizen participation to derive an overall index of governance quality. This index is then related to the degree of fiscal decentralization. Given the positive correlation between all of the governance quality component indexes and the composition of government expenditures, the positive relationship between fiscal decentralization and governance quality is unsurprising. What may be surprising is the strength of this correlation: if one assumes that the mix of national and subnational expenditures is an explanatory variable for governance quality, the resulting ordinary least squares regression yields an R^2 of 0.38 (the coefficient on subnational expenditures was 53.07, with a standard error of 10.99).

Causality

The relationship between the level of decentralized expenditures and governance quality appears to be strictly increasing, but clearly there must be some form of Laffer curve. It is easy to construct cases where complete decentralization of expenditures would lead to lower quality governance than where there is a mix of national and subnational expenditures. However, the data do not show that even the most highly decentralized governments have increased decentralization at the expense of lowering the quality of governance. This suggests that highly centralized countries can improve their governance quality through more decentralized expenditures without the risk of engaging in excessive decentralization.

In conclusion, recent discussions on the appropriate level of decentralization of fiscal expenditures have largely been theoretical or anecdotal (for example, see Prud'homme 1995 and Sewell 1996). The decentralization side of this debate cites efficiency gains from greater voice for local constituents while the centralized side cites efficiency gains from economies of scale (often from consolidating human or physical capital). The conclusion of the value of greater decentralization was informed by examining the relationship of fiscal decentralization to various individual and composite measures of quality of governance. At an empirical level, it appears that governance quality may be enhanced by greater decentralization. It should be noted however, that this analysis is a macroeconomic one and cannot be applied to specific expenditures. Even at the theoretical level, the appropriate mix of national and subnational roles and thereby expenditures differs by sector (or, even by project).

Reservations

As a starting point, we accept the caveats offered by the authors of the individual indexes that we have used. These caveats generally note that the indexes are meant to convey a general placement of countries rankings rather than precise assessments of country's relative performance. In addition, the authors generally acknowledge the potential for errors in individual rankings, since many of the indexes rely on subjective judgments or limited surveys. It can be argued that aggregation may offset the statistical biases associated with the techniques and biases of the individual indexes. A larger issue is less an econometric one than a theoretical one, relating to the weights applied to each component index. Our approach of applying equal weights to each component index is open to criticism that one component, say citizen participation or social development, should be weighted more heavily than another, say economic management. Making adjustments to these weightings would influence the rankings of individual countries, but our preliminary impression is that such adjustments would not affect the general trends noted here.

Omissions

Many of the indexes used in the governance index did not cover all of the countries that we have included in our sample. In cases where index numbers were not available (see table 2.5), we sought assessments of the relative performances of missing countries from World Bank staff. The majority of missing cases were from Africa, although indexes of government orientation were also missing for Central Europe. Estimates for missing values were made by senior members of the World Bank's Operations Evaluation Department (OED).

Of the 80 countries for which we were able to construct the governance index, subnational expenditure data were available for only 40. These countries[2] are fairly well distributed across per capita income groups and geographic regions, although developed countries are more strongly represented in this group than the larger group for which the governance index was calculated.

TABLE 2.5   Omissions from Original Indexes

Index	Omitted (%)
Political Freedom	6
Political Stability	28
Judicial Efficiency	28
Red Tape	28
Corruption	20
Human Development	0
Gini Coefficient	19
Outward Orientation	0
Central Bank Independence	30
Debt / GDP Ratio	21

Conclusion

Discussions and policy work regarding the role, scope, and effectiveness of government have typically taken place in the absence of empirical measures of governance quality. This chapter introduces a measurement that will allow both theoretical work and policy issues to be discussed in the framework of a concrete definition of governance quality. The definition we have used could easily be modified to reflect different beliefs about the relevance of the components used in this index. The index could also be narrowed or broadened to reflect differences in beliefs about the role and scope of government.

The application of this index to the decentralization debate shows that the polarization of opinion in the absence of hard empirical evidence can be overcome with the use of an appropriate standard of reference such as the one used here. The use of this index allows us to reach unambiguous conclusions regarding the net positive effects of fiscal decentralization on public sector performance in a majority of countries.

Notes

1. See Huther and Shah (1998) for an earlier version of this paper. Subsequently a vast literature has emerged following Huther and Shah methodology but providing a more comprehensive coverage of governance indicators.
2. Argentina, Australia, Austria, Belgium, Brazil, Canada, Chile, Colombia, Czech Republic, Denmark, Finland, France, Germany, Hungary, India, Indonesia, Iran, Ireland, Israel, Italy, Kenya, Malawi, Malaysia, Mexico, Netherlands, Norway, Pakistan, Paraguay, Philippines, Poland, Romania, South Africa, Spain, Sweden, Switzerland, Thailand, Uganda, United Kingdom, United States, and Zimbabwe.

References

Blair, Harry. 1996. "Supporting Democratic Local Governance: Lessons from International Donor Experience—Initial Concepts and Some Preliminary Findings." Paper presented at the American Political Science Association Meetings, San Francisco, CA, August 29–September 1.

Blair, Harry, and Gary Hansen. 1994. *Weighing in on the Scales of Justice.* USAID Program and Operations Assessment Report 7. Arlington, VA: USAID Development Information Services Clearinghouse.

Boadway, Robin, Sandra Roberts, and Anwar Shah. 1994. "The Reform of Fiscal Systems in Developing and Emerging Market Economies: A Federalism Perspective." Policy Research Working Paper Series 1259, World Bank, Washington, DC.

Bomfim, Antulio, and Anwar Shah. 1994. "Macroeconomic Management and the Division of Powers in Brazil: Perspectives for the 1990s." *World Development* 22 (4): 535–42.

Crook, Richard, and James Manor. 1994. *Enhancing Participation and Institutional Performance: Democratic Decentralization in South Asia and West Africa.* London: Overseas Development Administration.

Cukierman, Alex, Steven Webb, and Bilin Neyapti. 1992. "Measuring the Independence of Central Banks and Its Effect on Policy Outcomes." *World Bank Economic Review* 6 (3): 353–98.

Deininger, Klaus, and Lyn Squire. 1996. "Measuring Income Inequality: A New Data Base." *World Bank Economic Review* 10 (3): 565–91.

de Soto, Hernando. 1989. *The Other Path: The Invisible Revolution in the Third World.* New York: Harper & Row.

Gurgur, Tugrul, and Anwar Shah. 2002. "Localization and Corruption: Panacea or Pandora's Box." In *Managing Fiscal Decentralization,* ed. Ehtisham Ahmad and Vito Tanzi, 46–67. London and New York: Routledge Press.

Hansen, Gary. 1996. *Constituencies for Reform.* USAID Program and Operations Assessment Report No. 12. Arlington, VA: USAID Development Information Services Clearinghouse.

Haq, Mahbub ul. 1995. *Reflections on Human Development.* New York: Oxford University Press.

Humplick, Frannie, and Azadeh Moini-Araghi. 1996. "Optimal Structures for Decentralized Provision of Roads." *Journal of Infrastructure Systems* (September): 127–38.

Huther, Jeff, and Anwar Shah. 1998. "Applying a Simple Measure of Good Governance to the Debate on Fiscal Decentralization." Policy Research Working Paper 1894, World Bank, Washington, DC.

———. 2000. "Anti-Corruption Policies and Programs: A Framework for Evaluation." Policy Research Working Paper 2501, World Bank, Washington, DC.

Huther, Jeff, Sandra Roberts, and Anwar Shah. 1997. "Public Expenditure Reform under Adjustment Lending: Lessons from World Bank Experiences." Discussion Paper 382, World Bank, Washington, DC.

IMF (International Monetary Fund). 1995a. *Government Finance Statistics Yearbook.* Washington, DC: IMF.

———. 1995b. *International Finance Statistics.* Washington, DC: IMF.

Landon, Stuart. 1996. "Education Costs and Institutional Structure." Department of Economics Research Paper 96-4, University of Alberta, Edmonton, Canada.

Mauro, Paolo. 1995. "Corruption and Growth." *Quarterly Journal of Economics* 109: 681–712.

McLure, Charles E. 1995. "Comment on Prud'homme." *World Bank Research Observer* 10 (2): 112–17.

Meenakshisundaram, S. S. 1996. "Rural Development through Decentralized Governance—An Indian Experience." Paper for the World Bank Conference on Environmentally Sustainable Development, Rome, September 25–27.

Picciotto, Robert. 1995. "Putting Institutional Economics to Work." World Bank Discussion Paper 304, World Bank, Washington, DC.

Prud'homme, Rémy. 1995. "On the Dangers of Decentralization." *World Bank Research Observer* 10 (2): 201–10.

Saknini, Humam, Steven James, and Munir Sheikh. 1996. "Stabilization, Insurance, and Risk Sharing in Federal Fiscal Policy." Unpublished working paper. Ottawa: Department of Finance.

Sewell, David. 1996. " 'The Dangers of Decentralization' According to Prud'homme: Some Further Aspects." *World Bank Research Observer* 11 (1): 143–50.

Shah, Anwar. 1994. *The Reform of Intergovernmental Fiscal Relations in Developing and Emerging Market Economies.* Washington, DC: World Bank.

———. 1995. "Design of Economic Constitutions." *Canadian Economic Journal,* 29 (Suppl. 1): 614–18.

———. 1998a. "Balance, Accountability, and Responsiveness: Lessons about Decentralization." Policy Research Working Paper 2021, World Bank, Washington, DC.

———. 1998b. "Indonesia and Pakistan: Fiscal Decentralization—An Elusive Goal? In *Fiscal Decentralization in Developing Countries,* ed. Richard M. Bird and François Vaillencourt, 115–51. New York: Cambridge University Press.

Shah, Anwar, and Mark Schacter. 2004. "Combating Corruption: Look before You Leap." *Finance and Development* 41(4): 40–43.

Shah, Anwar, Theresa Thompson, and Heng-fu Zou. 2004. "The Impact of Decentralization on Service Delivery, Corruption, Fiscal Management, and Growth in Developing and Emerging Market Economies: A Synthesis of Empirical Evidence." *CESifo Dice Report* 2 (Spring): 10–14.

Sheikh, Munir A., and Stanley L. Winer. 1977. "Stabilization and Nonfederal Behavior in an Open Federal State: An Econometric Study of the Fixed Exchange Rate, Canadian Case." *Empirical Economics* 2 (3): 195–211.

Tanzi, Vito. 1996. "Fiscal Federalism and Decentralization: A Review of Some Efficiency and Macroeconomic Aspects." In *Annual World Bank Conference on Development Economics, 1995,* 295–316. Washington, DC: World Bank.

Transparency International and Gottingen University. 1996. "Corruption Index." http://www.gwdg.de/~uwvw/icr.htm.

UNDP (United Nations Development Programme). 1996. *Human Development Report 1996.* New York: Oxford University Press.

Wonnacott, Paul. 1972. "The Floating Canadian Dollar." American Enterprise Institute for Public Policy Research, Washington, DC.

World Bank. 1992. *Governance and Development.* Washington, DC: World Bank.

———. 1994. *Governance—The World Bank's Experience.* Washington, DC: World Bank.

———. 1996. *Global Economic Prospects and the Developing Countries.* Washington, DC: World Bank.

Annex 2.A: Sources and Quality of Data and Explanations Regarding Development of Component Indexes

Sources of Data

Various indexes used to create the governance quality index are described below:

- *Political Freedom (Haq 1995).* This index measures four factors that reflect an individual's ability to exercise political freedom: a country's political process, its statutory freedoms, an individual's ability to exercise freedom of expression, and the degree to which discrimination is tolerated.
- *Political Stability, Judicial Efficiency, Red Tape (Mauro 1995).* These indexes, developed by Business International Corporation, are unavoidably subjective. These indexes were developed with an investor's perspective in mind. This perspective may lead to different assessments of, say, judicial efficiency than an index with a less pecuniary perspective. These indexes, which we have not been updated, are based on older data than the other indexes—1980–83.
  - *Corruption (Transparency International and Gottingen University 1996).* This index, frequently updated, is based on survey results from several risk assessment consulting groups, the Global Competitiveness Report, and the Institute for Management Development.
  - *Human Development Index (UNDP 1996).* This index, published by the United Nations Development Programme, measures life expectancy, adult literacy, enrollments in primary, secondary, and tertiary education institutions, and per capita GDP in purchasing power parity terms.
  - *Gini Coefficients (Deininger and Squire 1996).* These estimates of income equality are based on household surveys, which are presented by the authors as a substantial improvement over previous work in both data quality and coverage.
  - *Outward Orientation (World Bank 1996).* This index uses an initial assessment of outward orientation made for 1980–83 and modifies it according to the speed of integration index calculated for 1990–93. The factors composing the index are a population-adjusted trade ratio, the country credit rating by Institutional Investor, foreign direct investment as a share of GDP (in PPP terms), and the share of manufacturing that is exported.
  - *Central Bank Independence (Cukierman, Webb, and Neyapti 1992).* This index is compiled from examination of 16 statutory aspects of central bank operations, including the terms of office for the chief

executive officer, the formal structure of policy formulation, the bank's objectives (as stated in its charter), and limitations on lending to the government.

● *Debt-to-GDP Index. Compiled from IMF (1995a, 1995b)* using data from most recent year available.

Quality of Indexes

For detailed information on the component indexes used, we refer those interested to the original works for discussions of the index strengths and weaknesses. In cases where the indexes have been produced for several years (HDI and Gini coefficients), the authors have had time to respond to criticisms of the initial versions. The indexes used from Mauro (1995) were constructed by a commercial organization, Business International Corporation, which sells updated versions. Presumably, the version made public by Mauro is old enough that its commercial (and, perhaps, academic) value is low. Unfortunately, an updated version was out of the range of our research budget.

The political freedom index created by Haq is new both in the sense that there are no previous versions and in that it addresses a topic that had previously not been subjected to formal indexing. The corruption index is updated annually and reflects the results of several surveys on bureaucratic honesty. The outward orientation index is an updated version of an index first created in the mid-1980s. The central bank independence index is relatively new and represents the legal characteristics of a country's central bank. As the authors note, there is often a discrepancy between the statutory independence of a central bank and its independence in practice. The authors attempted to capture this effect, by developing a second index that measures the frequency of turnover of heads of central banks. This second index has not been incorporated into this paper because of the small number of countries covered.

Note that although all of these indexes have been published in the past three years, the data from Mauro (1995) and from Cukierman, Webb, and Neyapti (1992) are somewhat older. This may bias results for, or against, specific countries that have experienced rapid change since the early 1990s. The Mauro indexes, for example, have assessments of Liberia and Nigeria that, given more recent events, seem high. The indexes have not been adjusted to reflect these changes, in order to preserve the internal consistency of these indexes.

Adjustments to Indexes

The following adjustments were made to the indexes that are components of the Governance Index:

- Political Freedom: mean shifted to 50.
- Political Stability, Red Tape, Judicial Efficiency: mean shifted to 50.
- Corruption: unchanged.
- Human Development Index: mean shifted to 50.
- Gini Coefficients: 10 – sqrt(Gini), mean shifted to 50.
- Outward Orientation: ln (speed of integration index) used as percentage change, then applied to initial index; mean shifted to 50.
- Central Bank Independence: mean shifted to 50.
- Debt-to-GDP Index: 2 – debt-GDP, mean shifted to 50.

Means were shifted as follows: Initial index number × 50 / Average of initial index.

Annex 2.B: Composite Indexes

Composite indexes are shown in the table below.

Country	Citizen participation	Government orientation	Social development	Economic management
Good Governance				
Switzerland	67	86	65	85
Canada	64	83	66	72
Netherlands	65	86	66	69
Germany	62	74	64	85
United States	66	80	64	71
Austria	65	73	65	78
Finland	66	83	65	60
Sweden	66	83	65	59
Australia	61	83	63	65
Denmark	65	83	64	60
Norway	68	84	64	54
United Kingdom	61	78	66	62
Ireland	60	74	63	67
Singapore	59	86	60	59
New Zealand	64	88	64	48
Japan	62	76	64	52
France	64	65	62	52
Czech Republic	59	54	62	66
Belgium	62	72	66	40
Malaysia	54	59	54	64
Israel	52	75	61	45
Trinidad and Tobago	59	53	58	58
Korea, Rep. of	51	52	62	63
Greece	60	47	63	52
Spain	56	52	66	48
Hungary	57	52	62	48
Costa Rica	62	46	58	51
Uruguay	64	53	56	45
Italy	59	43	63	52
Chile	49	69	57	42
Argentina	57	46	55	52
Fair Governance				
Jamaica	57	50	49	52
Romania	50	48	55	49
Panama	54	58	55	37
Venezuela, R. B. de	55	36	57	55
South Africa	52	56	42	50
Poland	55	54	60	32
Mexico	49	42	54	48

(continued)

Country	Citizen participation	Government orientation	Social development	Economic management
Saudi Arabia	32	48	55	63
Jordan	49	58	52	36
Peru	44	53	48	46
Oman	40	41	50	62
Ecuador	51	42	53	46
Colombia	47	40	55	50
Tunisia	46	40	51	53
Russian Federation	54	32	59	46
Brazil	50	37	51	48
Turkey	48	38	48	50
Sri Lanka	46	51	49	36
Paraguay	46	43	46	44
Philippines	44	36	46	52
Zimbabwe	46	63	37	34
Thailand	43	30	56	50
India	50	37	35	53
Côte d'Ivoire	53	58	29	37
Papua New Guinea	54	29	36	52
Poor Governance				
Egypt, Arab Rep. of	45	34	45	37
Morocco	38	52	40	32
China	38	25	46	56
Kenya	42	36	34	44
Honduras	45	37	39	33
Indonesia	40	24	48	46
Cameroon	42	42	35	32
Nicaragua	46	44	40	24
Nepal	45	39	29	35
Pakistan	41	24	36	38
Nigeria	44	22	32	41
Ghana	34	31	37	26
Zambia	38	24	31	25
Togo	37	22	30	27
Uganda	40	24	27	24
Yemen, Rep. of	28	28	26	31
Senegal	39	22	26	27
Sierra Leone	36	22	18	31
Malawi	31	28	25	20
Iran, Islamic Rep. of	20	14	52	29
Zaire	32	18	28	22
Rwanda	14	20	29	29
Sudan	18	22	29	16
Liberia	11	32	24	18

Source: Authors' calculations.

3

Assessing Local Government Performance in Developing Countries

MATTHEW ANDREWS AND ANWAR SHAH

Decentralization is common in many developing countries. Local governments are becoming more numerous in such countries and are increasingly required to play larger roles in providing services, alleviating poverty, and facilitating development (Mitlin 2000). Given the important role local governments are being called to play, central governments and development organizations are starting to ask how well they are doing (and how they can be improved). The problem with asking such questions is that criteria for evaluating local governments in developing countries remain poorly formed: What does a "good" local government look like in the developing world? What factors should one consider when evaluating local governments in such settings?

This chapter is written to address such questions, with the aim of identifying criteria for evaluating local governments in developing countries. It takes a mixed practice-theory approach to identifying such evaluation criteria. The practice element builds on existing evaluations practice at the local level in developed countries such as the United States, which typically focuses on issues of legal conformance and fiscal health. The theory dimension introduces concerns about responsiveness, efficiency, and accountability, with the potential for gains in these areas underlying dominant arguments in favor of decentralization and local-level governance. The approach recognizes that local governments in developing countries face their own special issues, and that evaluation criteria identified for use in such settings must be easily accessible, facilitating an observation-based analysis (and requiring limited resources).

Evaluation Criteria

Local government evaluation practice in developed countries generally focuses on issues of conformance and fiscal health. The conformance focus manifests in evaluations of whether local entities conduct their operations within the legal parameters set for them, and whether they adopt processes required (either by law or by some other professional standard setting entity, such as the Governmental Accounting Standards Board [GASB]). The fiscal health emphasis is reflected in evaluations of resource use in local government, with the usual focus being the level of fiscal discipline evident in financial management processes.

The main evaluation mechanisms in these local governments are embedded in financial and accounting management systems and in the process of fiscal evaluation undertaken by outside rating agencies in countries such as the United States. The influence of such mechanisms and the prevalence of this kind of evaluation leads Foltin to say that local governments in the United States have "focused principally on financial reporting and other financial matters . . . and legal compliance" (Foltin 1999, 43). Even recent evaluations in the United States and beyond, designed to emphasize performance, tend to analyze conformance to specific best-practice internal management processes and fiscal outcomes (examples include the Government Performance Project and the Local Government and Public Service Reform Initiative work in Central and Eastern Europe).

Legal and process conformance and fiscal health are important criteria for evaluating local governments in developing countries as well. Given that local entities are created by law and use public resources to fulfill their duties, it is important that they operate within the parameters of legislation and ensure an adequate level of fiscal health and discipline. Where local-level evaluations have been undertaken in the developing world, these considerations have often been the dominant (and often the only) criteria (as reflected in a 1993 evaluation conducted by the Harvard Institute for International Development in Indonesia [HIID 1993]).

Relying on this dominant practice is problematic, given that theoretical arguments in favor of decentralization and the formation of local governments identify potential decentralization gains in other areas of interest, government responsiveness, efficiency, and accountability to citizens (Tiebout 1956; Oates 1972; Shah 1998). Issues related to these areas also require evaluation, especially in developing countries, where local governments are often created in response to low responsiveness, efficiency, and accountability in central governments. In such situations local governments are required not only to operate according to legislation and manage their finances well, but also to provide the right services (in response to citizen need), in the right (or most efficient) way, and with the highest degree of accountability to constituents.

Combining the five focal areas yields the following broad criteria for evaluating local governments in developing countries: conformance to legislative and process requirements, fiscal health, responsiveness, efficiency, and accountability to citizens. All five can be further broken down into more specific criteria relevant to the developing country experience in general. To ensure that the approach taken in this chapter is pragmatic and facilitates observation-based analysis, such specific criteria are introduced with reference to examples of effective and ineffective local governments in developing countries.

Evaluating Conformance to Legislation and Process

Local governments in developed and developing countries come into being because of legislative action. Legislation defines the powers, functions, and responsibilities of local governments. As such, academic and practitioner local government evaluations in developed and developing countries appropriately derive their foundational evaluation criteria from legal (and quasi-legal) sources. These criteria typically concentrate on local government conformity with legislation (and other formal requirements) regarding the setting and upholding of bylaws, the generation and collection of revenues, the following of process requirements in resource disbursement, and the provision of services.

There are numerous studies of local-level legislative activity in countries such as the United States, generally investigating whether municipalities pass the kinds of laws they are meant to (and usually focused on local-level policing and the regulation of private markets). Such studies have also been extended to the developing world, with researchers evaluating whether municipalities set and uphold the laws they are required to, and whether they use their law-setting powers to facilitate development in their jurisdictions. A positive example of such analysis relates to the setting of legislation in Cebu City in the Philippines (UNESCO 2001). The city passed Ordinance 1344 to creatively facilitate the development of low-cost housing, allowing the use of a trust fund generated from the sale of city-owned lots exclusively for shelter and its related expenditures. The city also used its law-setting ability to increase the participation of vendors' associations in market management (which is recognized by the Revised Market Code). Finally, the city minimized red tape that was hampering service delivery by instituting the Systems and Procedures Rationalization in Government (SPRING) regulations. Halfani (1997) provides an example of a municipality not fulfilling its legal role effectively. He writes that "a large sphere of urban life" in Nairobi "has operated outside the regulatory and directive authority of the formal system" (188) because the municipality failed to set and uphold laws as required. In such situations the failure of the local government to comply with its de jure role can lead to social instability and disorganization in commercial activities.

The legal mandate faced by municipalities also relates to their revenue-raising activities. Laws typically limit both the kinds of revenues that local governments can raise and the ways in which they can raise different revenue types. In the United States evaluators must commonly ask whether governments are raising revenues in a legally sustainable way (such that the method of revenue raising does not clash with legislation). The Proposition 13 debate in California, for example, examined whether the process of collecting property taxes (and valuing property) was legal, or whether it contravened equal treatment clauses in the national constitution. In developing countries legislation tends to shape revenue-raising abilities of local governments. Local governments are required to adhere to such legislation. In the Republic of Korea, for example, local governments are given access to certain taxes (mostly regulation- and property-based) and are disallowed from using any kind of sales or income tax to raise revenues (Shin and Ha 1998). In South Africa local governments have a set of tax and user-charge instruments identified in law and face a limit on lending. Section 10 of the 1996 Local Government Transition Act states that municipal loans are not backed by provincial or national governments: "Any money borrowed by a municipality in accordance with this subsection and the interest thereon, shall be the financial obligation of the municipality concerned and shall be chargeable to and payable from the revenues and assets of that municipality" (South African President's Office 1996, Section 10 G 8(c)). It is important to identify whether governments in such situations raise revenues in accordance with such limitations, because if they do not, then their revenue-raising performance will not be sustainable.

Similarly, local government budgeting and procurement processes are typically shaped by national-level legislative requirements (or formal regulations developed by quasi-legislative agencies). In the United States formal regulations emanate from the GASB and other entities, requiring certain kinds of budgeting processes and reporting standards. This is also the case in developing countries, with an example coming from the 1991 Philippines Local Government Code. Chapter 3 of the Code outlines requirements for the budgeting and financial reporting process in local governments. Section 314, for example, requires (among other things) that local government budgets provide summaries of financial statements that set forth income and expenditures during the preceding year, estimates of income for the ensuing year (determined within legal parameters), estimated expenditures required to carry out all local government functions in the year, all essential facts regarding long-term obligations and the indebtedness of the local government unit, and other financial statements and data deemed necessary to "disclose in all practicable detail the financial condition of the local government unit" (Government of the Philippines 1991, Section 314 b.3.vii). In this situation it is important to ask whether municipalities complied with the requirements.

Similar process requirements in developing countries relate to planning and participation. In Cebu City in the Philippines, the city government responded positively to such requirements and adopted various schemes to give substance to partnerships in accordance with the Local Government Code. The most common is the special project contractual type of arrangement. For instance, the Cebu People's Multi-Purpose Cooperative serves the needs of microenterprises (Etemadi 2000; UNESCO 2001).

Contrasting experience to this positive evidence of legislative conformity comes from Dhaka and Bangladesh (Islam and Khan 1996). The Dhaka Metropolitan Area governments faced significant legislation requiring planning and participation, but the municipalities in the area are recorded as not having any planning program and not being very participatory. Similarly, in Bangladesh about 120 municipalities have a mandate to propose and implement plans, but none of them has any planning department or even an official urban planner. Another negative example comes from Bolivia, where the Law of Participación Popular was intended to change national and local power structures by requiring the participation of poor groups in resource allocation decision-making processes. Andersson (1999) conducted a social study involving interviews of local officials and citizens, and found that participation has not yet happened in the municipality of Caiza.

Apart from the processes of budgeting and resource allocation, local governments also face legislated mandates regarding the type of service toward which they have to allocate resources. Legislation typically identifies such functional responsibilities along with requirements related to service quality and standards. In this light, the South African Local Government Transition Act of 1993 provides a basic reference point for evaluating municipal performance by identifying the following as duties of local governments: "Water supply, sewerage purification, electricity if so agreed by all the individual local government bodies, refuse removal, roads and stormwater drainage, health services, emergency services, financial administration, and any other service agreed upon" (Section 7 (c)(i)(aa)). Local government studies in this setting typically begin by asking, "Are the local governments providing these services?" The general answer to such a question is yes, with most governments at least fulfilling the basic services mandate (providing water supply, sanitation, and electricity services). But legislation in South Africa and other countries often stipulates the functional responsibility further, specifying who should receive services and what standard services should be met. The South African Constitution commits to providing water, electricity, and sanitation to all, for example, while most local governments typically serve fewer than two-thirds of their constituents. Mitlin (2000) suggests that many local governments in developing countries would fail on a legislative requirement for a full-service provision: "It is clear that in most urban centers, local governments fail to meet many of their responsibilities to large sections of the population within their jurisdiction" (3).

This line of questioning is seen in the United States, where theoretical and practical evaluations of local government often ask whether local entities (school boards) provide the appropriate standard of education to all citizens. It is also pertinent in countries such as Tanzania, where local governments have a legal role in providing primary schooling (Therkildsen 1998). Local governments are required to do more than provide primary education: They are bound by a national mandate to provide the same standard education for all citizens. "Good performing" local governments provide such standard education according to such mandate, while "poor performing" local governments provide varying quality of education.

Legal conformance in areas such as service provision, budget process development, revenue-raising activity, and local regulatory activity thus provides a foundation for evaluating local governments. This kind of evaluation can also be useful in providing guidance as to temporal limitations, and complexities and even inconsistencies with the institutional setting in which local government find themselves (and which will factor into any evaluation). This knowledge can help evaluators to determine why a local government is performing as it is, and to provide appropriate advice for remediation or improvement. In South Africa, for example, local governments failed to provide services to all citizens in 1996 because territories were expanded in that year (thus creating a temporal limitation on local governments' abilities to abide by legislation). In Tanzania the provision of education is considered problematic, in that legislation simultaneously devolves significant responsibility to local governments so that they can shape education provision to local needs, and then requires the standardization of provision (Therkildsen 1998). In Nairobi, the poor regulatory performance of the city is explained as the result of a "disabling" legal context that limited resource access for the municipality and made it difficult for such to abide by legal requirements (Halfani 1997).

Evaluating Fiscal Health

Fiscal health factors are closely related to the legislative criteria for evaluating local governments. In most settings, local governments are required to manage their fiscal matters carefully, ensuring that they do not overspend and that their expenditure is in line with their mandate (as it is generally represented in the budget or as it is stipulated in national-level policy documents or legislation).

In countries such as South Africa such requirements are legislated, with municipalities and districts allowed to spend money only in accordance with agreed-upon budgets, and not allowed to run a deficit on their operating accounts. Municipalities that overspend are considered poor performers because they create a fiscal burden for their constituents (reducing their ability to allocate resources to services in future periods because of debt-servicing commitments). Municipalities that spend differently from their mandate are also considered poor performers, because their budget implementation does not match their stated objectives (unless, of course, there are valid reasons for the difference between the budget plan and implementation).

The basic criteria for identifying poor fiscal health on the expenditure side are widely known and easily observed from standard financial statements and budgets: high (and sustained) deficits and debt, poor allocations (with significant resources going to administration rather than to capital maintenance, for example), and a disjunction between planning allocations and implementation. In terms of these criteria, the literature and popular press are flush with examples of poor-performing governments. The 1998 White Paper in South Africa (DPLG 1998, Section A, 2.2) reflects on this: "Combined with service backlogs, collapsed or deteriorating infrastructure, and deteriorating creditworthiness and borrowing capacity, municipalities are experiencing financial stress, and in some instances crisis." Press reports connected to this statement relate the fact that, by September 1997, local governments in South Africa owed R 10 billion to various lending institutions and service providers such as Eskom (the electricity producer) (Kihato 1998). As further reflected in the press reports, this kind of debt led municipalities such as Nelspruit (the capital of Mpumalanga province) to suspend capital projects and caused a 58 percent reduction in Johannesburg's capital budget, resulting in "the provision and maintenance of infrastructure [being] affected dramatically" (Kihato 1998).

Not all governments are poor performers in this category, however. Two large cities in South Africa, Durban and Cape Town, were initially given strong favorable evaluations by policy makers and in the popular press because of their low deficits, high capital and service expenditures, and strong adherence to stated budgetary goals. Both municipalities have recently been experiencing some financial difficulties, however, running deficits and displaying fiscal vulnerability. This shows the time-specific nature of the fiscal health evaluation criteria, which can portray a healthy city in one year (with low deficits, for example) and a vulnerable city the next (with high deficits, for example).

The fiscal health criteria are also only as reliable as the budget and financial reporting process that determines the financial figures. In countries such as China, local government off-budget revenues and expenditures were extremely large in the mid-1990s, introducing "a degree of non-transparency in the fiscal process" (Arora and Norregaard 1997, 20) and yielding deficits and allocations figures unreliable in judging true fiscal health. Evaluators in such instances are required to examine not only the figures reflecting fiscal health on the expenditure side, but also the processes by which expenditures are reported. Niesner (1999, 32) describes this evaluation requirement thus: "Check compliance with accounting controls—whether rules had been followed, procedures had been established, proper accounting had been made, and controls were in place and functioning."

In tandem with the requirement that governments maintain discipline on the expenditure side, the literature also stresses that fiscally healthy local governments should have their own reliable revenue sources (Bird 1993; Oates 1993). An evaluation of this aspect of fiscal health requires analyzing the size of the local revenue base (the potential local resources available to the government) and the revenue effort on display (the actual local resources raised as a percentage of the potential). As with other aspects of the fiscal health evaluation criteria, there is a strong overlap with legislation in this area. Legislation often determines the size of the revenue base by defining tax and user-charge abilities of local governments. Local initiatives within such legislated parameters tend to determine performance in terms of revenue effort, however. It is not uncommon to find local governments collecting revenues inefficiently in developing countries—for example, using outdated modes of property evaluation or measurement of service access (such as electricity use).

Governments that perform well in terms of the revenue criteria of the fiscal health factor are identified as those that maximize the size of their revenue base while ensuring that they do not create social inefficiencies when levying taxes or user fees (Bird 1993). Examples of such governments include those in South Africa that have developed debtor follow-up mechanisms and indigent debtor policies to ensure that all constituents pay for services received as they are able and Cebu City's use of computerized assessment and appraisal procedures related to property taxes. Further examples include Abidjan's establishment of neighborhood committees to engage the resources of communities in addressing economic and infrastructure problems (DPLG 2000)[1] and the government partnership with community-based organizations for tax collection in the Sikasso commune in Mali (Attahi 1997).[2] In all these examples the municipalities are seen to be addressing their need for a strong local revenue source by enhancing their abilities to access the revenue base (through creative administrative and managerial methods).

A further way in which municipalities are seen to do this is through passing legislation that improves the functioning of their tax or fee mechanisms. In Kenya, local governments changed their system of having multiple business licenses to having one single business permit so as to simplify their licensing process. The move resulted in an expansion of the tax base (with all economic activities now included in the instrument) and a streamlined licensing process (reducing their own collection costs as well as those of businesses). The tax has enhanced their fiscal status by increasing revenues (Devas and Kelly 2001).

These examples show that fiscal health is about both the recorded numbers on financial statements and the processes underlying such numbers. Both the numbers and processes are generally accessible to evaluators and form a conventional source of evaluation information. Together with conformance to legislation, the fiscal health criteria are commonly used to evaluate governments in the developing world. Decentralization literature holds, however, that a fiscally healthy local government, one that spends responsibly and has a reliable and sizeable local revenue source, can be considered effective only if it uses such resources in responsive, efficient, and accountable ways (Oates 1972, 1993; Shah 1998).

Evaluating Responsiveness

Proponents of decentralization argue that, in a democratic context, these reforms lead to greater responsiveness to constituent demands, with local candidates having to please voters (who are indeed their neighbors). Oates (1993) builds the case for decentralized finance on the presumed responsiveness of local governments to their constituents' welfare. These perspectives underlie a large portion of the theoretical argument in favor of decentralization: Local governments are more likely to provide the right services than are higher-level governments. They also offer a practical appeal in the developing country context, where local governments are often created in reaction to the low levels of responsiveness by central governments. But literature and practical experience show that not all local governments are responsive to their constituents, even if they conform to legislation and maintain high levels of fiscal health (Oates 1993).

In a municipal case from South Africa, for example, observers found that spending "decisions are often directed by a bureaucratic agenda and citizens' inputs are limited," constraining the potential for local government responsiveness (Foundation for Contemporary Research 1999, 45). In the Bolivian context, Andersson (1999) observes that administrators see poverty reduction as a hindrance to other economic development objectives and ignore the demands of *campesinos* (peasants) (Mörner 1987; Harris 1995). In both cases the lack of local government responsiveness (especially to the poor) results from the structure of local government processes and manifests in suboptimal spending activity at the local level. Such processes and outcomes constitute the criteria for assessing responsiveness performance in local governments in developing countries.

Given the experience in the literature, two aspects of the local government's process of service provision require specific attention in any evaluation of responsiveness: the level of local political influence on allocation decisions and the level of civic participation in the decision-making process. The extent of the poverty focus in local government allocations in developing countries is identified as a key outcomes indicator of responsiveness.

The literature shows that local-level responsiveness is eroded by a high level of political influence from the central government on the decisions of the local government about service provision. Benjamin (2000) finds that higher-level government political and administrative appointments created a hierarchical structure in Bangalore that made local governments more responsive to central and regional government demands than they were to the needs of local constituents. Devas and Korboe (2000) have a similar finding in their study of Kumasi in Ghana, where local political and administrative representatives were strongly influenced by the central government, with the chief executive of the district and 70 percent of the local assembly appointed by central entities. They also found that the Kumasi local government was not very accountable or responsive to its own citizens. In this light, Mitlin (2000, 8) notes that the "influence of links with higher levels of government on local governments" seriously impedes the responsiveness of local entities.[3] In terms of such studies, it is apparent that local-level responsiveness is enhanced where politicians and administrators are appointed locally through regular democratic processes, resources are sourced locally, and political representatives are required to involve citizens in allocation decisions and implementation monitoring activities (Blair 2000).

According to such criteria, the county of Pérez Zeledón in Costa Rica provides an example of a high evaluation case (at least in terms of service responsiveness processes). A county representative championed the development of a program giving local citizens direct authority over discretionary funds allocated to them from higher levels of government (Breslin and Campbell 1999). These discretionary funds were traditionally used by representatives to develop lines of patronage and clientelism in their communities, but they are now channeled directly to district councils for local allocation. The district councils have to show evidence of direct consultation with their citizens when using the funds. This requirement is a shift from the old top-down approach of deciding spending allocations (Breslin and Campbell 1999). The literature suggests that the resource allocation process is more responsive and communities can see work being targeted and completed (Optiz 1998; IADB 2000). There is evidence that administrators are receiving more precise demands for actual results and public entities in the county are more responsive and output oriented than in other counties, borne out in lower relative response times to disasters.

The Pérez Zeledón case speaks to the importance of community participation in enhancing the responsiveness of local governments. Mitlin (2000) argues that participatory local governments tend to be responsive governments as well. She cites a number of cases of model participatory programs at the local level in which citizen voice was elicited from all parts of the local community (not just the wealthy) and where local politicians and administrators took citizen comments seriously (by recording and responding to them all, for example). These include the healthy cities program in León, Nicaragua; the environment and development programs in Ilo, Peru, and in Colombia; and the participatory budgeting programs in Belo Horizonte and Porto Alegre, Brazil.

The Porto Alegre case is an excellent example of a participatory program that enhances local government responsiveness. The participatory budget in Porto Alegre (the capital of the state of Rio Grande do Sul) involves citizen representation on a Budget Council and a Budget Forum. Community representatives discuss the budget in these settings, with their contributions taken up by a specially developed administrative unit, the Planning Cabinet (Gaplan), which processes community demands and transforms them into government plans. A Community Relations Coordination Committee works with Gaplan to maintain active records of participation and ensure that the community and its representatives receive feedback on the manner in which their demands affect plans. The number of citizen interactions with government through this process increased from 1,000 in 1989 to 10,000 in 1993, with 64.5 percent of participants classified as poor.

This case can be contrasted with conventional forms of participation in local government structures in developing countries that often fail to enhance responsiveness (especially to the poor). In South Africa, for example, local governments are required to involve citizens in budgeting processes, but seldom do so effectively (Putu 2001; Andrews 2003). In the Lichtenburg municipality, where poverty levels were above 50 percent in 1996, case reports state that although participatory mechanisms were in place, administrators selectively ignored citizen inputs emerging from public meetings: "Problem perceptions, which were not in line with facts and figures or the professional judgment of officials and councilors, were excluded" (DCD-GTZ 1999: North West Province Study, 4). A similar story emerges from the Thaba Nchu local government, where the participation approach was mostly seen to "reflect a compliance approach" with information collected from disadvantaged groups becoming "lost" in the process (DCD-GTZ 1999: Free State Study, 17, 18). In such cases, although poor communities had the mechanisms to participate, their participation was muted and did not empower them or increase their municipality's responsiveness to their needs.

Apart from those process aspects that distinguish responsive local governments from nonresponsive local governments in developing countries, the literature also emphasizes evaluating responsiveness in terms of the pro-poor perspective evident in budget allocations. Poverty is a constant in the developing world, and responsiveness to local need necessarily implies responsiveness to poverty-related issues in such settings. In this regard Mitlin (2000) observes that all municipalities in the developing world play a major role in providing services that are critical for the poor, but that "The critical role of basic services in reducing poverty is often forgotten or dismissed" (5). Authors such as Mitlin (2000) and Porio (1997) identify a number of indicators of the pro-poor perspective in local governments, including the amount spent on housing and the rehabilitation or upgrading of slums and squatter areas, the amount spent on developing new infrastructure for provision of basic services (such as water, electricity, and sanitation) and in providing such services in poor areas, and the locally financed activities aimed at stimulating small, informal commercial enterprises (such as the provision of accommodation for hawkers or the improvement of street trading facilities).

These indicators are generally open to evaluation in a practical sense, with observers being able to see the results of local government interventions in poor areas. Where it is not evident that local governments are providing services in poor areas (or developing infrastructure for such), or where local governments are repressing informal traders, it is obvious that the government has not adopted a pro-poor attitude. In the developing world context this is tantamount to saying that the local government has adopted a stance of limited responsiveness (being responsive to elite demands rather than general constituent demands). In situations where governments detail their fiscal allocations processes, such observation-based evaluation can be supplemented with references to budgets and financial statements. An NGO called DISHA (Developing Initiatives for Social and Human Action) was able to access and analyze provincial budgets in Western India to identify expenditures going to poor groups, largely because the provincial budget was very detailed and legislation allowed civic access to such detail (DISHA 2000). In their evaluation process, they initially found that the provincial government was very unresponsive to the needs of the poor.[4]

Evaluating Efficiency

As with responsiveness, theory presents potential efficiency gains as a major reason why governments should decentralize. Oates (1993, 240) states, "The basic economic case for fiscal decentralization is the enhancement of economic efficiency." Similarly, Arora and Norregaard (1997, 4) state, "An important rationale for establishing a decentralized government . . . is to improve economic efficiency."[5] Simply put, the argument is that local governments not only are more likely than higher-level governments to provide the right services, but also are more likely to provide these services in the right way. But not all local governments provide services efficiently. The city of Bamako in Mali was known to have particularly inefficient public sanitation systems, for example, with 90 percent of the expensive individual drainage systems being nonfunctional and most residents tipping liquid waste onto public streets

(DPLG 2000). This kind of waste could be identified through active evaluation of efficiency.

Local government efficiency has a number of components, including cost efficiency and competitiveness. The decentralization literature assumes that local governments will provide services at a lower cost than larger governments and in a competitive way, because of the presence of alternative service providers (including other local governments) (Tiebout 1956). This assumption is particularly based on the argument that citizens can voice their disapproval of inefficient service provision (through voice mechanisms) or can exit inefficient jurisdictions (in favor of other jurisdictions or nongovernmental producers in their own jurisdiction). Efficiency can be evaluated either by examining the costs and competitiveness of fiscal outcomes, or by examining the voice and exit mechanisms in place in local governments (and the effect they have on production and provision behavior).

A study shows, for example, that the efficiency of Bamako's cesspool operations improved significantly in the 1990s, with records of decreased service costs and improved service quality (and competitiveness) (DPLG 2000). In the 1990s the municipality decreased the cost of drainage by 80 percent and built 1,800 new cesspools (DPLG 2000). These efficiency and related productivity gains, as reflected in easily identifiable outcomes, mirror those reported on in the best U.S. city government experiences. In the case of residential street sweeping in San Diego, for example, service regularity increased in the late 1990s from once a year to between five and ten times a year, with costs decreasing at the same time (Andrews and Moynihan 2002). The gain is even greater in terms of commercial sweeping services (whereby roads in commercial areas are cleaned). The efficiency gains in this setting are easily identified because the city directly compares costs and service access with private alternatives.[6]

Local government efficiency can also be evaluated in terms of the processes used in service production. San Diego's efficiency gains are largely related to the fact that the city adopted a managed competition initiative to stimulate competition between city service departments and private firms offering similar services (Andrews and Moynihan 2002). In doing so, the local government clearly identified the exit options citizens enjoyed (with citizens able to use private alternatives instead of the city entities). Competitive pressure arising from such identification led to the city adopting an approach to benchmarking its performance against private alternatives, which facilitated internal service improvements. Similarly, Bamako's efficiency gains were the result of a creative production arrangement between the city and an NGO called Jigui (DPLG 2000). The NGO proposed that residents be responsible for 37 percent of the costs of cesspool construction, and that 63 percent be covered through a government special development fund. It played a coordinating role with the community and managed the cesspool operations. In creating this collaboration, the Bamako city government created the capacity for alternative service provision (by the NGO) as well as a civil society source of commentary about the efficiency of government service provision. The new exit and voice options stimulated a more competitive performance in providing service.

Other examples of local governments producing services through processes that enhanced efficiency include Cebu City, Buenos Aires, and Ahmedabad. Cebu City developed a process of comparing service performance in city projects (similar to a benchmarking process) and allocated extra resources to projects that performed well, and to NGOs with a track record of delivering in areas related to poverty alleviation (Etemadi 1997). The Ramón Aboitiz Foundation Inc. was subcontracted to manage relief and rehabilitation work in the aftermath of Typhoon Ruping, for example, while the NGO Pagtambayayong was brought in to rehabilitate urban poor districts. Buenos Aires privatized water and sanitation services to Aguas Argentinas, automatically creating an alternative service provider (Hardoy and Schusterman 2000). Although the privatization had its problems (with the city not structuring the agreement to include an incentive for the private firm to serve poor people), it still reflected an attempt to improve government efficiency. The city of Ahmedabad adopted innovative service provision arrangements and financing when it involved itself in a number of strategic partnerships in urban development. One of these is with the Slum Networking Project, which worked with slum dwellers as partners to redevelop a street (Dutta 2000). In this case the creative service provision arrangement improved efficiency and facilitated greater responsiveness to the needs of poor constituents (the government was able in this instance to produce the right services in the right way).

Evaluating Accountability

Alongside improved responsiveness and efficiency, enhanced accountability is often seen as an expected gain from decentralization. Bird (1993) identifies accountability gains as a central theme in localist arguments. These gains are largely expected because decentralization shifts government authority closer to the people (Shin and Ha 1998). As with responsiveness and efficiency, however, accountability gains are not always evident in local governments. Such gains require evaluation to establish an effective view of the quality of local governance.

The word *accountability* is most often used in relation to governance processes as it refers to political accountability to citizens.[7] In terms of decentralization theory, local-level representatives are meant to be more accountable to their constituents. The theory assumes that local constituents have the ability to call such representatives to account for their actions and for their performance, and to discipline or reward representatives accordingly. This is only possible where political representation is highly localized, however, and citizens have information about government performance and voice and exit channels that can effectively be used to ensure the accountability of their representatives. This is not the case in many governments, where citizens typically lack information about performance and the mechanisms necessary for voicing a response.

Governments commonly internalize information and elevate the knowledge of technical, managerial, and political elites over the local "time-place" knowledge of grassroots actors and constituents. Such transparency-reducing approaches (and the devices associated with them) underscore an official and unofficial limit on citizen information access—information is not provided to social groups because their input is not valued or required in the governance process—and legitimizes the exclusion of citizens (especially poor citizens) from decision making. It reinforces an inward, managerial model of governance and prohibits local-level accountability.

Cases where local government accountability has improved in recent years are remarkably different, exhibiting high levels of information dissemination to society at large. Information is disseminated through NGOs in some cases (as in Bangalore's Report Card [Paul 1996] and DISHA's [2000] budget demystification activities). In other cases local governments themselves report on performance information or process detail in highly public venues (with Hong Kong being a prominent example [Lam 1997]). The 1991 Local Government Code in the Philippines requires that local governments report on performance, facilitating strong accountability links between citizens and their representatives. Section 316(h) of the Code requires local governments to

> conduct semi-annual review and general examination of cost and accomplishments against performance standards applied in undertaking development projects. A copy of this report shall be furnished to the local chief executive and the Sanggunian concerned, and shall be posted in conspicuous and publicly accessible places in the provinces, cities, municipalities and Barangays. (Government of the Philippines 1991, Section 316 h).

In such cases, access to performance information (especially when benchmarked against goals or comparable alternatives) facilitates a challenge by citizens against the "obscurantist and remote culture of the bureaucracy, and reinforces democratic notions regarding the obligations of government officials and elected representatives as public servants" (Jenkins and Goetz 1999, 605).

In order for citizens to hold local governments accountable, however, they need channels through which they can mount such challenges (and respond to information they receive). Strong monitoring and evaluation and voice and exit mechanisms facilitate this, and are notably lacking in many local governments (Paul 1992, 1996). The most basic of these mechanisms is the regular political choice process (in which citizens have an opportunity to voice their response to whatever evidence they have of their political representatives' performance). Local governments in countries such as Nigeria lack even this mechanism, with representatives appointed by central government and citizens limited in their ability to voice approval or disapproval for local government performance (Onibokun 1997). Political representatives in such settings are unaccountable to local citizens largely because the mechanisms that facilitate citizen influence are missing. In contrast, cities that would be candidates for a high evaluation on the accountability criteria have active electoral processes in place and/or other voice mechanisms that citizens can use to call their representatives to account for performance. Cebu City, for example, facilitates citizen engagement through rallies, forums, audiences with the mayor, participation in local planning bodies, and the creation of citizen monitoring entities (Etemadi 2000). Citizen voice is actively recorded in such settings, and in many cases there is evidence that local officials respond directly to those participating through such settings (to indicate how their input affected decisions or outputs in the governance process).

A final area in which the literature increasingly suggests that accountability requires evaluation relates to local-level innovation. In many local governments, privatization and other forms of service production are being pursued in rather unaccountable ways, leading to low levels of service provision for constituents. Benin City in Nigeria privatized a number of its services, including solid waste, for example. The privatized system left a lot to be desired, with regressive patterns of service access in evidence (Ogu 2000). The problem in Benin City lay not in the idea of privatization, but in the fact that the government appeared to view this kind of innovation as a way out of accountability (washing its hands of responsibility for provision following the privatization). The lesson is that innovative solutions to public sector problems need to be developed within the context of general accountability, and they should be evaluated in such context as well. This is particularly important in low-income areas, where market solutions to public problems need to be extremely well developed to avoid regressive effects.

Conclusion

This chapter asks the questions: What does a good local government look like in the developing world? What factors should one consider when evaluating local governments in such settings? In response five factors were identified as constituting the broad criteria on which evaluators of local governments should concentrate. Combining the discussion of each factor, a model local government would

- conform to legislation in process and structure
- maintain its fiscal health (in outcomes and processes)
- do the right things (be responsive)
- do them in the right way (with maximum efficiency)
- be accountable to its constituents (in processes and for its outputs and outcomes)

This view of local government is founded on practice and theory, and examples of good and bad local governments show some detail of what is meant in terms of each factor. Each of the five factors (legislative conformance, fiscal health, responsiveness, efficiency, and accountability) is multidimensional and requires evaluation in terms of both processes and outcomes. Such evaluation is argued to provide a more complete, applied, and appropriate view of local government quality in developing countries than other alternatives, which typically concentrate on legal conformance and fiscal health alone. The evaluation approach is also designed to facilitate observation-based evaluation, so that interested parties will be able to identify good local governments in the developing world by what they see.

Notes

1. In this case community committees work with the municipality to improve street cleaning, garbage collection, security services, road maintenance, street lighting, and collection of taxes and user fees associated with such service provision. They have collected $120,000 in fees and have mobilized $20,000 for specific projects, including infrastructure development.
2. In this case the community-based organizations assisted in tax collection, and the collection rate increased by 300 percent in 10 months.
3. Kharoufi (1997) provides a specific example of this effect in Morocco. The author writes that the hierarchical structure in which local governments are located significantly impedes responsiveness: "A multiplicity of agencies and commissions may be appointed to initiate projects which give little importance to local constraints or to the overall aspects of the urban renewal problem" (71).

4. DISHA's Participatory Budget Analysis program has demystified the process of governance through pro-active budgetary analysis involving pro-poor NGOs. The budget analysis has helped to keep government accountable for general money flows and policy decisions. The press and local activist groups have a device to assist them in understanding what government does, thus closing the power gap between informed bureaucrats and uninformed citizens (DISHA 2000).

5. Another reference emphasizing the importance of efficiency is provided by Bird (1993, 207): "Many developing countries are turning to various forms of fiscal decentralization as one way of escaping from the traps of ineffective and inefficient governance."

6. The information regarding San Diego's performance in these areas comes from an interview with Ed Plank in August 1998 as well as documentation provided by Mr. Plank.

7. Accountability in this sense means "holding individuals and organizations responsible for performance measured as objectively as possible" (Paul 1996, 37).

References

Andersson, Vibeke. 1999. "Popular Participation in Bolivia: Does the Law 'Participación Popular' Secure Participation of the Rural Bolivian Population?" Working Paper 99.6, Center for Development Research, Copenhagen.

Andrews, Matthew. 2003. "New Public Management and Democratic Participation: Complementary or Competing Reforms? A South African Study." *International Journal of Public Administration* 26 (8–9): 991–1015.

Andrews, Matthew, and Don Moynihan. 2002. "Why Reforms Don't Always Have to 'Work' to Succeed: A Tale of Two Managed Competition Initiatives." *Public Performance and Management Review* 25 (3): 282–97.

Arora, Vivek, and John Norregaard. 1997. *Intergovernmental Fiscal Relations: The Chinese System in Perspective.* Washington, DC: International Monetary Fund, Asia and Pacific Department and Fiscal Affairs Department.

Attahi, Koffi. 1997. "Decentralisation and Participatory Urban Governance in Francophone Africa." In *Governing Africa's Cities,* ed. Mark Swilling, 161–210. Johannesburg: Witwatersrand University Press.

Benjamin, Solomon. 2000. "Governance, Economic Settings, and Poverty in Bangalore." *Environment and Urbanization* 12 (1): 35–56.

Bird, Richard. 1993. "Threading the Fiscal Labyrinth: Some Issues in Fiscal Decentralization." *National Tax Journal* 46 (June): 207–27.

Blair, Harry. 2000. "Participation and Accountability at the Periphery: Democratic Local Governance in Six Countries." *World Development* 28 (1): 21–39.

Breslin, P., and D. Campbell. 1999. "Giving a Community the Authority to Distribute Public Funds Creates a Dynamic of Efficiency and Accountability." *Grassroots Development* 22 (1): 28–30.

DCD-GTZ (Department of Constitutional Development and German Technical Corporation). 1999. *Integrated Development Planning Pilot Projects Assessment Study.* Pretoria: South African Department of Constitutional Development.

Devas, Nick and Roy Kelly. 2001. "Regulation or Revenues? An Analysis of Local Business Licences, with a Case Study of the Single Business Permit Reform in Kenya." *Public Administration and Development* 21 (5): 381–92.

Devas, Nick, and David Korboe. 2000. "City Governance and Poverty: The Case of Kumasi." *Environment and Urbanization* 12 (1): 123–35.

DISHA (Developing Initiatives for Social and Human Action). 2000. Presentation D. Mistry, PREM Network, World Bank, Washington, DC.

DPLG (Department of Provincial and Local Government). 1998. "White Paper on Local Government." Pretoria, South Africa.

———. 2000. "Examples of Innovation in Local Government." http://www.local.gov.za/DCD/dcdindex.html.

Dutta, Shyam S. 2000. "Partnerships in Urban Development: A Review of Ahmedabad's Experience." *Environment and Urbanization* 12 (1): 13–26.

Etemadi, Felisa U. 2000. "Civil Society Participation in City Governance in Cebu City." *Environment and Urbanization* 12 (1): 57–72.

Foltin, Craig. 1999. "State and Local Government Performance: It's Time to Measure Up!" *Government Accountants Journal* 48: 40–46.

Foundation for Contemporary Research. 1999. *A Review of Integrated Development Planning in the Western Cape.* Cape Town, South Africa: Foundation for Contemporary Research.

Government of the Philippines. 1991. Local Government Code. Republican Act No. 7160. http://www.comelec.gov.ph/laws/lgc_b2t5ch3.html#sec314.

Halfani, M. 1997. "The Governance of Urban Development in East Africa." In *Governing Africa's Cities,* ed. Mark Swilling, 115–60. Johannesburg, South Africa: Witwatersrand University Press.

Hardoy, Ana, and Ricardo Schusterman. 2000. "New Models for the Privatization of Water and Sanitation for the Urban Poor." *Environment and Urbanization* 12 (2): 63–75.

Harris, Olivier. 1995. "The Sources and Meaning of Money: Beyond the Market Paradigm in an Ayllu of Northern Potosí." In *Ethnicity, Markets, and Migration in the Andes: At the Crossroads of History and Anthropology,* ed. Brooke Larson and Olivier Harris. Durham, NC: Duke University Press

HIID (Harvard Institute for International Development in Indonesia). 1993. "Incorporating Provincial Opinion in the Evaluation of Local Government Fiscal Capacity in Indonesia." Development Discussion Paper 472, HIID, Cambridge, MA.

IADB (Inter-American Development Bank). 2000. "Ensuring Transparency and Accountability in Hurricane Reconstruction and Transformation." http://www.iadb.org/regions/re2/consultative_group/groups/transparency_workshop_3.htm.

Islam, Nazrul, and Muhammed Mohabbat Khan. 1996. "Urban Governance in Bangladesh and Pakistan." In *Cities and Governance,* ed. Patricia L. McCarney: University of Toronto, ON: Centre for Urban and Community Studies.

Jenkins, Rob, and Anne-Marie Goetz. 1999. "Accounts and Accountability: Theoretical Implications of the Right-to-Information Movement in India." *Third World Quarterly* 20 (3): 603–22.

Kharoufi, M. 1997. "Governance of Urban Society in North Africa." In *Governing Africa's Cities,* ed. Mark Swilling, 37–84. Johannesburg, South Africa: Witwatersrand University Press.

Kihato, Caroline. 1998. "No Development without Money." *Weekly Mail and Guardian,* February 6. http://archive.mg.co.za/.

Lam, Newman M. K. 1997. "Transformation from Public Administration to Management: Success and Challenges of Public Sector Reform in Hong Kong." *Public Productivity and Management Review* 20(4): 405–18.

Mitlin, Diana. 2000. "Towards More Pro-Poor Local Governments in Urban Areas." *Environment and Urbanization* 12 (1): 3–11.

Mörner, Magnus. 1987. "The Indians as Objects and Actors in Latin American History." In *Natives and Neighbors in South America,* ed. Harald Skar and Frank Salomon. Göteborg: Göteborgs Etnografiska Museum.

Niesner, Helen. 1999. "Local Government Auditing—Improving the Performance of Government in the Next Century." *Government Accountants Journal* 48: 32–38.

Oates, Wallace. 1972. *Fiscal Federalism.* New York: Harcourt Brace Jovanovich.

———. 1993. "Fiscal Decentralization and Economic Development." *National Tax Journal* 46: 237–43.

Ogu, Vincent I. 2000. "Private Sector Participation and Municipal Waste Management in Benin City, Nigeria." *Environment and Urbanization* 12 (2):103–17.

Onibokun, P. 1997. "Governance and Urban Poverty in Anglophone West Africa." In *Governing Africa's Cities,* ed. Mark Swilling, 85–114. Johannesburg, South Africa: Witwatersrand University Press.

Optiz, S. 1998. "Community Participation in Rural Road Maintenance." *Gate Magazine* 3.

Paul, Samuel. 1992. "Accountability in Public Services: Exit, Voice and Control." *World Development* 20: 1047–60.

———. 1996. "Strengthening Public Accountability through Participation." In *Participation in Practice,* ed. Jennifer Rietbergen-McCracken. World Bank Discussion Paper 333, World Bank, Washington, DC.

Porio, Emma. 1997. "Urban Governance and Poverty Alleviation in Southeast Asia." In *Urban Governance and Poverty Alleviation in Southeast Asia,* ed. Emma Porio, 1–40. Quezon City, Philippines: Global Urban Research Initiative.

Putu, Mpho. 2001. "Ward Committees Will Encourage Community Participation." *Khanyisa,* Issue 0. Cape Town, South Africa: IDASA.

Shah, Anwar. 1998. *Balance, Accountability, and Responsiveness: Lessons about Decentralization.* Operations Evaluation Department, Country and Regional Evaluation Division. Washington, DC: World Bank.

Shin, Roy, and Yeon-Seob Ha. 1998. "In Search of Decentralization and Deconcentration: Local Autonomy and Fiscal Reform in Korea." *Journal of Public Budgeting, Accounting and Financial Management* 10: 192–218.

South African President's Office. 1996. Local Government Transition Act Second Amendment, No. 97 of 1996. Pretoria: Government of South Africa.

Therkildsen, Ole. 1998. *Local Government and Households in Primary Education in Tanzania: Some Lessons for Reform.* Center for Development Research Working Paper 98.6. Center for Development Research, Copenhagen.

Tiebout, Charles. 1956. "A Pure Theory of Local Expenditures." *Journal of Political Economy* 64 (5): 416–24.

UNESCO (United Nations Educational, Scientific, and Cultural Organization). 2001. *Partnerships for Poverty Alleviation in Cebu City.* MOST Clearing House for Best Practices. http://www.unesco.org/most/bppover.htm.

4

Results Matter

Suggestions for a Developing Country's Early Outcome Measurement Effort

HARRY P. HATRY

The manager of a soccer team needs a running score of the game. The manager needs this to help identify whether a change in strategy or other action is needed and, subsequently, to find out whether those changes resulted in the desired results (outcomes).

The manager of a private business needs regular feedback on the business's profitability so the manager can determine whether actions are needed and, subsequently, whether those actions led to the desired results.

Similarly, managers in any government and any government agency, whether at the national or the local government level, need regular feedback on the quality and outcomes of services to citizens.

What Is Outcome Measurement?

Outcome measurement is the regular measurement and reporting of the outcomes (results) of public agency programs. Measurement should be done at least annually but preferably more frequently, such as quarterly. The agencies might be national government agencies or subnational agencies. Outcome measurement has also begun to be used in some countries by private, nongovernmental organizations (NGOs) to track the outcomes of their services.

Outcome measurement includes the measurement of program results, and the quality of the way in which the service is delivered (such as how long it takes customers to get the service). Sometimes the term *outcome measurement* is also used to include the measurement of the efficiency with which the service is provided. The term *efficiency* is defined as the ratio of the amount of input to the amount of product produced. Inputs can be expressed in monetary units or amount of employee time. The word *product* traditionally refers to the amount of physical output of the agency's programs (such as the number of meters of roads repaired). In outcome measurement, however, it means relating the amount of input to the amount of outcome produced. This provides indicators such as expenditures per meter of roads improved to a satisfactory, or better, condition.

Why Measure Outcomes?

Outcome measurement serves a number of basic and vital governmental purposes:

- It helps service managers apply whatever resources they have to problem areas identified by the outcome information, to get the best use from limited resources.
- It provides information to public officials as to the extent to which the program is "winning" or "losing," thereby helping provide improved services to citizens—by motivating public employees to continually improve the quality and outcomes of the services they are delivering.
- It identifies the extent to which service quality and outcomes have changed after service improvement actions have been taken.
- It helps in budgeting, so that resources are allocated in ways most likely to produce the maximum benefit to citizens.
- It makes public agencies more accountable for results to elected officials and the public.
- It can increase the public's trust in the government.

Obstacles to Outcome Measurement in Developing Countries

Developing countries usually have many obstacles to implementing outcome measurement. They include the following:

- Very limited funds are available for services and for outcome measurement.

- Data processing technology is highly limited (both hardware and software), requiring the use of manual procedures, which can be inaccurate and considerably more time-consuming.
- Staff members typically (especially in operating agencies) have little formal training and expertise in the quantitative techniques needed for outcome measurement.
- At the highest levels, government officials may have little understanding and appreciation for the importance of obtaining feedback on service quality and outcomes.
- Government personnel may have quite limited experience in obtaining input from their citizens (the customers of their services). Input is needed initially to help identify what service characteristics should be measured and, subsequently, to obtain customer feedback on service quality and the results of services received by customers.
- Developing countries typically rely on multiple donors who may have different interests and degrees of support for outcome measurement.

Despite all these limitations, most developing countries are likely to be able to, and should, implement at least a rough version of outcome measurement—even governments who exercise tight control over their populations should undertake outcome measurements, if they are truly interested in the welfare of their citizens and not solely concerned with retention of power. (The latter governments might restrict the reporting of the findings. However, as long as they seek to make services as helpful to citizens as possible, these governments should also implement an outcome measurement process.)

Regardless of how poor a country is, as long as its government is providing services to the public, public agencies should attempt to do that job as well as possible—that is, to produce as high a quality of service and outcomes as possible. To do this, agencies need objective, valid, and reliable information on how well they are doing in delivering quality services. Clearly, outcome measurement cannot require so many resources that a service suffers rather than improves. The key issue is what can be done at low cost to undertake such measurement, without compromising the ability to obtain at least roughly accurate outcome information. That is the subject of the rest of this chapter.

The key point is that whatever service a public agency is providing, it almost always can improve on the quality and outcomes of the service—without additional resources. Outcome information should enable agencies to make improvements and also to better justify their requests for resources.

Basic Steps in Implementing an Outcome Measurement Process

To implement outcome measurement, agency personnel should first carefully identify the mission and objectives of each of the agency's services. From these mission statements and objectives, the agency should identify the outcomes and indicators to be used to measure these outcomes. Tables 4.1, 4.2, and 4.3 provide examples from programs aimed at education, welfare of children, and street cleanliness. Each provides a statement of objectives, a list of

TABLE 4.1 Outcome Indicators for Elementary and Secondary School Systems

Objective: Provide children with education that leads to learning that in turn produces young adults who are able to work and live in a modern society.

Outcome indicators	Data sources
1. Attendance/absenteeism rates—number and rate of student-days	School records
2. Attrition/dropout rates	School records
3. Number of actual student-days	School records
4. Percentage of students promoted to the next grade	School records
5. Number of students graduated or promoted	School records
6. Results of academic test scores	Tests
7. Percentage of students achieving a specified amount of test score gain during the school year	Tests
8. Number of disruptive incidents of violence on school grounds	School records
9. Percentage of parents rating their children as having improved in, or having good or excellent work and study habits	Survey of parents
10. Percentage of students who, years after completing x years of schooling (e.g., two years), either are continuing their education or are employed	Survey of students

Source: This list is abstracted from GASB 1989. (*Service Efforts and Accomplishments Reporting: Its Time Has Come for Elementary and Secondary Education.* Norwalk, Connecticut: Governmental Accounting Standards Board).

TABLE 4.2   Outcome Indicators for Youth Welfare

Objective #1: Assure the physical and emotional well-being (safety) of children

End outcome indicators	Data sources
1. Number and percentage of child (a) "serious" injuries and (b) deaths	Agency Records
2. Number and rate of reported (a) abuse and (b) neglect by first-time parents	Agency Records/Trained Observer Ratings
3. Number and rate of identified (a) re-abuse and (b) re-neglect	Agency Records
4. Number and percentage of children indicating "severe" emotional disturbance	Trained Observer Ratings
5. Percentage of children reporting "substantial" fear because of in-home factors (e.g., because of physical or mental problems in their current place of residence)	Survey of children
6. Number and percentage of children in the system that subsequently had to be removed from a residence because of safety concerns (including cases in which the decision was to leave in own home)	Agency Records/Trained Observer Ratings
7. Number and percentage of safety-related "serious" health problems	

Intermediate outcome indicators	Data sources
8. Percentage of children in the system that have "adequate" immunizations	Agency Records
9. Number of cases in which needed "needed" intervention was delayed beyond a specified "appropriate" length of time—broken out by reason category, such as "no space was available."	Agency Records

Objective #2: Encourage/support/ensure proper development of children, including health, education, and social skills.

End outcome indicators	Data sources
1. Number and percentage of children who developed illnesses, or other health conditions that deterred development or reduced ability to	Agency Records

(continued)

TABLE 4.2 Outcome Indicators for Youth Welfare (Continued)

End outcome indicators	Data sources
function normally. (For school-age children, an indicator such as "number/percentage who had over x days absences for sickness" might also be used)	
2. Number and percentage of children who met normal growth curves and height/weight expectations	Agency Records
3. Number and percentage of children who displayed "age-appropriate" social skills	Agency Records
4. Number and percentage of pre-school children who "achieved school readiness," such as indicated by tests, etc	Tests/Trained Observer Ratings
5. Number and percentage of children who progressed in school according to "normal" development, such as by being promoted and/or passing all courses	Agency Records
6. Number and percentage of children with at least one "severe" school delinquency problem in the past school year	Agency Records
7. Number and percentage of children who dropped out of school before completing x years	Agency Records
8. Number and percentage of children who obtained "basic life skills" and "self-sufficiency," such as indicated by performance in the children's last years of school on selected skills tests, e.g., reading, writing, math, vocational skills, etc.	Tests/Trained Observer Ratings
9. Number and percentage who became "self-sustaining," "independent" young adults after they became adults. (This indicator requires follow-up surveys of youth, perhaps one or two years after they completed school, to determine if they have a regular job or are in post-school education.)	Survey of young adults
10. Number and percentage who indicate a reasonable level of self-esteem (such as indicated by various self-esteem scales developed for children of various ages)	Tests

Intermediate outcome indicators	Data sources
11. Number and percentage of children who have been "fully" immunized	Agency Records
12. Number and percentage of children who have had "regular" medical/dental exams	Agency Records

TABLE 4.3   Outcome Indicators for Solid Waste Collection

Objectives and principal effectiveness measures for solid waste collection

Overall Objective: To promote the aesthetics of the community and the health and safety of the citizens by providing an environment free from the hazards and unpleasantness of uncollected refuse with the least possible citizens inconceivable.

Objectives	Quality characteristics	Outcome indicators*	Data sources
Pleasing aesthetics	Street, alley and neighborhood cleanliness	1. Percentage of (a) streets, (b) alleys, the appearance of which is rated satisfactory (or unsatisfactory)	Trained observer ratings
		2. Percentage of (a) households, (b) business rating their neighborhood cleanliness as satisfactory (or unsatisfactory)	(a) Household Survey (b) Business Survey
	Offensive Odors	3. Percentage of (a) households, (b) businesses reporting offensive odors from solid wastes	(a) Household Survey (b) Business Survey
	Objectionable noise incidents	4. Percentage of (a) households, (b) businesses reporting objectionable noise from solid waste collection operations	(a) Household survey (b) Business Survey
Health and Safety	Health	5. Number and percentage of blocks with one or more health hazards	Trained observer ratings
	Fire hazards	6. Number and percentage of blocks with one or more fire hazards	Trained observer ratings
	Fires involving uncollected waste	7. Number of fires involving uncollected solid waste	Fire department records
	Health hazards and unsightly appearance	8. Number of abandoned automobiles	Trained observer ratings

(continued)

TABLE 4.3   Outcome Indicators for Solid Waste Collection (*continued*)

Objectives	Quality characteristics	Outcome indicators*	Data sources
	Rodent hazard	9. Percentage of (a) households, (b) businesses reporting having seen rats on their blocks in the past three months	(a) Household survey (b) Business Survey
	Rodent bites	10. Number of rodent bites reported per 1,000 population	City or county health records.
Minimum citizen inconvenience	Missed or late collections	11. Number and percentage of collection routes not completed on schedule	Sanitation department records
		12. Percentage of (a) households, (b) businesses reporting missed collections	(a) Household survey (b) Business survey
	Spillage of trash and garbage during collections.	13. Percentage of (a) households, (b) businesses reporting spillage by collection crews	(a) Household survey (b) Business survey
	Damage to private property by collection crews.	14. Percentage of (a) households, (b) businesses reporting property damage caused by collection crews	(a) Household Survey (b) Business survey
General Citizen satisfaction	Citizen complaints	15. Number of verified citizen complaints by type per 1,000 household served	Sanitation department records
	Perceived satisfaction	16. Percentage of (a) households, (b) businesses reporting overall satisfaction with the solid waste collection service they receive	(a) Household survey (b) Business survey

*Officials who wish to focus on the amount of dissatisfaction may substitute "unsatisfactory" for the term "satisfactory" in many of these measures.

outcomes that arise from the objectives, and specific indicators for each outcome. Potential sources of data for each outcome and types of data collection procedures are also included. Data sources and collection procedures are discussed in the next section.

Basic Outcome Measurement Procedures and Their Costs

Examples of procedures that governments in developing countries can use to obtain basic information on service quality and outcomes are given below.

Counts of Major Incidents

Probably the first outcome data that most governments and their agencies track on a regular basis are counts of key incidents, ones that are of major importance to the government. They are obtained—where possible—from agency records. These include counts such as

- the incidence of various diseases, by category
- the incidence of infant mortality, by cause
- numbers of crimes reported to law enforcement agencies, by category
- numbers of vehicle traffic accidents, injuries, and deaths, by cause
- educational achievement levels, such as the number of children completing specific numbers of years of schooling
- pollution content of sources of drinking water supply

These are examples of data that most governments seek to collect. Developing countries, however, may not have systematic procedures in place for collecting and processing such information, at least not from all locations throughout the government's jurisdiction. Establishing these data collection procedures can be a problem for some developing countries but should be attempted. Even if data sources are not fully reliable, establishing even rudimentary procedures for data collection is desirable and appropriate. Indicators such as those listed above are basic quality of life indicators for the citizens of any country or city. Even rudimentary manual systems are preferable to not attempting any systematic data collection at all.

Initially, the effort might be concentrated in major population areas because of difficulties in obtaining data from outlying rural areas. A system that processes data solely from a country's largest cities is preferable to one that completely neglects the information. Such data should drive many decisions about the allocation of scarce resources.

Customer Feedback Surveys

Surveying customers can be a very useful tool in governing. It is a major way to obtain credible, reasonably accurate feedback from customers of government services. Surveys need to be undertaken in a reasonably sound, professional manner. Customer surveys can provide various types of information for outcome measurement, including the following:

■ Ratings from citizens of their overall satisfaction with individual public services (thus providing data for such outcome indicators as the percentage of surveyed customers who rated a particular service as either "excellent" or "good" rather than "fair" or "poor")

■ Ratings from customers of the specific characteristics of those services, such as their timeliness and helpfulness (thus providing data for outcome indicators such as the percentage of surveyed customers who rated a particular service characteristic, such as timeliness, as either "excellent" or "good" rather than "fair" or "poor")

■ Factual information about citizens' conditions, attitudes, and behavior, such as citizens' health, earnings, use of public services (such as public transit), and extent of crime victimization, and the extent of extra payments (bribes) needed to obtain services (thus providing data for outcome indicators such as the percentage of citizens who have been a crime victim at least once during the past six months)

■ Reasons why citizens had problems with specific services (asked of respondents who gave negative responses on questions about their experiences with particular services), thus providing useful information about problems that need attention

■ Suggestions for improving services, which may provide specific guidance to public managers

■ Demographic information on the population surveyed (thus helping identify which population groups have had particular problems with services so that attention can be directed toward them)

Annex 4.A provides an example of a customer survey questionnaire used in Uganda.[1] It includes questions about the quality of services received by citizens and about corruption experienced by citizens.

Citizen surveys, if properly done, provide reasonably representative feedback. This is unlike other sources of citizen feedback, such as open meetings, group discussions, and tabulations of complaints received by an agency (because only some people attend such meetings, and only some people are willing or know how to complain).

For some services an agency would survey samples of all households (for services that most households can be expected to have first-hand experience with). For services that serve only small proportions of the population, only those who have been customers of the service need to be surveyed (such as families that have received maternal health care, or farm families that have received technical assistance on farming practices). Surveys can be done of individuals, households, or businesses. Businesses are likely to be customers for many public services.

A principal use of surveys of customers is to obtain regular feedback in order to track trends and to assess the extent of improvement after the government has changed its service delivery approach.

Can developing countries afford to undertake such surveys, especially on a regular (for example, annual) basis? Surveys conducted on a regular basis may not be feasible for many developing countries without external support. Large-scale independent surveys using professional survey firms usually are not cheap.

Donor organizations such as the World Bank have in the past supported such surveys. For example, the World Bank has sponsored service delivery surveys in a number of countries. These surveys have provided feedback from representative samples of citizens on perceptions of the quality of individual services and on the extent of corruption these citizens have encountered in attempting to obtain public services.

Other possible sources of help for customer surveys are NGOs that have an interest in the measurement of one or more services. NGOs might provide interviewers, data entry, or assistance in tabulation, data analysis, and report preparation.

A less expensive option is for the government to undertake the surveys itself. In countries where labor is available and inexpensive, a government may find it feasible to use temporary or permanent personnel to do the survey interviews. The public agency, however, will still likely need some outside assistance in developing the questionnaire and a reasonably representative sampling plan, to ensure that they are unbiased.

After the questionnaires have been completed by respondents, the public agency will need to process that information and tabulate it accurately. In developed countries and some developing countries, such processing and tabulation can be done with computers, using either manual or automatic entry of data from the questionnaires. If such equipment is not available to the agency, tabulations will need to be made manually. This is considerably more time-consuming and is likely to lead to more mistakes.

To contain survey costs, public agencies usually need to survey only small samples of the customers who they serve. It is not likely to be feasible for a large agency to try to survey the full population of the nation or a city, other than in very special, infrequent, circumstances, such as 10-year censuses.

In developed countries, agencies sometimes place tight precision requirements on survey results. These precision requirements mean large samples are needed. Such precision is unlikely to be needed by developing countries (and may even be excessive in developed countries). For example, requiring that surveys provide a 95 percent confidence that the survey data are within two or three percentage points of the true value for the population will likely require considerable extra cost that is excessive and unnecessary. Governments and their agencies can build their survey capabilities over time. The earlier years may involve smaller samples and more approximate procedures than would be preferable. However, it is better to be roughly right than precisely ignorant.

Focus Groups

If small, representative sample surveys are infeasible, the government can fall back on a procedure that does not provide statistical credibility but can give some useful citizen feedback. This method is the use of focus groups with customers of particular services. In this procedure, the agency invites a small number of customers, perhaps 10 to 15, for a two-hour session. At the session, participants are asked about their experiences with the service, how they would rate the service on various characteristics, and why they gave those ratings. They can also be asked for suggestions for improving the service. Government officials may believe that these citizens will only ask for more (costly) service. However, participants are also very likely to discuss options that do not require additional resources.

The agency might hold a number of such meetings in various locations to obtain a variety of viewpoints. The sessions should include, to the extent possible, persons with various demographic characteristics, such as some sessions with participants who are very poor and other sessions with richer citizens. Both rural and urban areas should be represented. In most developing countries, many ethnic groups receive services. The meetings should include each such major ethnic group, probably in different sessions.

The findings from focus group meetings are primarily qualitative, not quantitative. Nevertheless, the information obtained should provide feedback to the agency on how well it is delivering the service and where improvements seem necessary. Users of focus groups need to understand that these sessions do not provide statistically reliable data, such as that obtainable from systematic surveys of representative samples of customers.

Trained Observer Assessment of Key Physical Conditions

Public agencies should monitor and track the condition of key facilities that are their responsibility. This applies to conditions such as the following:

- road "rideability"
- condition of water and sanitation facilities and equipment
- condition of hospitals and long-term care facilities
- condition of school buildings and schoolrooms
- cleanliness and sanitary condition of streets and neighborhoods
- presence of rats and insects
- exterior condition of homes

To make these measurements, the agency needs to develop a well-defined rating scale, one that identifies in specific terms each rating category for each condition that the agency wants to monitor. A number of agencies have used rating scales that use photographs to represent different levels of road conditions, street cleanliness, and schoolroom and housing conditions. To develop a photographic rating scale, the agency would

- take many photographs of a variety of conditions of the facilities that it wants to assess
- select photos that represent each of perhaps three, four, or five rating categories (using a scale that rates conditions, such as from "excellent" to "poor")
- test the procedures with personnel who are likely to do the ratings

Trained observer ratings can usually be done by low-cost personnel. These personnel might be permanent staff members, temporary employees, contract personnel, or volunteers. The agency needs to provide adequate training in the use of the rating scale to each person who is to make the observations.

The data from the ratings of all, or a sample of, facilities are then aggregated to provide overall totals. This procedure also provides reasonably reliable outcome measurements on the condition of individual facilities. Thus, the procedure can be used to identify where to best allocate limited resources (such as to facilities where the need seems to be greatest and the greatest pay-off in the use of scarce resources can be obtained).

The feasibility of this procedure in a developing country depends on the extent to which low-cost personnel are available to do the ratings. This is not a sophisticated procedure. The tabulations of the information can be done manually, but with less accuracy than if the public agency is able to use automated programs. Annex 4.B provides more detail on the procedures for trained observer assessments.

Measurements of Extent of Corruption

Corruption in the delivery of public services is a major concern today for many countries and donors. Wherever money is involved, some corruption will likely occur. Governments need to take steps to reduce it to the extent possible. To track the success of anticorruption efforts, governments (through their anticorruption agencies) need to track the extent to which corruption is occurring. Thus, indicators of the extent of corruption at particular points in time should be part of performance measurement systems in developing countries.

Annex 4.C is a sample set of indicators that appears appropriate for an anticorruption agency to track on a regular, annual basis. Such measurement is most likely to be feasible in countries whose leaders are actively pressing for corruption reduction and that have an independent audit or inspector-general office. The data for many of these indicators would come from anticorruption agency records. Each government will need to establish procedures for recording the needed data. Few of these indicators are likely to be costly to collect. However, because of their sensitivity, some are likely to be controversial.

Obtaining data on this last group of indicators in annex 4.C (19–22) requires surveys of household and businesses. The questionnaire shown in annex 4.A includes questions that ask respondents about their personal experiences with corruption, thus providing data for indicators 19–22 in annex 4.C. As discussed earlier, citizen surveys require special resources. In that discussion, we noted ways to keep costs to a low level. Surveys covering corruption issues probably have a greater need to be undertaken by a professional organization outside the government, to provide credibility. The government can fund the survey as long as it does not impose undue constraints on it. Funds might also come from donor agencies. As noted earlier, the World Bank has sponsored a number of these. Also, as noted earlier, an NGO might be willing to sponsor the survey effort.

These surveys should be of a representative sample of households. A separate survey can be done of a representative sample of businesses. Businesses themselves sometimes cause the corruption; therefore, some responses from businesses would be expected to be dishonest. Nevertheless, governments can probably learn much from the overall responses. The assumption here is that most businesses would prefer not to be involved with corruption activities. An important element of surveys that ask respondents about their experiences with corruption is to ensure the confidentiality of responses. This may be difficult in some countries if the survey sponsors are not able to use a credible and professional survey organization.

These surveys do not capture all aspects of corruption, only those of which sampled citizens and businesses have first-hand knowledge and are willing to include in their responses. Businesses are not likely to identify their own corruption attempts, such as incidents of bribery between government personnel and private sector individuals or organizations. Corruption indicators 1–18 in annex 4.C cover only incidents that come to the attention of the government. The household and business surveys reach out to citizens and businesses to obtain information that is not reported.

Measurements of Response Time

Some governments that have established a performance measurement process started with indicators of response time. Response time is the time from when a request for service was made until the time the service organization provided a response. Response time data are particularly important for emergency services, such as citizen requests for police and fire agency assistance relating to crimes, fires, and emergency health care needs. Also, citizens usually have a significant concern about response times for many other services, such as the time required to get registered, to receive assistance payments, to obtain permits, and to receive a response on any application to the government.

Response times on individual service requests are subsequently aggregated to provide indicators such as average response time or percentage of requests for which the response time exceeded X hours. The quantity X would be selected by the agency as its standard.

Tracking response times may appear simple at first glance. However, it is likely to be more time-consuming than it appears. An operating agency needs to record the time that each request for the service was initially received and then, again, record the time when the service was provided. In developed countries, automatic recording devices are used for fire and police responses to calls for services. In developing countries, use of such automated devices may be a long time off. In the meantime, however, an agency can establish manual procedures. Staff members would record these times and subsequently collect and tabulate those times manually. This procedure is complicated by the need to match up the starting and service delivery times for individual requests. If a substantial time (such as several days, or even several hours) usually occurs between requests and service provision, care needs to be taken to match the time of the response to the time of the particular request.

Response time measurement is particularly critical for some services (such as any emergency service). For most other services, response time measurement is likely to be secondary compared to the other measurements described above. Although response times are important to customers (and therefore should be tracked so that improvements can be made), such data do not tell anything about the outcome of the service the customers received— only how long it takes to get the service.

Data Quality Control

An important issue for any outcome measurement process is maintaining the integrity of the data so that they are reasonably accurate and credible to outsiders, such as to elected officials, citizens, and members of the media.

With manual data collection or tabulation procedures, the opportunities for inaccuracies and data manipulation are particularly high. Methods to reduce the potential for inaccuracies and manipulation are needed. One need is to provide an atmosphere in which data findings are not threatening to employees if the data do not look good. A second need is for adequate training of those responsible for providing and tabulating the data in order to avoid mistakes and misinterpretations. Finally, and probably most important for credibility to those outside the agency, the government's audit office can be made responsible for reviewing at least samples of the data and periodically reviewing data collection and tabulation procedures.

These steps will help encourage public agencies to increase their care in data collection and tabulation and will help reduce the temptations for manipulation. They will also help identify poorly implemented data collection, tabulation, and reporting procedures so that improvements can be made.

Using Outcome Data

An early section of this chapter identified why outcome data should be collected and the major purpose of it. That included helping to determine budget allocations and helping service managers improve their programs.

Outcome-based budgeting (or performance-based budgeting, as it is more popularly called in developed countries) is still very much in its developmental stage. For most outcomes, the relationships between the amount of inputs (funds or staff time) and outcomes is not known. (For example, how much more funding would be required to increase customer satisfaction levels for a particular service by five percentage points?) Nevertheless, if outcome data are available to an agency, the data should be useful in identifying where improvements are likely to be most needed. For example, if poor outcomes occur for a particular demographic group and not for others, this would suggest that more attention should be given to the service provided to that group.

Regular outcome data are likely to be of considerable use to public managers for deciding on actions throughout the year. This will be particularly so if the data are collected periodically throughout the year, such as every month or every three months. For example, New York City has tracked street cleanliness throughout the city for many years. Its sanitation department uses that information to allocate its cleanup crews. This has led to substantial reductions in the number of areas with very dirty streets. Another example: if dropout rates have been increasing in schools in some locations or with some demographic groups, the managers might look to determine the causes and try to alleviate them to the extent possible.

A major use of the data is for review: managers can hold "how are we doing?" sessions with their staffs shortly after each performance report has been prepared and disseminated. Such meetings can be an excellent way to obtain input from staff members on what is causing problems identified in the latest report and to obtain suggestions for corrective actions. In later sessions, staff members would look to see the extent to which actions taken have led to the outcome improvements sought.

As indicated earlier, a major use of outcome data is to examine trends over time, whether between months or quarters or across years. Such information helps managers and their agencies determine whether they are winning or losing the game.

A final point is that performance report formats can have a substantial impact on the use and usability of performance information. Reports need to be clear, concise, attractive, and understandable. An excellent way to display outcome data is to map the results by geographic location (region, district, neighborhood) to indicate those locations most in need of improvement. Maps are easy to understand and are visually attractive. For example, on a map an agency might shade the areas of a city to display different levels of cleanliness of each portion of a city—the darker the shading, the dirtier the streets.

The city can use the data to allocate its street crews. By examining the shading from previous reporting periods, the reader can readily assess the changes that have occurred over time. Data from later years might show, for example, a steady decline in the number of dirty areas. Data from any source (trained observer ratings, customer surveys, or agency records) can be displayed with maps—as long as the data can be geographically coded.

Final Note

A major issue that has caused problems in developed countries, and likely will in developing countries, is the misunderstanding that outcome data from an outcome measurement system automatically indicate that the agency, and its managers, are primarily responsible for the observed outcomes. If the outcomes are not as good as expected, higher-level officials (and the media) jump to the conclusion that it is the fault of the agency. This puts agency personnel very much on the defensive, resulting in fear and the temptation to manipulate and misuse the data.

Public officials at all levels and members of the media need to be informed that, as with the score of a soccer game and the bottom-line profits of a private business, outcome data indicate only results. They do not indicate why the results occurred. Many factors outside the control of agency managers usually affect outcomes. For example, world economic conditions, unusual weather conditions, and actions by customers can affect many outcomes—and be beyond the control of the agency.

Outcome measurement information raises important questions that agency officials need to address. Agency officials then need to identify reasons why outcomes are less than expected and undertake needed improvement actions.

In developing countries, scarce funds will almost inevitably be a major reason for a significant part of outcome problems. Nevertheless, public agencies in developing countries are still responsible for squeezing the most out of their resources. They need to use their scarce resources as wisely as possible to produce services whose quality and outcomes are as good as possible. Effective and efficient use of available resources, however small an agency's resources may be, should be the objective of public agencies and their personnel. Regular, reliable measurement of service quality and outcomes should be a major tool of public agency managers in helping produce the most effective and efficient use of scarce resources.

Annex 4.A: Household Questionnaire

1. What is the sex and age of the household head?
2. Note sex of respondent.
   What is the relationship of the respondent to the household head?
3. What is the level of education of the household head?
4. What is the occupation of the family head?
5. How many members of the household are there altogether?
   What is the age and sex of each one, starting with the youngest?
   <For people under 20, record whether in primary school or not>
   <Ask the following questions for each child in primary school (up to 4 children in primary school).>
   <Ask for children registered for UPE and in government-aided schools.>
6. What class is the child in?
7. How many times (if any) has the child had to repeat a class?
8. What payments have you made for the child's education during the past year?
   Books/pens etc.
   Uniforms/shoes
   Travel to school
   Official school fees
   Extra tuition payment to the school
   Extra payments directly to teachers
9. How satisfied are you with the teaching (apart from extra private tuition) that the child is receiving at school?
   <satisfied>
   <neither satisfied nor dissatisfied>
   <dissatisfied>
10. How long ago did any member of this household last have a contact with:
    The central police?
    The judiciary (magistrates courts and above)?
    The URA?
    The government health services?
    The local administration? (including LA police, LC courts, local tax)
    <Write answer in months (if less than one year) or years since beginning of last contact>
    <Ask questions 10–33 for the LAST contact for EACH ONE of the services contacted>
    <If none of the services ever contacted, skip to Q34>
11. Which service was it?

12. What is the sex and age of the person having the contact with the service?
13. Did you contact this service? Or why did they contact you?
14. How did you first make/have contact with the service to help you through your dealings with them?
15. How did you first make/have contact with the service?
    (personal contact/letter/telephone/through friend or relative)
16. Did you have a contact in the service to help you through your dealings with them?
17. How long did it take for your problem to be attended to?
    <n/a if service made through the contact>
    <in hours if less than one day, in days if one day or more>
18. Have your dealings with the service been completed?
19. How long did it take to complete dealing with your problem?
    <if not yet completed, put time taken up until now; in days if less than
one month, otherwise in months>
20. If you visited the service in your dealings with them, how many visits did you (or other members of the household or someone acting for you) make?
21. How satisfied were you with the speed of service?
    <satisfied>
    <neither satisfied or dissatisfied>
    <dissatisfied>
22. How satisfied were you with the behavior of the staff of the service toward you?
    <satisfied>
    <neither satisfied or dissatisfied>
    <dissatisfied>
23. When you first contacted the service, what information were you given by the service about how to use it?
    (none/spoken/written/spoken and written)
    <if none, skip to Q25>
24. How helpful was the information given by the service?
    <very helpful>
    <somewhat helpful>
    <not at all helpful>
25. Did you know how to make a complaint about the service?
26. Did you actually make a complaint about the service?
27. How many different staff did you meet in your dealings with the service?
28. Did you use the help of a broker or agent in dealing with the service?

29. How much did you have to pay the broker?

30. Did you have to pay anything extra, in money or goods, (apart from official charges) to people in the service to get your problem dealt with?
<if no, skip to Q33>

31. Did the person(s) concerned ask you for money or goods or did you pay on your own initiative?

32. How much did you have to pay extra to service workers to get your problem dealt with?

33. If you did not make any extra payments to service workers:
Were you asked for any extra payment, in money or goods, but you refused?
Did you offer any extra payment but it was refused by the service worker?

<FOR ALL HOUSEHOLDS>

34. What do you think about the practice of paying extra (bribes) to service workers in order to get a service in favor?

35. What forms of corruption do you think happen in this district?

36. How much of a problem do you think there is with corruption in public services in this District?
<very much>
<somewhat>
<not at all>

37. Has this problem gotten better, stayed the same or gotten worse in the last two years?
<better>
<the same>
<worse>

38. Which government departments or agencies in this district are the most corrupt, in your opinion?
<allow up to three answers>

39. Which departments or agencies are the least corrupt?
<allow up to three answers>

40. What do you think the national government should do to solve the problem of corruption in public services?

41. What do you think the local government in this district should do to solve the problem of corruption in public services?

42. What do you think communities themselves could do to help solve the problem of corruption in public services?

43. Have you heard of the Inspectorate of Government (the IGG)?
    <if 'No,' skip Q44–46>
44. What does IGG do?
    <allow up to three answers>
45. Have you ever made a complaint to the IGG?
46. How satisfied were you with the way the IGG dealt with your complaint?
    <satisfied>
    <neither satisfied nor dissatisfied>
    <dissatisfied>

Source: The questionnaire was sponsored by the World Bank and Uganda. The results are reported in "Uganda National Integrity Survey 1998: Final Report" (August 1998), CIET International.

Annex 4.B: Trained Observer Procedures

Trained observers can be used to rate a variety of important outcomes that can be documented by the eyes or other physical senses of an observer. Its familiar form is in inspection functions, such as for buildings, health, and food safety. A key requirement for performance measurement is that the rating scales and procedures provide reasonably accurate ratings.

A high degree of accuracy can be maintained if the procedures provide

- a well-defined rating system
- adequate training and supervision of the observers and the process
- a procedure for periodically checking the quality of the ratings

Trained observer ratings—if properly done—reduce the subjectivity in assessing physical conditions such as street cleanliness. Ratings scales, if properly developed, provide trained observers with specific criteria against which to assess conditions in a reliable manner. Without such common criteria to assess conditions, different observers will likely come up with different ratings for a condition. Well-defined rating scales reduce the subjectivity in condition assessments.

The goal is for different observers, at different times, to give approximately the same ratings to similar conditions.

Applications of Trained Observer Ratings

For observer ratings to be applied to a particular outcome, the outcome should

- be measurable by physical observation—through any of the five senses: sight, hearing, smell, taste, or touch (though most applications in the public sector, thus far, have used sight)
- be one that can be rated on a scale that identifies variations in condition

Examples of Outcomes for Which Trained Observer Ratings Have Been Used to Provide Data

- cleanliness of roads and alleys
- condition of roads
- condition of parks
- condition of facilities such as schools, nursing homes, and hospitals
- condition of housing

- Quality of food provided in publicly supported facilities (taste, smell, and sight can be used)
- Ability of handicapped clients to perform activities of daily living, after receiving public service

Advantages of Trained Observer Procedures

- They can provide reliable, reasonably accurate ratings of conditions that otherwise are difficult to measure.
- The data can be used to assist programs in allocating their resources throughout the year, if the ratings are done periodically (for example, the New York City Sanitation Department has for many years regularly used trained observer ratings of street cleanliness to help allocate its street cleaning crews).

Disadvantages of Trained Observer Procedures

- These are labor-intensive procedures that require personnel time to do the ratings.
- Ratings need to be periodically checked to ensure that the observers are adhering to the procedures.
- Program personnel may not be comfortable with using this procedure, as it is not very common.

Types of Trained Observer Rating System

Several types of rating systems can be used by trained observers. These include ones that use

- written descriptions only
- photographic rating systems that use photographs as the rating scales
- other visual scales such as scales that use drawings or videos rather than photographs
- combinations of these types.

Each type is briefly described below.

Trained Observer System Using Only Written Descriptions

This is the simplest type of rating system. It depends solely on written descriptions of each grade used in the rating scale. These rating descriptions need to be quite specific about what constitutes each particular rating, to maintain the accuracy of the ratings.

An abbreviated example of a written scale for "building (or street) cleanliness" is the following:

- Rating 1: *Clean.* Building (street) is completely or almost completely clean; a maximum of three pieces of litter per floor (block) are present.
- Rating 2: *Moderately Clean.* Building (street) is largely clean; a few pieces of isolated litter and dirt are observable.
- Rating 3: *Moderately Dirty.* Some scattered litter or dirt is present.
- Rating 4: *Dirty.* Heavy litter or dirt is present in several locations throughout the building (along the block).

A written rating scale has three advantages:

- It is the simplest form of rating scale.
- It is the most familiar procedure, the one usually used by public agencies, which use trained observer ratings, such as for inspections.
- It can also help agencies identify resource allocation needs, by specific locations where problems are present.

Table 4.B.1 illustrates an additional, very important, use for such outcome information. The City of Toronto used these ratings of street conditions to help determine what repairs were needed in each location—as noted in the right-hand column.

Disadvantages of written rating systems are as follows:

- The written information for each rating grade needs to be very specific in order to ensure reasonable accuracy, so that different raters will give approximately the same rating for a particular condition.
- Because each grade on the rating scale needs to be defined very clearly, the program is likely to have to spend a considerable amount of time developing the ratings.
- This procedure can be used to measure outcomes only if the outcome can be expressed as a physically observable condition.

Trained Observer Systems Using Photographic Scales

Photographic scales can be very useful in providing clear definitions for each rating grade. Preselected photos are used to represent the various grades on

TABLE 4.B.1 Toronto Road Condition Rating Scale

Rating	Condition	Description	Comments
9	Excellent	No fault whatsoever	
8	Good	No damage, normal wear and small cracks	Recently constructed work
7	Fair	Slight damage, crack fill or minor leveling required	Average rating for city of Toronto pavements and sidewalks
6	Repair	10% of complete replacement cost	Pavement requires preventive overlay. Level of tolerance for city of Toronto pavements
5	Repair	25% of complete replacement cost	Eligible for reconstruction program
4	Repair	50% of complete replacement cost	Condition Rating 4- Level of Tolerance for city of Toronto curbs and sidewalks
3	Repair	75% of complete replacement cost	Total reconstruction probably indicated
2	Repair	More than 75% of complete replacement cost	Requires complete reconstruction
1	Impossible to repair		

the rating scale. Each trained observer is given (and trained in the use of) a set of photos, perhaps four photos for each grade on the scale.

Trained Observer Systems Using Other Visual Scales

Visual rating scales can also use drawings or sketches that represent each grade on a rating scale. Figure 4.B.1 is an example of a rating scale using sketches to represent conditions of school buildings, in this case, the condition of schoolroom walls. This was used by the New York City school system to track the physical condition of its schools and to help make decisions about repairs.

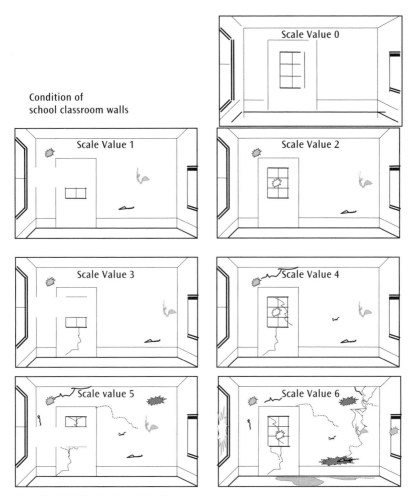

Source: New York City Department Education.

FIGURE 4.B.1 New York City Trained Observer Rating Scale

Annex 4.C: Examples of Performance Indicators for Tracking Anticorruption Efforts

Many of the following indicators should be broken out by such characteristics as type of complaint/incident; severity of complaint/incident (such as the amount of funds involved or the level of suspected official involved); district; source of the case; organizational unit responsible for initially handling the case; and the difficulty or complexity of the case (for example, whether it was of considerable, medium, or low difficulty or complexity).

1. Number of corruption complaints received and found after preliminary investigation to have merit. Note: Corruption complaints should exclude other kinds of complaints, such as delays or mistakes in making pension or other payments that are not due to corruption-related elements. These are very important but different problems. This number will be affected by efforts to get citizens and businesses to report corrupt activities. This is likely to be a problem for at least the first year or two of a program to encourage more citizens and businesses to report incidents of corruption.
2. Number and percentage of corruption complaints received that were not investigated.
3. Number of cases for which sufficient evidence was obtained to be prosecuted and an arrest made.
4. Number and percentage of cases for which a reasonable penalty was assessed and carried out; that is, number and percentage of cases investigated that were successfully resolved.
5. Number and percentage of cases not prosecuted because of poor practice in investigation, such as evidence gathering.
6. Number and percentage of cases not successfully prosecuted because of poor practice during the prosecution stage.
7. Monetary value of missing or misused supplies and equipment found during audits.
8. Percentage of public leaders who have not publicly declared their assets.
9. Amount of funds recovered through (a) administrative action or (b) legal action.
10. Value of money recovered, and property seized and confiscated for corrupt practices.
11. Number and percentage of cases lost.
12. Percentage of complaint cases whose time from receipt of complaint until the investigation was started exceeded X days.

13. Percentage of complaint cases whose time from receipt of complaint until the investigation was completed exceeded Y days.

14. Percentage of complaint cases whose time from receipt until case was finally resolved in the courts (not counting time for appeals) exceeded Z days.

15. Number of government employees removed for corruption activities.

16. Number and percentage of government cases overturned on appeals.

17. Percentage of substantive recommendations made to individual agencies and departments (in special studies) that were implemented by the agency or department.

18. Number of cases that could not be investigated because of lack of personnel or funds (perhaps broken out by district).

19. Percentage of citizens, households, and businesses in a representative survey who reported that they had made extra payments for one or more services (broken out by service and district).

20. Percentage of citizens, households, and businesses in a representative survey who reported that they believed that corruption in their district was less than it was 12 months ago.

21. Percentage of citizens, households, and businesses in a representative survey who reported that they would make a complaint (such as to the inspector general or other public official) if asked for a bribe.

22. Number of citizens, households, businesses that in a representative survey reported that they had (a) seen or heard one of the radio or TV spots on corruption, had examined an anticorruption brochure, or had participated in a workshop or seminar on corruption; and (b) had taken some action called for by the material presented (such as reporting bribe requests from public officials).

Implementing a Trained Observer Process

The following are steps needed to implement a trained observer process:

1. Decide what conditions should be rated.
2. Develop a rating scale for each condition. Use photographs and written guidelines as appropriate.
3. Determine which locations or clients should be rated, when, and how frequently. Ratings can be applied to all or to selected ones. If you have only enough resources to rate some locations, choose them by using random sampling so that the locations or clients chosen are representative.
4. Select and train observers. You can use program personnel or even school students and volunteers. More technical ratings, such as ratings of safety hazards, will require persons with more professional training.
5. Test the scale and the observers on a small number of locations to ensure that reasonably trained raters will give approximately the same ratings.
6. Establish procedures for supervising the observers, recording the data they collect, and transcribing and processing data.
7. Conduct the ratings at the desired frequency.
8. Develop and disseminate reports on the findings. The reports will be more informative if they show the number and percentage of locations that fall into each rating category. Avoid reporting only average scores, which can hide important distribution information. Also, in reports, show changes in the ratings from previous periods.
9. Establish procedures for systematically checking the ratings of trained observers to ensure quality control and the accuracy of the process. For example, the supervisor might periodically check a small sample of ratings done by each observer.

The following are additional steps needed for a photographic rating system:

1. Take a large number of photographs in locations representative of the range conditions to be rated. These photos should show the actual types of conditions that the program wants to assess.
2. Select a set of familiar labels, each representing a condition that the program expects to find (such as clean, moderately clean, moderately dirty, and dirty, for observations of cleanliness). Select a panel of judges composed of persons with varied backgrounds who are not associated with the measurement activities. Ask the judges to sort the photographs into groups that represent each condition.

3. For each condition level, select the four or five photographs that most judges identified as representing that level. These photographs can then be used as the rating scale.
4. Train the observers in the use of the photographic scale. Field test the scale with trained observers to determine whether there is sufficient agreement among them on the ratings. If not, revise the procedures.
5. Develop the final scale. Package copies of the selected photographs in a kit for each trained observer.

Small handheld computers that can be programmed so that trained observers can electronically record their ratings (as soon as the ratings are made) are becoming available at low prices. Such tools can considerably reduce the amount of clerical work needed later. For example, the city of New York has been using such procedures to regularly report on the condition of city buildings (including schools)—to meet legislative requirements. An NGO, the Fund for the City of New York (a private public interest organization), has used handheld computers to collect data on a number of physically observable conditions in samples of locations within New York City. The conditions observed include, among others, defective street signs, abandoned cars, the presence of rodents or pests, and defective street lights. This information is used to identify specific and summary conditions in various city community districts.

5

Delivering Local/Municipal Services

HARRY KITCHEN

Municipal and local services may be delivered in a variety of ways. Alternatives range from complete public provision to complete private provision or a mix of these two, including public-private partnerships.

Public sector provision ranges from responsibility resting with the local council or city hall to responsibility assigned to some kind of independent or quasi-independent special-purpose body or local government enterprise.[1] Private sector alternatives include contracting out, franchises, grants, vouchers, volunteers, self-help organizations, and nonprofit agencies.

This chapter will examine and evaluate these options by concentrating on the incentives and efficiency implications inherent in each structure (Kitchen 1993) rather than on cataloging their frequency of use.[2] Where possible, it will also provide a brief summary of the empirical evidence on cost differences under these alternative structures.

Public Sector Alternatives

This section compares service delivery through a separate local government body or enterprise with delivery by the local government itself.[3]

Local/Municipal Responsibility

Local or municipal governments are directly responsible for a range of public services for which fees or prices tend not to be used. Local streets and roads, street lighting, fire and police protection, and neighborhood parks are almost always funded from local taxes, grants from senior governments, and other locally generated revenues. In many countries, local or municipal governments are also responsible for services for which they charge user fees or prices—water, sewers, recreation, public transit, and so on. For all municipal services, local government staff and personnel generally share accounting, auditing, and legal services, municipal employees, and capital equipment. As for governance, local councils are responsible for making policy decisions for all services, including the trade-off between spending on one service rather than another.

Local Government Enterprises

The universe of what constitutes a local business enterprise covers a wide range. There is no single and uniform definition, but it is generally the case that each body or enterprise is responsible for the provision of a marketable good(s) or service(s)—one that has characteristics of a private good and for which a fee or price per unit can be charged. This explains, at least in part, why electricity, water, sewers, and public transit are often (but not always) the responsibility of local government enterprises or special-purpose bodies, and why local streets and roads, street lighting, sidewalks, fire protection, and neighborhood parks—services that have characteristics of public goods and for which specific fees or charges per unit cannot be imposed—are the responsibility of local governments themselves.

Each enterprise generally operates as a separate functioning business entity—sometimes independent of the locally elected council and sometimes under some kind of governing control or affiliation with the locally elected council. Each tends to be responsible for only one service (water or electricity or sewer and so on). Usually, each body has its own independent or quasi-independent (from the local council) governing body that is responsible for all policies affecting the enterprise. Each has its own accounting and financial system, frequently has its own work force and capital equipment, and is responsible for monitoring and reporting on its own activities.

In New Zealand, North America, and Europe, local government enterprises are responsible for relatively few local services. Furthermore, almost all of them are provided in an environment where there are generally no alternatives or no competitors. These services often include one or more of the following: electricity, telephone, water and sewers, municipal airports, and social housing. In other countries, by contrast, local government enterprises are responsible for many more services. A number of them may compete with the private sector. For example, subnational governments in the Russian Federation have long looked to state enterprises to finance many essential services. In 1992, it was estimated that 40 percent of subnational budgetary outlays in Russia came from enterprise contributions (Martinez-Vasquez 1994). In most one-company towns, the percentage was much higher, sometimes reaching almost 100 percent. At the subnational level in Russia, for example, revenues from local enterprises are important because they help finance basic services that might not be funded if left to the local tax base (Bahl and Wallich 1995). A similarly important revenue-generating role for local government enterprises has been reported for Colombia (Bird 1984).

Local government enterprises may be separated into those that operate in an environment where there are no competitors and those that openly compete with the private sector. For the former, there is only one supplier—a public sector monopolist. Water and sewers in a municipality, for example, are the responsibility of one agency—a separate utility or business enterprise, sometimes under the direct governance of the municipality and sometimes under the governance structure of a special-purpose board or commission that tends to have features and characteristics similar to those of a separate business entity. Similarly, electricity is the responsibility of one agency, as is public transit, and so on. Furthermore, services with high infrastructure costs such as water, sewers, and electricity have characteristics of a natural monopolist.[4] Others, such as public transit, may not benefit from economies of scale over their entire output (not a natural monopolist) but are, nevertheless, provided in a protected setting. In short, there is no competition for many of these services (electricity, water, and sewers) and limited and indirect competition for others (cars competing with public transit, for instance).

For publicly provided goods or services that compete with the private sector, there is the question of whether the public sector should be involved at all. In response, there is no solid economic rationale for public sector provision, although such provision has been defended on the basis of generating revenue for the local government. Examples include public sector involvement in bakeries, paint shops, flower shops, sports clubs, mushroom growing, and handicraft businesses in Russia (Kurlyandskaya, Nikolayenko, and Golovanova 2001).

Why Are Local Government Enterprises Used?

A variety of arguments have been advanced in defense of using special-purpose bodies or local government enterprises for specific services.

First, in some countries or some provinces, states, or regions within countries, legislated requirements stipulate that specific services must be the responsibility of a separate body or enterprise, generally under a governing structure called a commission, board, or utility. This is the case for municipal electricity distribution in Ontario, Canada, where all policy decisions are made by either a private corporation or a municipally appointed board of directors operating at arm's length and independently of the local council.

Second, where local governments are free to choose their governing structures for the provision of local goods and services, tradition often plays a role in relying on separate enterprises; that is, it has always been done that way and there is no reason to change.

Third, these bodies have been defended on the grounds that appointed or elected officials governing single-purpose enterprises will make better decisions than directly elected municipal politicians who must make decisions, choices, and trade-offs over a vast range of local government functions. A single-purpose governing council, the argument goes, is more likely to consist of experts and therefore able to make better decisions when compared with locally elected politicians and government officials, who have heavy workloads and insufficient time to plan, administer, and oversee all governing functions. This argument is supported by those who assert that financially independent public utilities are generally well run, honest, and efficient, while utilities governed by local councils are alleged to be markedly worse in each of these respects and likely to be run at a financial loss.

Fourth, enterprises are used in some countries as a way of escaping rigid controls (by a senior level of government) that apply to what and how local governments spend, who it employs for what, how much it pays people, which revenues it can access, on what terms it may borrow, and the like.

Fifth, local government enterprises may be preferred in those countries where senior levels of government share in local tax revenues but do not share in revenues generated by local enterprises (Martinez-Vazquez and Boex 2001).

Sixth, these bodies are used in some countries to provide employment.

Seventh, there is a perception in the minds of many politicians and a large proportion of the population that local business enterprises are more efficient and accountable in their operation because they are run more like a business—they sell a product, deliver it, retain the revenue, and cover all costs—when compared with other municipally provided services that are not sold for specific fees, charges, or prices.

Finally, local politicians and administrators sometimes prefer business enterprises because there tend to be fewer citizen complaints about revenues generated from the sale of goods and services by what is deemed to be a business enterprise than from increasing local taxes to raise the same amount of money. More bluntly, it seems to be more acceptable politically to set up a local business enterprise and sell a good or service to raise revenues than it is to raise local taxes. Generating revenues from the sale of goods and services by local government enterprises may also be preferred if municipal governments face legislated restrictions on their ability to raise taxes.

Criteria for Evaluating Local Enterprises

To evaluate the role for these bodies and how they should be structured, one needs a set of criteria. For this purpose, the following are appropriate: allocative or economic efficiency, accountability, transparency, and ease of administration.[5] Issues of fairness are important but of little relevance in this discussion. Fairness is associated with the way in which specific services are funded ("benefits received" arguments[6]) or with income distribution issues ("ability to pay" arguments[7]), not with the agency (enterprise or local government) responsible for the service.

Economic (Allocative) Efficiency

This efficiency is achieved within the local public sector when all service responsibilities are organized and allocated so that society gets the greatest possible gain from the use of all resources (inputs) at its disposal. In other words, if reliance on local government enterprises leads to the use of fewer resources than would be required if the same service were provided directly by local government, then it would be more allocatively efficient[8] to provide the service by a local enterprise because society would be better off collectively. If, however, the existence of one or more enterprises provides barriers or impediments to efficient local public sector decision making and leads to a greater use of resources (waste), local enterprises could be deemed to misallocate resources and be more costly to society collectively.

Accountability

In the provision of local public sector services, accountability is achieved when the customer or taxpayer is able to identify who is responsible for what and is able to link the governing unit responsible for the service directly to its funding. Where there is only one governing unit, taxpayers know who is responsible for what and who to contact if they wish to have an impact on decision making. Where there are a number of local governing units responsible for a diverse range of services, customers or taxpayers may become confused and not know who is responsible for what and how to have an impact on decision makers.

Transparency

Transparency is achieved when citizens or taxpayers have access to information and decision-making forums, so that the general public knows what is happening and is able to judge whether it is appropriate. Vehicles or instruments for enhancing transparency should include legislation that requires public sector decision makers to consult with and report to the public annually on planned activities; enforcement of regulations by officers; and purchasing of inputs through contractual arrangements with internal staff or the private sector. This legislation could include the annual publication of local public sector performance measures, thus providing local citizens with information for making intermunicipal efficiency and effectiveness comparisons. All this effort is intended to mitigate the risk of corruption by making information statutorily available and by ensuring that all public policy decisions are made in an open and transparent manner.[9]

Ease of Administration

Ease of administration is an extension of the criteria of efficiency and accountability. The easiest system to administer is one that is not confusing and does not require an unnecessary amount of time and effort in consultations, correspondence, and meetings in reaching decisions.

Do Local Government Enterprises Play a Unique Role?

Does a local government enterprise perform a service delivery role or function that cannot be performed at all or cannot be performed as efficiently by the local government (local or municipal council) directly? Using the criteria listed above, some light may be shed on this question. At the outset, it is asserted that the best and most socially desirable governing structure is achieved when locally elected councilors have decision-making responsibility for all local goods and services regardless of how they are delivered.[10] Perhaps this is illustrated best by pointing out a variety of problems—real and potential—that frequently emerge when some local public sector decision-making powers are the responsibility of local government enterprises. For example, if a local government enterprise can make policy decisions and has funding control over specific goods and services, and if it operates independently or semi-independently of the locally elected council that is responsible for a range of other goods and services, there is less incentive or possibility that local public sector efficiency, transparency, and accountability will be achieved. As well, if additional resources and time are wasted on reaching agreements and coordinating policies between these competing governing units, the system will be more expensive to administer than it should be.

As noted earlier, support for local government enterprises rests, partially at least, on the assertion that individuals appointed or elected to an enterprise's governing board can govern more efficiently and effectively than locally elected politicians, who are responsible for a range of local public sector goods and services. These services, it is argued, must be kept free from political interference. This approach to municipal government as basically corrupt and unrepresentative of consumer demands, however, is a poor principle upon which to organize municipal service responsibility.

Furthermore, arguments supporting removal from politics seem to be an attempt to substitute special politics for general politics, or a withdrawal from the struggle to change the political decisions of the community. And if politics is understood in the pejorative sense of partisan or personal patronage and influence, the independence of local government enterprises does not guarantee freedom from spoils but rather opens possibilities for methods of self-enrichment of their own. Technical specialists in many functions and their respective supporting groups of citizens may believe that their function is so important to the general welfare and the methods involved so technical that their objectives can be accomplished only if they are protected against interference by nonprofessionals (Bird 1980). Practical politics, however, involves compromise in the decision-making process. Experts and special interest groups should be available for advice on such decision making, but they need not be responsible for policy. In cases in which the proponents of an activity find the existing political situation distasteful, the tempting alternative of avoiding involvement must be resisted in favor of seeking basic political improvements.

Another dubious contention by advocates of local government enterprises is their assertion that funding specific goods and services from user fees or charges or through public sector prices is more business-like, and therefore preferred, if conducted by an independent or semi-independent business enterprise rather than if funded in the same manner but under the governance of a locally elected council. Such an argument overlooks the essentially political nature of decision making with regard to many services supported in whole or in part by user charges or public sector prices. There is no reason why a user-supported service cannot be operated on a business-like and self-sustaining basis under a department at city hall.

The existence of a number of independent and semi-independent enter-prises complicates local government to the point where citizens cannot under-stand its structure or determine who is responsible for what. The weakening of the municipal council through the removal of some responsibilities, com-bined with the inability of citizens to understand government (who is respon-sible for what), results in a loss of accountability, a lack of transparency, and reduced public interest in local government. As the municipal organization becomes more diffuse it becomes less accessible to political control. Also, the agencies into which local government is fragmented are often only indirectly responsible to the public, particularly if their members are appointed. Frag-mentation of government into separate enterprises further complicates the problems of administrative integration and coordination.

Bringing all governance and policy-making decisions for local enterprises under the governing responsibility of the local council (day-to-day manage-ment should be left to the managers, regardless of the governing structure) has been criticized, however, because local politicians in some countries appar-ently use these enterprises as places of employment for relatives, friends, and cronies. If governing responsibilities for enterprise operations were left with local enterprises, it has been suggested that these potentially inefficient and unfair employment practices could be minimized. There are at least two rea-sons why this might not be true. First, there is nothing inherent in either the governing structure of a local government enterprise or local council opera-tion to suggest that either agency is more or less susceptible to this type of employment abuse. Second, where this is a problem, its resolution should involve the implementation of fair, effective, and transparent employment policies that prevent this kind of nepotistic behavior.

Of the enterprises that exist, many enjoy considerable autonomy and financial independence. In fact, there is a tendency for them to become little governments in themselves with the inherent characteristic that they are inde-pendent and in no way subordinate to the elected municipal politicians. This can lead to an environment over which residents and taxpayers have little control and which is, hence, politically inefficient. For those that are funded partially by grants or local taxes, there is often no direct link between the policy-making body (that is, the body making the expenditure decisions) and the revenues (local taxes) that are collected by municipal councils and must be used to fund the agencies. Whenever expenditure and revenue decisions such as these are made independently, the system is likely to be less accountable or transparent[11] and unable to allocate its resources efficiently across all competing municipal services. When agencies are fully funded from sales of their output, there is greater likelihood that they will become independent and more removed from the governing decisions of the local council.

When a large number of independent single-purpose enterprises exist, coordination of inter-related activities is difficult and, in some instances, impossible to achieve (Kitchen 1989). Attempts by locally elected politicians to provide services are frequently thwarted or made more difficult because of decisions made by these independent enterprises over which the politicians have little, if any, control. For example, actions taken by electrical utilities, water and sewer utilities, and public transit authorities may conflict with the council's overall planning effort.

This institutional structure, which may be referred to as a *localized monopoly,* creates a potential impediment to the pursuit of competitive forces if municipal councils are prevented from making all decisions affecting the local municipality in the most accountable, transparent, and efficient manner. This may happen, for example, when a municipality defers all decisions on spending and funding until a local government enterprise has determined its level of spending and funding. For example, a decision by a separate water utility (enterprise) to replace or rehabilitate a water line or sewer main (underground services) may affect a municipality's timing for resurfacing or improving a local road or street (aboveground services). This, is turn, may affect the way in which the municipality allocates its resources to other municipal services (in terms of both timing and its choice of competing alternatives).[12] Similarly, if a decision by a local enterprise to borrow in order to finance the rehabilitation or provision of new capital infrastructure crowds out or inhibits the local council's ability to borrow for other capital projects (perhaps because of debt limits), then resources are not allocated efficiently.

In general, where municipal councils are directly responsible for a service, there tends to be greater pressure toward public accountability (Kitchen 1975) and political responsibility. Greater public accountability leads in turn to greater pressure to reduce costs,[13] improve efficiency, and justify expenditure increases. When compared with governance under a municipal council, most enterprises are free from the limelight of major municipal elections and consequently further removed from these important political pressures. The elections of commissioners, where elections rather than appointments occur, are generally dull affairs that go virtually unnoticed by the public and often result in acclamations. Voter apathy develops in municipal elections but the general desire to control costs at city hall extends to all departments, whereas such pressure is less frequently exerted on a separate enterprise.

Partly for this reason, many governing boards for local enterprises slip into the "rubber stamp syndrome" and allow policy decisions to stem from dominant, technically competent managers.

Connected with the idea of political accountability is the financial flexibility available to each type of organization. A sufficient degree of political leverage and direct accountability to the public must be maintained over the governance of local public services; otherwise, strong temptation exists for these organizations to engage in unwarranted expansion or to invest in new assets that are far out of line with investment in other municipal functions. Municipal council operations appear to satisfy such a condition much more than separate local enterprise operations, and the latter's financial freedom may permit greater indulgence in empire building (Kitchen 1975) and wasted expenditures.

An important source of economies available to operations run by a municipal council and often not available to single-purpose enterprises comes from the opportunity for certain personnel, facilities, and capital equipment to be engaged in multiple functions. First, municipally provided services may share office space at city hall, whereas separate enterprises are generally established in separate buildings. Second, a municipally governed service easily shares administrative and operational tasks with other departments at city hall (for example, accounting and legal services), whereas separate enterprise operations tend to set up their own administrative and operational facilities. In the latter structure, economies of scale and cost savings are less likely to be achieved than in the former structure. Third, opportunities exist for pooling capital equipment and labor in city-governed operations. Doing so permits a reduction in idle hours for capital and labor through the opportunity to transfer equipment and personnel to different functions as needs arise. As with many of its departments, city hall can achieve economies of scale in the use of unspecialized personnel and equipment. This source of savings is more important for smaller municipalities than for larger ones, because the smaller-scale operations are much more likely to encounter indivisibilities in capital and labor inputs. Local government enterprises, however, have a tendency to acquire a separate complement of labor and equipment. These inputs are not used, as a rule, for other municipal government functions. In many instances, especially for capital equipment, there is considerable downtime and lack of use of some of the capital equipment (Kitchen 1975).[14]

In summary, the economic and political arguments in support of independent and autonomous or semi-independent and semi-autonomous local government enterprises are generally weak. Such enterprises do not appear to contribute anything that is unique. Their existence creates or has the potential for creating decision-making problems and unnecessary costs both for local governments and for local residents. Elimination of local government enterprises should improve the extent to which local public sector efficiency, accountability, and transparency could be improved. Certainly, it would remove the confusion over who is responsible for what and allow local councils to set priorities and weigh and consider the trade-offs necessary in making decisions on the relative merits of spending on water and sewer systems, roads, public transit, police, firefighting, local parks, and other such services.

All of this discussion assumes, of course, that we are operating in a best world and that the current decision-making structures could be changed. Unfortunately, change may not be possible for many enterprises and in many countries. Local government enterprises are solidly entrenched in local public sector services. And they will continue to be used, even though they have declined in importance in some countries over the past decade[15] largely because of the types of decision-making problems described above.

Governance of Local Government Enterprises

Even though arguments in support of local government enterprises are not strong, these enterprises will continue to be responsible for a range of local goods and services in many countries. The discussion here, then, will concentrate on policies designed to improve the efficiency, accountability, and transparency of the governance structure of these agencies.

Governance refers to the political body responsible for making all policy decisions. It does not refer to the day-to-day management of local government or its enterprises,[16] and it does not refer to service delivery because that may be handled in a variety of ways. Because a major objective of the local government sector should be to design an overall governance structure that, in principle and as closely as possible in practice, meets the criteria described earlier, it is best achieved if all decision-making powers of the local public sector are left with a democratically elected local council. In effect, then, a case exists for governing all special-purpose bodies by the same body that governs city hall. Doing so creates an environment in which it would be easier to coordinate all municipal services and functions. It would also minimize conflicts between the policies of local enterprises and the policies of local councils. In principle, a system in which local councils have responsibility for making decisions on the appropriate trade-offs to be made for all local expenditures reduces the possibilities of conflict between local agencies seeking to promote special interests and the municipality attempting to hold the line on taxes, restricting expenditures, or altering expenditure choices among those services over which it does have substantial control.

Putting all decision-making powers on municipal public policy—including those that are politically sensitive and those that are not so politically sensitive—under council control should improve local accountability and responsiveness to the tax-paying public (Municipality of Metropolitan Toronto 1988; Stenning and Landau 1988). When one stops to think about it, an independent body in charge of a basic service such as water, sewers, electricity, police, and the like, that can set its own rates or determine its own property tax requirements, determine its own policies, and formulate and approve its long-range plans, has considerable control over the range of other municipal services, over how a community is governed, and over how and where it develops residentially, commercially, and industrially.

Private Sector Provision

The most obvious private sector delivery option is contracting out, but it is not the only option. Private sector involvement may also include the use of franchises, grants, vouchers, volunteers, and self-help (Savas 1982; Hatry 1983). Public-private partnerships have recently grown in interest as an acceptable option for funding services, especially where there may be substantial capital or infrastructure costs. Because each option is a unique way to deliver services, the potential efficiency strengths and weaknesses are discussed below.

Contracting Out

In the United Kingdom, local authorities are now required to enter into competitive tendering for the provision of municipal services. In New Zealand, legislation introduced in the early 1990s had a significant impact on the way services are provided, but it does not go as far as requiring competitive tendering. In New Zealand, service delivery exclusively by local council departments declined from 70 percent in 1989 to 26 percent in 1994, while delivery by business units rose from 2 percent to 18 percent (Department of Internal Affairs 1994). The core services of water supply, sewage systems, stormwater control, and drainage are delivered by business units in more than 50 percent of the councils, while the majority of councils that provided legal services, refuse collection, commercial forestry, and refuse disposal use external providers (Pallot 1998).

Because the current fashion is to advocate privatization of local public services, primarily through contracting out, the efficiency advantages of this action should be noted. In essence, it is alleged that contracting out through competitive tendering improves the competitive environment and leads to lower per unit operating costs for the delivery agent. Contractors face incentives to be efficient and sanctions if they are not. Contracting need not be only to the private sector; indeed, it could equally apply to enterprises and governments that contract from each other and for nonprofit and voluntary organizations as well (Bish 1986).

Contracts are typically awarded through a competitive tendering system in which the lowest bidder is normally chosen. In addition, some jurisdictions have adopted a policy whereby regions, counties, or cities are subdivided and contracts tendered for a series of subregions or areas for those services where economies of scale do not exist. The purpose is to encourage smaller firms to bid on contracts—a situation that would not arise if all contracts were large—and to permit, in some cases, municipal crews to compete with the private sector in securing a contract. This provides a stimulus for increased competition and ultimately, cost savings and greater efficiency. In fact, in some cities in the United States, it is not uncommon to see municipal government employees competing with the private sector for responsibility for service delivery. Where this has happened, considerable cost savings and efficiency gains have followed—along with enhanced service levels (Goldsmith 1997, 1998).

The most successful contracts tend to be those based on outputs that can be measured (solid waste, recycling, and the like) primarily because it is easier to monitor the quality of the output. As well, writing contracts in terms of outputs rather than inputs leaves the contractor free to organize the operation to attain output goals or targets in the most efficient way possible (Bish 1986).

Many local government politicians and administrators who are not strong advocates of contracting out have argued that service quality is inevitably lower in the private sector. This concern over quality deficiency has led to suggestions that a monitoring system be established to ensure that quality is maintained at an acceptable level. There is no a priori reason to believe, however, that public sector monitoring will be any more effective or efficient than a policy of competitive tendering for service delivery on a relatively frequent basis (annually, biannually, or every three years, for instance). Tendering, by itself, can create an incentive for a firm to maintain quality if it wishes to be a candidate for continuation of its contract at the time of rebidding.

Most of the empirical work on contracting out suggests that per unit operating costs are lower in privately run operations. Although the bulk of these studies have been completed in the United States and Europe

(Borcherding, Pommerehne, and Schneider 1982; Hike 1992), similar studies have been conducted in other countries. In New Zealand, for example, cost savings from contracting out are reported to range from 45 percent to 60 percent in the case of refuse collection in Dunedin to 15 percent to 30 percent for other services in Dunedin and Christchurch (Douglas 1994; Williamson 1994). In Canada, a number of studies on a variety of services (solid waste collection, recycling and disposal, public transit operations, and electrical utility maintenance) provide similar results (table 5.1). Similar results have been noted in an examination of private sector involvement in three urban services (waste collection, water supply, and electricity supply) in developing countries (Batley 2001). A further study that compiled the results of 203 separate studies on contracting out (without regard to whether public sector units were invited to bid) concluded that savings on the order of 20 percent were most frequently reported without any sacrifice in the quality of service (Domberger and Jensen 1997). Finally, a critical assessment of several studies concluded that the private sector is more efficient in refuse collection, fire protection, cleaning services, and capital-intensive wastewater treatment, while results are less conclusive for water supply and railways (Tang 1997).

Briefly, the conclusion of these studies is that most of the efficiency gains from contracting out have resulted from an increased scope for competition rather than from the fact that the service was provided by a private contractor (Bish 2001; Donohue 1989; Johnson 1988). In addition, the results suggest that where economies of scale are not prevalent, the creation of delivery zones creates a more competitive environment than exists when there is only one delivery agent for an entire municipality (Bartone 2001). Introducing or increasing rivalry, however, may not be possible without the existence of some private ownership. In other words, some degree of privatization through contracting out may be a necessary but not sufficient condition for substantial performance improvements (Vickers and Yarrow 1991).

Although most of the studies have concentrated on contracting out individual services, there is some experience in the United States with cities that contract out most service responsibilities. These cities have formed an Association of Contract Cities and are concentrated in California. This group has generated a highly competitive local service environment with a vast network of producers and contract arrangements. Cities buy and sell to one another, and private firms compete actively among themselves and with government producers for contracts (Bish 1986; Frontier Centre for Public Policy 1997). One empirical analysis of these contract cities indicated that they received services at lower cost than the noncontract cities in Los Angeles County (Deacon 1979).

TABLE 5.1 Private versus Public Sector Delivery in Canada

Services studied: author/year	Delivery alternatives	Results
Bus Service: Kitchen (1992)	Municipal dept. versus privately contracted service in Ontario municipalities.	Significantly lower costs per km. under privately contracted operation
Electric Utility Maintenance: Kitchen (1986)	Utilities contracting out utility maintenance vs. in-house maintenance in Ontario municipalities.	Contracted-out service significantly less expensive.
Refuse Collection: Kitchen (1976)	48 Canadian cities—municipal versus privately contracted firms.	Municipal suppliers more expensive than private firms.
McDavid, Richards & Doughton (1984)	Comparison of costs before and after Richmond, B.C. switched from private to public collection.	Residential solid waste collection fell from $46.24 per household in 1982 to $30.63 in 1983.
McDavid (1985)	Survey of private collection versus municipal collection of residential solid waste in 107 Canadian municipalities.	In municipalities with sole delivery agents (public versus private), collection was 51% more expensive in municipal operations. In municipalities with a mix of public and private, the public sector was 12% more expensive. Differences attributed to much higher productivity in private operations.
Tickner & McDavid (1986)	Detailed survey information on outputs, inputs and costs for private vs. public collection of residential waste obtained from 100 municipalities.	On average, private collectors were 28% less expensive.

(continued)

TABLE 5.1 Private versus Public Sector Delivery in Canada (*continued*)

Services studied: author/year	Delivery alternatives	Results
McRae (1994)	Comparison of charges for collection of commercial/industrial solid waste in 3 communities on Central Vancouver Island.	Depending on the size of container and frequency of pickup, municipal services were between 16% and 67% higher than private sector prices.
McDavid and Eder (1997)	327 questionnaire responses to survey on solid waste collection services in Canadian municipalities.	For all of Canada, government collection was 22.3% more costly per household than private contractors.
McDavid (2001)	327 questionnaire responses to survey on solid waste collection services in Canadian municipalities	–On average, public producers have higher costs than contracted private producers; –In municipalities where collection is split between private and public, both have lower costs than the national average and private producers are lower than public producers; –Municipalities that competitively bid their solid waste collection contract enjoy significantly lower costs per household.
Landfill Sites: McDavid and Laliberte (1998)	Comparison of operational cost of 72 public and private landfill sites across Canada.	Operational costs of privately run operations was lower—$15.75 per tonne compared to $23.48 per tonne.
Residential Recycling: McDavid and Laliberte (1999)	Private versus public sector comparison of 132 recycling agents	Net cost per tonne is virtually identical for public and private producers except in 7 communities where public and private producers compete directly. Here, substantial cost savings were reported for private producers when compared with public producers.

While potential cost reductions seem to be prevalent from increased competition, it is well understood that unions are generally opposed to contracting out (see Dijkgraaf, Gradus, and Melenberg 2003, 554; Canadian Union of Public Employees 1985). In particular, they are concerned about their members losing jobs and the extent to which contracting out would undermine the union, fragment the workforce, sidestep provisions of collective agreements, and reduce labor costs with resultant profit-taking opportunities for businesses (see Cassidy 1994). In addition, the cost savings and increased efficiencies noted in the empirical studies are not universally accepted because, it has been alleged, they fail to consider some important cost items. In particular, the critics have argued that contracting out results in additional costs due to time and money spent on drafting, negotiating, and monitoring a contract.[17] The contractee must train and oversee the contractor's employees to ensure productivity; and additional costs are incurred in laying off employees after their services have been contracted out (see Sauter, Weisman, and Percy 1988). Further concerns have arisen because employees do not identify with the company and because they have multiple clients and are not able to give priority to the current client (Cassidy 1994).

Offsetting these concerns and criticisms, however, are a number of advantages: greater flexibility for management in allocating human resources; greater productivity and efficiency, particularly if workers are paid on the basis of incentives; increased ability to hire specialized expertise when needed; reduced turnover; and greater variety for the employee (Cassidy 1994; Dijkgraaf, Gradus, and Melenberg 2003).

Franchises

A franchise exists when a private firm provides a service to residents within a specific geographic area and when the supplier is paid (price or user fee) directly by the users (customers or clients). Franchises may be exclusive (one producer) or nonexclusive (many producers).

If services are provided by exclusive franchises, prices may have to be regulated.[18] Further regulations may be imposed to guarantee that quality standards or performance measures are met and that all consumers within a specific area (served by the franchise) have access to the service if they pay for it. For exclusive franchises that are largely capital intensive, not tendered on a frequent basis, and not subject to competitive forces (such as water and wastewater), adherence to performance standards is essential[19]—along with carefully drawn-up contracts spelling out the terms and conditions of the agreement. For services that are not capital intensive (refuse collection, for example), frequent tendering for the right to provide the service (similar to contracting out) should assist in maintaining the necessary competitive forces to ensure high quality and low cost.

For services provided by nonexclusive franchises, price regulation and monitoring activities would likely be less needed. The attractiveness of this organizational structure is mainly a function of the number of firms involved and hence the degree of competition created. The larger the number of firms is, the more competitive is the environment and hence, the greater is the incentive for improving efficiency, lowering costs, and providing quality services.

A possible problem with franchise operations is that some users (perhaps low-income families) may discontinue consumption of certain services. If users view the price of the service as being too high, they may decide to do without it or to find a substitute. This has occurred primarily in smaller communities, where solid waste collection has been privatized and franchised. Not only could this lead to unsanitary conditions and impose externalities on those who pay, it could lead to lower-quality service or greater costs for existing users if economies of scale disappear. Use of a franchise operation in lieu of contracting out, therefore, may not be desirable on the grounds of efficiency, especially for services from which negative externalities might be created because individuals choose not to use the service.

Where franchises are considered, a franchise agreement between the local council and the supplier is critical. It is the core legal document by which both parties are bound and which can be enforced. This agreement should include, among other items,

- terms of payment for a franchise fee
- principles and practices to follow in setting prices
- all standards and performance measures that are to be met
- a list and description of all financial and performance reports that are to be provided on a regular basis to the local council and the public
- procedures to follow in renegotiating standards and conditions in the agreement
- for services where ownership of capital assets are retained by local council, the conditions for their return at the end of the agreement period

Grants for Specific Services

Grants are often provided by local governments for various community groups and activities, including volunteer groups, charitable organizations, recreational and cultural activities, and special boards such as arena boards and library boards. Some of these grants are ad hoc while others are provided annually, although applicants for annual grants are often required to apply each year. On efficiency grounds, grants are justified if the service delivered through the grant-receiving agency is provided less expensively or more efficiently relative to provision by the municipal government directly. For example, if the grant is to a volunteer organization, it may be less expensive to deliver the service through this type of organization than through some body or organization at city hall.

Grants to boards involved in the production of a service are typically made to cover all or a portion of operating costs (library boards, for instance). Once again, on efficiency grounds, this policy may be appropriate if the service can be provided less expensively than under the responsibility of local government directly. Implicit in this statement, of course, is the condition that the budgets for these boards must be determined by the local council in competition with the range of other services provided by local government.

In reality, local government grants are almost never given to improve productive efficiency. They are generally given for one of two reasons: first, to appease specific groups who are persuasive in appealing to the social conscience of local councils to support their causes; or second, to provide a particular service through a special board (library board, for example) that is at least one step removed from direct council responsibility.

Vouchers

Vouchers are yet another way of privatizing the provision of public services, with their distribution coming directly from municipal governments to citizens deemed to be eligible for a particular service. The user then submits the voucher to the private provider of his or her choice. The provider, in turn, forwards the voucher to the government for payment (which, in all likelihood, would be a constant dollar amount per voucher of the same type).

Determining the cash value of the voucher (that is, the value that the government pays to each firm) is particularly important, because the value could affect the production and delivery efficiency of the provider. The quantity and quality of the service supplied must be stipulated. For example, if the cash value of the voucher is set equal to the average cost of each unit delivered by the firm or if it equals a weighted average of costs incurred by all firms, the scheme may penalize more efficient producers. To overcome this problem, the per unit cash value should equal the average cost of the most efficient supplier. The advantage of this payment schedule is that a highly efficient firm can lower its costs to governments and, in turn, to taxpayers.

A system of vouchers can provide incentives for diversity and hence, a large number of producers—thus increasing the choice available to residents. For this reason, the delivery of services such as day care, homemaker services, foster homes, and group homes could be well suited to a voucher system. Vouchers are frequently used for public transportation for welfare recipients and the disabled, and sometimes for medical expenses.

A potential offshoot of increasing the choice for voucher holders is the increase in service quality and efficiency that should follow. This outcome, however, would depend on the effectiveness of the information network established among voucher holders. If the network is effective, the existence of competitive forces should lead to improvements in service quality and should lower delivery costs. Reduced delivery costs, however, may be partially offset by increased monitoring and administration costs—to prevent voucher forgery, for example.

Although this approach may encounter some administrative and monitoring problems, experimentation with a voucher system for certain services ought to be encouraged. Initially, vouchers might be tried in those areas where the government is providing assistance to nongovernmental agencies, such as social services for low-income families.

Volunteers

Volunteers are used by governments in many countries to deliver specific services. One typically observes unpaid help in places such as libraries, hospitals, and teachers' aid programs, where volunteers are normally assigned to tasks that might not otherwise be undertaken.

Smaller municipalities in Canada and the United States frequently have volunteer fire departments or a mix of volunteer and professional firefighters. In fact, one study on 104 municipal fire departments in Canadian municipalities in 1981 and 1982 concluded that fire departments employing a mix of full-time and part-time (volunteer) firefighters in communities up to 50,000 people enjoyed the benefits of lower fire service costs without sacrificing effectiveness (McDavid 1986). In communities of more than 50,000 people, effectiveness tended to diminish with a mixed force. As well, the effectiveness of an entirely part-time fire department was reduced because the firefighters took longer, on average, getting to fires.

Since existing labor is usually not replaced (at least in the first instance) by volunteers, one cannot presume that the use of volunteers will lower delivery costs immediately. Indeed, there may be some administrative costs in maintaining a volunteer staff; for example, training programs, guidance, and general coordination requirements consume regular staff members' time.

Although costs may be lower in the short run, the dependence on volunteers may also lower costs in the long run, especially if volunteers serve as substitutes for paid employees. Further cost savings arise, in both the short and the long run, if the use of volunteers permits extra service or longer hours of service—as with volunteer library assistance, for example. Whether this use improves the quality of existing services greatly depends on the quality of the volunteers and the perception of recipients (the use of volunteers in hospitals, for example, may be perceived to improve the quality of hospital care).

A potential problem in using volunteers arises if they are available only at selected times (weekends or evenings, for instance) or if they are not dependable—which they may not be because they are not paid to perform. Further problems and costs might be incurred if a system of continuous recruitment is necessary in order to staff the volunteer program.

Self-Help Groups

The self-help concept is closely related to the concept of using volunteers. Self-help programs are designed so that individuals or neighborhoods provide services for themselves. Typical examples in North America include "neighborhood watch" and "block parent" programs, or flooding and maintaining outdoor ice-skating surfaces in neighborhood parks. These programs have grown in popularity over the past few years. In some of the larger municipalities, residents on certain streets or in certain neighborhoods have collectively organized (and provided funds) for the purpose of hiring security firms to reduce the incidence of crime and generally improve safety for local residents. Here, the service is provided and paid for directly by the users.

Whether self-help groups (for many services) are willing to organize on their own is a debatable issue and, of course, is likely to depend on the severity of the reason for organizing in the first instance. For example, citizens are more likely to organize for protection purposes than for maintaining a neighborhood park. Unless it can be proven that delivery costs will fall or service quantity and quality will rise for the beneficiaries (for example, through improved security), individuals are unlikely to agree to undertake the activity. In addition, there is the obvious problem of operating a delivery system if free riders emerge. This problem is likely to be more apparent if large setup costs are involved in establishing certain services. Given these potential problems, efficiency gains will be maximized only if the majority of residents within a given jurisdiction agree to cooperate.

Conversely, if governments are able to convince established groups or neighborhoods to convert to self-provision as a substitute for rather than an addition to existing public services, then significant savings in the delivery of specific services might be realized. These savings, however, may be offset or partially offset by increased personnel costs associated with their delivery.

Further problems and increased costs may arise if self-help groups decide, after a short period, to terminate their activity and revert to public provision of the service, possibly by increasing pressure on local politicians to supply the service through the local public sector. Clearly, such indecision could create inefficiencies and higher costs. To avoid these costs partial government assistance may be required—not only during the initial establishment stages but also on an ongoing basis. In fact, this is frequently the practice with maintaining outdoor neighborhood skating surfaces in municipalities in Canada: the local government often pays a small per diem honorarium to a resident of the neighborhood to ensure that the ice is maintained for local residents.

Private Nonprofit Agencies

A number of services have traditionally been provided by private nonprofit agencies in many countries. Common examples in North America include organizations such as Alcoholics Anonymous, the Salvation Army, and the United Way. If these organizations provide services that would otherwise be provided by local governments, cost savings may be observed. Three potential concerns arise, however, from dependence on the nonprofit sector. First, it may be difficult to ensure a high-quality service since that may depend on the quality of the people working for the agency. Second, without a reliable and ongoing source of funding, these organizations may not be a stable supplier of services. Third and perhaps more philosophically, there is the important issue of whether the public sector is relinquishing some of its public responsibility by relying on nonprofit agencies (with no or very little financial assistance from municipal governments) to provide services such as food banks and shelters.

Mix of Delivery Systems

In addition to the large number of purely public and purely private delivery systems, more and more services are being provided by a mix of these organizations. This mix may consist of provision by one government (level of government or department or local business enterprise) for another government or governmental agency, or it may consist of the private sector providing part of a service (generally through contracting out) for a government department or agency. This use of mixed delivery systems has increased substantially over the past decade. In some instances, this mix of delivery systems is designed to take advantage of savings that arise from economies of scale or scope in the provision of a number of services. These economies are attributed to efficiencies that may be gained from serving a larger population or geographical area. In other instances, however, this mix is used to overcome problems of diseconomies of scale because no municipal government is the most efficient size for providing all public services. As well, by introducing more competition into delivery systems, this mix may resolve concerns over efficiency problems created by monopolistic service providers.

Examples where one government contracts from an adjacent and generally larger governmental unit occur in matters such as road maintenance and repairs; operation and maintenance of municipal electric utilities; repair and servicing of public works vehicles; operation of transit services; accounting and legal administrative services; solid waste management; and the like. Most governmental construction projects, including buildings, roads, water and sewage lines, and certain professional services such as engineering design, consultants' studies, and legal advice, are contracted from the private sector.

Public-Private Partnerships

Although policy-making and funding decisions about public sector infrastructure must ultimately be the responsibility of the governing council, that does not mean the governing body must own the assets and deliver the services (see Savas 1987, chapter 6; Osborne and Gaebler 1992; Kolderie 1986; Wunsch 1991; Ostrom, Schroeder, and Wynne 1993; Batley 2001; Freire and Stren 1994; and World Bank 1994). Asset ownership and service delivery may be handled in a variety of ways including some type of public-private partnership.[20] The major implications of such partnerships are discussed in this section.

Over the past decade or so, there has been a growing interest in delivering public sector infrastructure through public-private partnerships (Hrab 2003a, 2003b), particularly for services that have substantial capital costs. To illustrate, 85 percent of government respondents to a survey by the Canadian Council for Public-Private Partnerships noted that their government was increasing its reliance on public-private partnerships (Martin 2001). Similar trends have been noted in other countries (Szalai 2001). This involvement can take different forms, including project initiation or planning, construction, operation, ownership, and financing. These public-private partnerships are a form of contracting out and involve the direct participation of one sector in a venture controlled by the other sector. Both partners contribute funds or services in exchange for certain rights or future income.

Public-private partnerships can take many forms, such as the following:

- The private sector operates the facility for a fee. The public sector retains responsibility for capital costs.
- The private sector leases or purchases the facility from the public sector, operates the facility, and charges user fees.
- The private sector builds or develops a new facility, or enlarges or renovates an existing facility, and then operates it for a number of years.
- The private sector builds the required infrastructure, operates the facility for some specified period of time, and then transfers it to the government.
- The private sector builds and operates the facility and is responsible for capital financing. The public sector regulates and controls the operation.
- The private sector builds the infrastructure and then transfers ownership to the public sector.

Public-private partnerships provide some advantages. In addition to providing a source of capital funds, they enable the public sector to draw on private sector expertise (Conference Board of Canada 2003) and skill in order to minimize costs. This advantage may be especially important to small municipalities, which may have greater difficulty than large ones in attracting expertise. Third, private sector involvement tends to lead to more innovative and efficient operations than if the public sector provides the service on its own (Probyn 1997).

Like most options, public-private partnerships also have disadvantages. First, there may be some uncertainty about whether the private sector will be able to carry out its role, especially if there is a risk of private sector bankruptcy in the provision of essential local services. Second, there is a potential loss of control to the private sector. Third, there may be a trade-off of upfront capital costs for future operating costs; for example, the annual cost of private sector financing of a project may turn out to be greater than the cost of public sector financing would have been (De Luca 1997; Probyn 1997). Finally, private sector financing may include government financial or credit backing, hence continuing to impose a potential burden on the public sector.

Experience with public-private partnerships suggests that, in general, most have produced cost savings (Slack 1996; Mann 1999), efficiency improvements, and expanded services, with the most notable improvements occurring in the presence of meaningful competition (Harris 2003; Hrab 2003a). Even where competition has not been prevalent and service provision has remained largely monopolistic, the evidence suggests that where the private sector bears the risk, private participation delivers better results that any credible public sector alternative (Harris 2003). It is also apparent that public-private partnerships are more appropriate for infrastructure that provides services with characteristics of private goods.

For a governing jurisdiction that may be considering a public-private partnership, the following questions should be asked and answered (Bartone 2001; Carr 1996):

- To what extent is it possible to describe objective standards and performance measures for the service?
- Is competition present—that is, are there two or more contractors able and willing to provide the service?
- Would it be possible to replace the private provider if the firm goes out of business or its performance is below standard?
- Has the asset in question been outsourced elsewhere?
- To what extent will the government be able to monitor the contractors' performance?
- What impact would outsourcing have on current employees?
- How much opposition might there be to privatization?
- Is private sector involvement in the asset in question legal?
- How much time will it take to structure and implement privatization?

If the answers to these questions suggest that a public-private partnership is appropriate, one further question remains and that is "What role should the government play?"

What Is the Role for Local Government?

Because public-private partnerships for most physical infrastructure projects are monopolistic and because they provide services that were or could be provided by the public sector, there is likely to be a role for local government. Local governments need not be involved in the construction of the asset nor should they be involved in the day-to-day management and delivery of services provided by this asset. Instead, the government should, through a carefully drawn-up contractual agreement, set the terms and conditions for service delivery, funding, and quality and establish performance standards or measures to be met. It could even set out the pricing structure to be used (volumetric pricing for water and sewers, tolls for roads, user fees for solid waste disposal, and so on). In addition, government involvement might consist of setting up a price regulatory system or introducing monitoring practices that could include the establishment of performance measures.

Price Regulation

Although private sector providers are likely to oppose price regulatory schemes (Mann 1999), support for price regulation is founded on the premise that it is necessary to protect consumers and taxpayers from inefficient and unfair price increases when decisions about service responsibility and funding are made in an environment in which there is no competition (KPMG and CMS Cameron McKenna 2002). Setting up a regulatory system is a complex task, however. When should prices be regulated? Who should regulate them? How should they be regulated?

- *When?* Current practice in many countries is inconsistent when it comes to local price regulation. For example, prices are regulated for specific local government services (electricity, for instance), but not for other services in the same countries (water and sewer, public transit). The rationale behind this differential treatment is far from clear. The practice appears to be based on tradition and what is done elsewhere as opposed to any solid economic rationale. Presumably, however, the case for price regulation is strongest in instances where competitive pressures both in terms of decision making (lack of opportunity for local council to make decisions on the trade-offs for all local goods and services) and production and delivery are weakest, as in noncontestable markets.
- *Who?* Should regulation be the responsibility of the governing council or of an independent body set up by the governing council? Of these options, the use of an independent regulatory body operating at arm's length from all levels of government—with experts appointed jointly by local and senior levels of government and fully versed in financial, budgetary, and operational details—may best serve local citizens. Certainly, it may minimize the opportunity for public sector interference in the day-to-day activities of the private sector provider.
- *How?* What benchmark or criterion should be used in determining the appropriate price? Should the price be based on financial costs or eco-

nomic costs? Should it be based on a defined standard of service, and if so, what is that standard?

These are not easy questions to answer. In general, price regulatory schemes have two common prototypes: rate of return and price cap regulation (Szalai 2001). Where rate of return is used, the regulator defines a fair and reasonable profit level, and the company has the opportunity to increase the price to the point where its maximum profit level is reached. Because reasonable profit is counted as a percentage of the asset base, the company has an incentive to overinvest so as to increase its asset base and hence, its profit. Further concerns with this regulatory pricing scheme exist because there is little incentive for the provider to be efficient and vigilant in controlling costs, because providers are generally permitted to recover all costs. Monitoring this price is time consuming and expensive because it would require regulators to check the usefulness of all investments so that unnecessary ones could be dropped from the asset base—a formidable task, to say the least.

Price cap regulatory schemes concentrate on creating incentives for the enterprise to increase efficiency.[21] This scheme adjusts the regulated price each year by the rate of inflation minus the rate of the expected efficiency gain. If the company reduces its costs through technological innovation or production efficiencies, it earns extra profit. If it does not, it incurs a deficit. A major difficulty with this scheme is establishing a measure of efficiency. The practice has been to compare relevant performance indicators for a company or utility with similar indicators from companies or utilities in other municipalities or to take the average for all similar enterprises within a country, adjusted for geography and other factors that affect cost. The difference between a specific provider and the comparator group may be called the *efficiency deficit* (gap). Where a deficit arises, it is not always expected that it will be corrected immediately. It may take a few years, with a condition that a specific percentage of the deficit be removed each year. For example, the water regulator in the United Kingdom requires that less efficient companies close 50 percent of the gap yearly. Again, such regulation, to be effective and efficient, requires a high degree of knowledge and competence on the part of the regulator.

Where the costs are less than expected under price cap regulation, owners of the physical infrastructure will earn unexpectedly high profits. One solution here is to give each customer a refund (at the end of the fiscal year) equal to that customer's share of the profit (this could be referred to as a *patronage dividend*). Another possibility, although less preferable economically because it would reward those customers who did not consume the service in the year when the profit was earned, would be to use the profits to reduce prices in the following year.

Monitoring

Where public-private partnerships are used, governments may also wish to monitor the activity and performance of private sector providers through the use of performance measures. Although performance measures are relatively new for the public sector or for private providers of services for the public sector, their importance is widely recognized and has been for some time (Hatry 1999). A performance measure, if correctly set, records the output, rather than the input, of spending on specific programs or services.

Implementation of a performance measurement system has a number of advantages. It allows providers and consumers to compare performance over time and across similar agencies and municipalities—referred to as *benchmarking*. It strengthens accountability because consumers and taxpayers are in a better position to evaluate the services provided given the cost of producing them and, therefore, are in a better position to judge whether service provision is effective and efficient. It enhances transparency because citizens will be able to observe and monitor activities more closely. Performance measures reinforce managerial accountability (Solano and Brams 1996) and often provide an incentive to stimulate staff creativity and productivity. Finally, performance measures help providers develop budgets on the basis of realistic economic costs and benefits rather than historical patterns (incrementalism).

Performance measures are also used for determining the effectiveness of service delivery. Effectiveness measures the extent to which an activity contributes to the achievement of the stated goals, objectives, or targets. For example, an activity such as building a road may be very efficient in terms of cost per kilometer, but its effectiveness will depend on the usefulness of the road in providing convenience, safety, and economy for vehicular transportation. When a direct evaluation of the benefits arising from local services is not possible, the demand for services that are subject to quality standards could be measured through citizen surveys, studies of local economic conditions, reports on the number of applications, tallies of requests or complaints received, or expert evaluations. In this way, a measure of the value of the service provided can be estimated. Thus, effectiveness will measure the success not only of doing things, but also of doing them to citizens' satisfaction.

Performance measures are now required for a wide range of services in all municipalities and their agencies in Ontario, Canada. More than 100 municipalities across North America now participate in a municipal performance measurement program developed by the International City/County Management Association (Ontario Ministry of Municipal Affairs and Housing 2003). These municipalities share their performance measurement results with each other annually. Sharing information on performance measures should help improve the efficiency, accountability, and transparency of private sector partners, as long as the results are reported to users on an annual basis. This reporting could take a variety of forms, including mailings to all users and residents through property tax or utility bills, notices in local newspapers, and postings on municipalities' Web sites.

Summary

Municipal services may be delivered in a variety of ways. Alternatives range from complete public provision to complete private provision to a mix of public and private provision, including public-private partnerships. For public sector provision, the economic and political arguments in support of independent and autonomous or semi-independent and semi-autonomous special-purpose bodies are generally weak. These bodies do not contribute anything that is unique. Their existence creates or has the potential for creating decision-making problems and unnecessary costs both for local governments and for local residents. Eliminating special-purpose bodies and transferring their responsibilities to the municipal council should improve the extent to which local public sector efficiency, accountability, and transparency could be improved. Certainly, doing so would remove the confusion about who is responsible for what and allow local councils to set priorities and weigh and consider the trade-offs necessary in making decisions on the relative merits of spending on water and sewer systems, roads, public transit, police, firefighting, local parks, and other services.

Although private sector provision of municipal services is generally interpreted as contracting out or entering into public-private partnerships, it also includes the use of franchises, grants for specific services or functions, vouchers, volunteers, self-help groups, and private nonprofit agencies. Privatization does not mean that governments should forego ownership of municipal services. Indeed, they should retain the right to set standards and specify conditions and should generally retain overall responsibility through the use of contractual arrangements. The private sector's role is to deliver services according to the specifications and conditions laid out by government.

A number of studies at the municipal level compare the costs of delivering services through the public and private sectors. In each study, the cost comparison is between local government provision and provision by contracting out to the private sector. In virtually all cases, significant per unit cost savings have been observed for private sector provision. This saving, it is argued, is due to competitive forces present in private sector delivery but generally absent in public sector delivery.

Overwhelming as the empirical evidence may be, it has not silenced some critics. Perhaps the strongest criticism has come from public sector unions, which feel particularly vulnerable because of possible job losses and reduced bargaining power. Nonetheless, contracting out has the potential for increasing management's flexibility in managing human resources, for increasing productivity (especially if incentives are built into payment schemes), for improving a manager's ability to hire specialized expertise when needed, and for lowering the public sector's payroll costs.

Although there has been relatively limited discussion and application of the role of franchises, grants, vouchers, volunteers, self-help programs, and private nonprofit agencies in delivering public services, these instruments or organizations may become important in the future, especially if governments reduce or discontinue some services. Similarly, there is increasing evidence that public-private partnerships will grow in importance.

As for the future of private sector delivery of public services, the debate will continue. There will be advocates for greater privatization, as there will be critics. In reality, however, political pressure to reduce government expenditures and reduce or restrict increases in taxes and user fees will force governments to resort to private sector delivery in one form or another, for a variety of what are currently referred to as municipal services. In fact, this shift is even legislated or mandated in some countries.

Notes

1. Special-purpose bodies and local government enterprises have similar structures and objectives and may be referred to as business enterprises or enterprises here.
2. It should be noted that there is no practical and useful way of cataloging the frequency of use of each option.
3. An earlier version of the material in the first part of this chapter appears in Kitchen (2001).
4. A natural monopolist is often depicted by local utility services (water, sewers, and natural gas, where it is a municipal responsibility). Their predominant characteristic for analytical purposes here is that they exhibit decreasing per unit costs over the entire range of output (economies of scale).
5. These are the same criteria that are used in evaluating municipal finance issues. Their application in local service delivery, however, differs somewhat from their application in local financing issues.
6. For a discussion of the benefit model of local finance, see Bird (1993).

7. For a discussion of income redistribution and how it should be handled, see Boadway and Kitchen (1999, chapter 8).

8. Economic efficiency is more than technical efficiency—the latter is a necessary but not sufficient condition for economic efficiency. Technical efficiency exists when a producing unit (firm, government, commission) operates in such a way that it is not possible to secure any additional output given the available inputs (labor, material, and capital) and level of technology. In other words, technical efficiency is achieved when the output per unit of input is maximized or the cost per unit of output is minimized. This, it should be noted, is not concerned with whether one good or service generates more or fewer net benefits than another good or service. It simply concentrates on the efficient employment of inputs in the production of a specific good or service. Finally, as the level of technology advances, a technically efficient production process leads to increased output with the same inputs.

9. This corresponds to IMF (2001).

10. For a discussion of the importance of distinguishing between decision making or governance and service delivery, see Savas (1987, chapter 6); Osborne and Gaebler (1992); Kolderie (1986); Wunsch (1991); Ostrom, Schroeder, and Wynne (1993); Batley (2001); Freire and Stren (1994); and World Bank (1994).

11. For a discussion of the importance of this linkage between revenues and expenditures, see Bossons, Kitchen, and Slack (1993).

12. Information was gathered from interviews with municipal officials in Ontario. Similar results have been observed for school board and police spending (both are under governing structures that are independent of the municipal council) in Ontario, where the expenditure decisions and ensuing property tax requirements of these two independent local bodies frequently crowd out municipal expenditures over which the municipal council has control. Crowding out, it is argued, occurs because municipal councils are reluctant to raise property taxes (for municipal expenditures) and incur the wrath of local citizens if expenditure decisions of school boards and police boards have resulted in higher property taxes for their specific services. See Tassonyi and Locke (1994) and Knapton (1993).

13. The results of Kitchen (1976) indicated that the costs of supplying water through a separate water utility or enterprise were significantly higher than the costs of supplying it by a department directly responsible to the municipal council.

14. Kitchen (1975); For a more recent illustration and discussion, see Armstrong and Kitchen (1997, 134–39).

15. In Ontario, reliance on utility commissions (local enterprises) for water provision declined from 112 separate utilities in 1990, to 41 in 2000, and 15 in 2001 (Sancton and Janik 2001, table 3).

16. In New Zealand, it is legislated that policy-making responsibilities of elected municipal councils must be decoupled from day-to-day management of the authority (Pallot 1998).

17. For a discussion on the proper design of contracts along with efficient monitoring systems, see David (1988).

18. For a discussion of price regulation, see the section on public-private partnerships later in this chapter.

19. Discussed under monitoring in the section on public-private partnership later in this chapter.

20. The use of public-private partnerships to finance capital infrastructure is discussed in Kitchen (2004).
21. For a more detailed discussion, see KPMG and CMS Cameron McKenna (2002, part V).

References

Armstrong, W. Douglas, and Harry Kitchen. 1997. "Peterborough County/City Municipal Review." Report prepared for the Joint Restructuring Committee of the City and County of Peterborough, ON.

Bahl, Roy, and Christine I. Wallich. 1995. "Intergovernmental Fiscal Relations in the Russian Federation." In *Decentralization of the Socialist State,* eds. Richard M. Bird, Robert D. Ebel, and Christine I. Wallich, 321–78. Washington, DC: World Bank.

Bartone, Carl R. 2001. "The Role of the Private Sector in Municipal Solid Waste Service Delivery in Developing Countries: Keys to Success." In *The Challenge of Urban Government: Policies and Practices,* ed. Mila Freire and Richard Stren, 215–23. Washington, DC: World Bank.

Batley, Richard. 2001. "Public-Private Partnerships for Urban Services." In *The Challenge of Urban Government: Policies and Practices,* ed. Mila Freire and Richard Stren, 199–214. Washington, DC: World Bank.

Bird, Richard M. 1980. *Central-Local Fiscal Relations and the Provision of Urban Public Services.* Canberra: Australian National University, Centre for Research on Federal Financial Relations.

———. 1984. *Intergovernmental Finance in Colombia.* Cambridge, MA: Harvard Law School, International Tax Program.

———. 1993. "Threading the Fiscal Labyrinth: Some Issues in Fiscal Decentralization." *National Tax Journal* 46 (2): 207–27.

Bish, Robert L. 1986. "Improving Productivity in the Government Sector: The Role of Contracting Out." In *Responses to Economic Change,* ed. David Laidler, 203–37, Vol. 27 of the *Royal Commission on the Economic Union and Development Prospects for Canada.* Toronto, ON: University of Toronto Press.

———. 2001. *Local Government Amalgamations: Discredited Nineteenth-Century Ideals Alive in the Twenty-First.* Toronto, ON: C. D. Howe Institute.

Boadway, Robin, and Harry Kitchen. 1999. *Canadian Tax Policy,* 3rd ed. Toronto, ON: Canadian Tax Foundation.

Borcherding, Thomas E., Werner Pommerehne, and Friedrich Schneider. 1982. "Comparing the Efficiency of Private and Public Provision: The Evidence from Five Countries." *Nationalökonomie Journal of Economics* 42 (Suppl. 2): 127–56.

Bossons, John, Harry Kitchen, and Enid Slack. 1993. "Local Government Finance: Principles and Issues." Paper prepared for the Ontario Fair Tax Commission, Toronto, ON.

Canadian Union of Public Employees. 1985. "Contracting Out: It's a Trend CUPE Must Continue to Oppose." *Facts* 7: 14–15.

Carr, Glenna. 1996. "Promoting Entrepreneurial Municipalities." Background paper for the Greater Toronto Area Task Force, Toronto, ON.

Cassidy, Gordon. 1994. "Contracting Out." Discussion Paper 94-06, School of Policy Studies, Queen's University, Kingston, ON.

Conference Board of Canada. 2003. *Defining the Canadian Advantage.* Ottawa: Conference Board of Canada.

David, Irwin T. 1988. *Privatization in America, Municipal Yearbook.* Washington, DC: International City Management Association.

Deacon, Robert T. 1979. "The Expenditure Effects of Alternative Public Supply Institutions." *Public Choice* 34: 381–97.

De Luca, Loretta, ed. 1997. *Labour and Social Dimensions of Privatization and Restructuring—Public Utilities, Water, Gas, Electricity: Part II Europe.* Geneva: International Labour Organization, Interdepartmental Action Program on Privatization, Restructuring, and Economic Democracy.

Department of Internal Affairs. 1994. "Territorial Authority Service Delivery 1993–1994." Wellington, New Zealand.

Dijkgraaf, Elbert, Raymond Gradus, and Bertrand Melenberg. 2003. "Contracting Out Refuse Collection." *Empirical Economics* 28: 553–70.

Domberger, Simon, and Paul Jensen. 1997. "Contracting Out by the Public Sector: Theory, Evidence, Prospects." *Oxford Review of Economic Policy* 4: 67–78.

Donohue, John. 1989. *The Privatization Decision: Public Ends, Private Means.* New York: Basic Books.

Douglas, M., 1994. "New Zealand Paths to Competitive Tendering." In *Introducing Competitive Tendering in Local Government in Australia,* 87–112. Melbourne, Australia: RMIT University, Department of Management, Foundation for Local government Education and Development Fund.

Freire, Mila, and Richard Stren, eds. 2001. In *The Challenge of Urban Government: Policies and Practices,* ed. 199–214. Washington, DC: World Bank.

Frontier Centre for Public Policy. 1997. "California Contract Cities." Policy Brief, Winnipeg, MB.

Goldsmith, Stephen. 1997. "Can Business Really Do Business with Government? The Answer Is Yes, Just Ask the Mayor of Indianapolis." *Harvard Business Review* (May–June): 110–21.

———. 1998. "Smaller Government Prescriptions for Big City Problems." *Fraser Forum* (September): 6–15.

Harris, Clive. 2003. *Private Participation in Infrastructure in Developing Countries: Trends, Impacts, and Policy Decisions.* Washington, DC: World Bank.

Hatry, Harry. 1983. *A Review of Private Approaches for Delivery of Public Services.* Washington, DC: Urban Institute Press.

———. 1999. *Performance Measurement.* Washington, DC: Urban Institute Press.

Hike, John. 1992. *Competition in Government Financed Services.* Westport, CT: Quorum Books.

Hrab, Roy. 2003a. "Private Delivery of Public Services: Public Private Partnerships and Contracting-Out." Research Paper 21, prepared for the Panel on the Role of Government in Ontario. http://www.law-lib.utoronto.ca/investing/index.htm.

———. 2003b. "Privatization: Experiences and Prospects." Research Paper 22, prepared for the Panel on the Role of Government in Ontario. http://www.law-lib.utoronto.ca/investing/index.htm.

IMF (International Monetary Fund). 2001. *Code of Good Practices on Fiscal Transparency.* Washington, DC.; IMF.

Johnson, Christopher, ed. 1988. *Privatization and Ownership.* London: Lloyds Bank Review.

Kitchen, Harry. 1975. "Some Organizational Implications of Providing An Urban Service: The Case of Water." *Canadian Public Administration* (Summer): 297–308.

———. 1976. "A Statistical Estimation of an Operating Cost Function for Municipal Refuse Collection." *Public Finance Quarterly* (January): 56–76.

———. 1986. "Local Government Enterprise in Canada." Discussion Paper 300, Economic Council of Canada.

———. 1989. *Report and Recommendations: A Review of Regional Government in Niagara.* Toronto, ON: Queen's Printer for Ontario.

———. 1992. "Urban Transit Provision in Ontario: A Public/Private Sector Cost Comparison." *Public Finance Quarterly* 20 (1): 114–28.

———. 1993. "Efficient Delivery of Local Government Services." Discussion Paper 93-15, School of Policy Studies, Queens University, Kingston, ON, Canada.

———. 2001. "Local Government Enterprise." World Bank, Washington, DC. http://www.worldbank.org/wbi/publicfinance/decentralization/fiscalfederalism_Russia.htm.

———. 2004. "Financing Local Government Capital Investment." Paper prepared for International Seminar on Local Public Finance and Governance, Dali, China, August 9–12.

Knapton, David. 1993. "Police Commissions: Do They Crowd Out Other Municipal Expenditures?" Honors economics essay, Trent University, Economics Department, Peterborough, ON.

Kolderie, Ted. 1986. "Two Different Concepts of Privatization." *Public Administration Review* 46: 285–91.

KPMG and CMS Cameron McKenna. 2002. "Analysis of Business Models and Their Applicability to Ontario." Study 7, Part IV, prepared for the Ontario SuperBuild Corporation, Toronto, ON.

Kurlyandskaya, Galina, Yelena Nikolayenko, and Natalia Golovanova. 2001. "Local Governments in the Russian Federation." Paper prepared for Local Government and Public Service Reform Initiative, Open Society Institute, Budapest.

Mann, Patrick C. 1999. "Financing Mechanisms for Capital Improvements for Regulated Water Utilities." Report prepared for the National Regulatory Research Institute, Ohio State University, Columbus.

Martin, Stephen. 2001. "Public-Private Partnerships: An Effective Tool for Providing Best Value." Paper presented at Managing the New Realities of Municipal Amalgamation conference, Toronto, ON, February 13–14.

Martinez-Vazquez, Jorge. 1994. "Budgeting in the Russian Federation." Draft report, Europe and Central Asia Department, World Bank, Washington, DC.

Martinez-Vazquez, Jorge, and Jameson Boex. 2001. *Russia's Transition to a New Federalism.* Washington, DC: World Bank.

McDavid, James. 1985. "The Canadian Experience with Privatizing Residential Solid Waste Collection Services." *Public Administration Review* 45 (4): 602–8.

———. 1986. "Part-Time Fire Fighters in Canadian Municipalities: Cost and Effectiveness Comparisons." *Canadian Public Administration* 29 (3): 377–87.

———. 2001. "Solid-Waste Contracting-Out, Competition, and Bidding Practices among Canadian Local Governments." *Canadian Public Policy* 44 (1): 1–25.

McDavid, James, and K. Anthony Eder. 1997. *The Efficiency of Residential Solid Waste Collection Services in Canada: The National Survey Report.* Victoria, BC: Local Government Institute, School of Public Administration, University of Victoria.

McDavid, James, and Verna Laliberte. 1998. *The Efficiency of Canadian Solid Waste Land-fills: National Survey Report,* Victoria, BC: Local Government Institute, School of Public Administration, University of Victoria.

———. 1999. *The Efficiency of Residential Recycling Services in Canadian Local Governments: National Survey Report.* Victoria, BC: Local Government Institute, School of Public Administration, University of Victoria.

McDavid, James, P. L. Richards, and B. E. Doughton. 1984. "Privatization of Residential Solid Waste Collection in Richmond, British Columbia." Unpublished paper. University of Victoria School of Public Administration, Victoria, BC.

McRae, James J. 1994. "Efficient Production of Solid Waste Services by Municipal Governments." Discussion Paper 94-11, School of Policy Studies, Queen's University, Kingston, ON, Canada.

Municipality of Metropolitan Toronto. 1988. "First Report of the Sub-Committee on Special Purpose Bodies." Metropolitan Toronto, ON, Canada.

Ontario Ministry of Municipal Affairs and Housing. 2003. *Municipal Performance Measurement Program.* Toronto, ON: Queen's Printer for Ontario.

Osborne, David, and Ted Gaebler. 1992. *Reinventing Government—How the Entrepreneurial Spirit Is Transforming the Public Sector.* Reading, MA: Addison Wesley.

Ostrom, Elinor, Larry Schroeder, and Susan Wynne. 1993. *Institutional Incentives and Sustainable Development: Infrastructure Policies in Perspective.* Boulder, CO: Westview.

Pallot, June. 1998. "Local Government Reform in New Zealand: Options for Public Management as Governance." Paper presented at the International Public Management Network Conference, Salem, OR, June 28–30. http://www.inpuma.net/research/papers/salem.

Probyn, Stephen. 1997. "Public-Private Partnerships on the Way to Nowhere." *Financial Post,* April 4.

Sancton, Andrew, and Teresa Janik. 2001. "Provincial-Local Relations and Drinking Water in Ontario." Issue paper commissioned by the Walkerton Inquiry.

Sauter, R. W., R. D. Weisman, and R. W. Percy. 1988. "Union View: Subcontracting the Work of Union Members in the Public Sector." *Labour Law Journal* 39 (8): 487–96.

Savas, Emanuel S. 1982. *Privatizing the Public Sector.* Chatham, NJ: Chatham House.

———. 1987. *Privatization: The Key to Better Government.* Chatham, NJ: Chatham House.

Slack, Enid. 1996. "Financing Infrastructure: Evaluation of Existing Research and Information Gaps." Canada Mortgage and Housing Corporation, Ottawa.

Solano, Paul L., and Marvin A. Brams. 1996. "Budgeting." In *Management Policies in Local Government Finance,* 4th ed., ed. J. Richard Aronson and Eli Schwartz, 125–68. Washington, DC: International City Management Association.

Stenning, Philip, and Tammy Landau. 1988. "The Niagara Regional Board of Commissioners of Police: Its Role and Accountability." Background study for the Niagara Region Review Commission, Niagara Falls, ON.

Szalai, Akos. 2001. "New Models of Privatizing Public Utilities: Highlights of Reform in Post-Soviet Countries." *Local Government Brief: The Quarterly Journal of Local Government and Public Service Reform Initiative* (Fall): 18–24.

Tang, Kwang-leung. 1997. "Efficiency of the Private Sector: A Critical Review of Empirical Evidence from Public Services." *International Review of Administrative Sciences* 63: 459–74.

Tassonyi, Almos, and Wade Locke. 1994. "Shared Tax Bases and Local Public Expenditure Decisions." *Canadian Tax Journal* 41: 941–57.

Tickner, Glen, and James McDavid. 1986. "Effects of Scale and Market Structure on the Costs of Residential Solid Waste Collection in Canadian Cities." *Public Finance Quarterly* 14: 371–93.

Vickers, John, and George Yarrow. 1991. "Economic Perspectives on Privatization." *Journal of Economic Perspectives* 5 (2): 111–32.

Williamson, J. 1994. "The Christchurch Case Study on Competitive Tendering." In *Introducing Competitive Tendering in Local Government in Australia*, 113–29. Melbourne, Australia: RMIT University, Department of Management, Foundation for Local Government Education and Development Fund.

World Bank. 1994. *World Development Report 1994: Infrastructure for Development.* New York: Oxford University Press for the World Bank.

Wunsch, James S. 1991. "Institutional Analysis and Decentralization: Developing an Analytical Framework for Effective Third World Administration Reform." *Public Administration and Development* 11 (5): 431–52.

6

Assessing the Performance of Health Services in Reaching the Poor

AGNES SOUCAT, RUTH LEVINE,
ADAM WAGSTAFF, ABDO S. YAZBECK,
CHARLES C. GRIFFIN, TIMOTHY
JOHNSTON, PAUL HUTCHINSON AND
RUDOLF KNIPPENBERG

This chapter presents information of relevance to planners and policy makers who are interested in evaluating the performance of their health systems in addressing the health needs of the poor. At issue are the manner in which countries allocate their limited resources to activities that benefit the poor, the efficiency with which a country's health system converts those limited resources into an effective supply of services that will maximize the health of the poor, and whether the poor use the available health services. One intent of this chapter is therefore to describe methodologies, sources of data, and indicators that can be used to analyze the performance of health services in improving the health, nutrition, and population outcomes of poor households.[1] Through such assessments, planners will be able to identify areas within the health sector that are operating inefficiently and inequitably, thereby allowing them to design the most appropriate strategies.

The chapter focuses primarily on the characteristics of the supply of health services depicted in the Health System and Related Sectors part of the framework in figure 6.1. It includes characteristics of the market, institutional factors and incentives affecting health care providers, and those factors that affect markets for health inputs such as drugs, equipment, and—perhaps most importantly—labor.

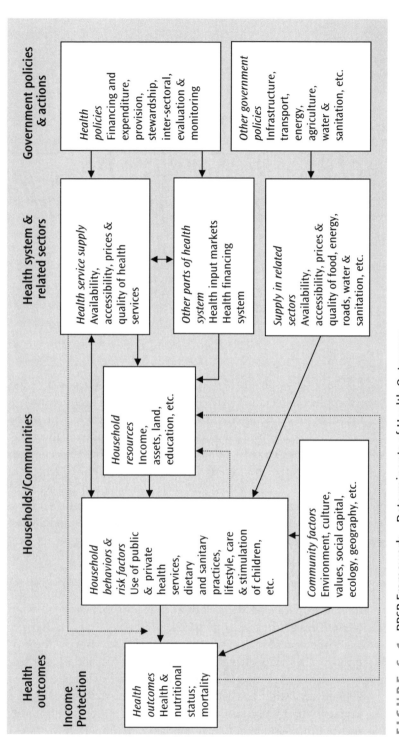

FIGURE 6.1 PRSP Framework—Determinants of Health Outcomes

Health service supply is shaped in part by government policies and actions, specifically the resources that a country has available and how a government prioritizes the health sector within its development program. Further, governments have choices about how to best allocate their resources within the health sector—between different types of health services, between different modes of financing and delivery, and between different levels of care—all of which have implications for improving the health of the poor.

The impact of the supply of health services on health outcomes, in turn, depends on factors at the household level (Mosley and Chen 1984; Vega and others 2000; Wolfe and Behrman 1982). Household and service supply factors combine to influence individual behaviors. The focus of this chapter is on addressing the problems of the supply side. However, evaluating health system performance necessarily entails having an accurate picture of what is happening with the poor, including assessing their level of service utilization and the barriers to service utilization (Cebu Study Team 1991; Wagstaff 2000b). Often the examination of barriers to care seeking is focused on the capacity of the poor to afford basic health services. In reality, whether the poor use health services is a function not just of affordability but of a wide variety of factors: accessibility, service quality (as measured by the availability of key personnel, supplies, and equipment and provision of appropriate treatment), household resources, and individuals' knowledge and awareness of what health services are needed and when (Wong and others 1987; Panis and Lillard 1994). The impact of health services in turn depends ultimately on how individuals and households transform the various health inputs, including health services, into actual outcomes (Mosley and Chen 1984; Schultz 1984; Acheson 1998; DFID 1999; Hughes and Dunleavy 2000).

In short, evaluating the performance of health systems in delivering services to the poor hinges on three related questions (depicted by the boxes in figure 6.1):

- Do health systems choose to do the "right" things, providing the services of greatest potential benefit to the poor and promoting policies that encourage use by the poor? (Government policies and actions)
- How well do those health systems provide the "right" things, with their limited resources? (Health systems and related sectors)
- Do the poor actually use health services, and does that use improve health outcomes? (Households and communities)

It is important to recognize that this overview does not cover all the possible issues, nor is it organized in a way that corresponds directly to economic theory. It is intended to be a practical guide, one that will permit an analyst in a relatively data-poor environment to understand where the main shortcomings are in the health financing arrangements and, in particular, how these shortcomings are related to the system's capacity to respond to the needs of the poor.

The focus of this chapter is therefore on the extent to which health, nutrition, and population interventions contribute to improving the health outcomes of the poor and reduce the consequences for their financial well-being of ill health or seeking care. The performance of health services is thus assessed according to the capacity to

- channel resources to the poor by funding pro-poor interventions
- reach the poor by providing key outputs that influence the availability of quality health services to be used in the household production of health
- minimize financial obstacles to the use of the interventions

This chapter is organized in terms of these three criteria. The next section looks at how decisions can be made about channeling resources to the poor. The second section provides a framework for assessing the capacity of a health sector to deliver services to the poor. The last section provides important information on evaluating whether the poor are benefiting from health services and identifying further impediments to improving health outcomes.

Channeling Resources to the Poor

Governments can perform several functions to improve the health outcomes of the poor. The first is to address a set of market failures inherent in health systems, namely ensuring provision of public goods and intervening to ameliorate the effects of catastrophic illnesses that can impoverish households in the absence of properly functioning insurance markets (Musgrove 1996; Filmer, Hammer, and Pritchett 1998). The second function is a socially determined one: to promote equity by ensuring that all members of society—the poor especially—have access to basic health services that permit a socially accepted minimum level of health.

The two functions are not mutually exclusive. Addressing market failures relating to public goods can have effects that disproportionately benefit the poor. The poor are by definition more vulnerable to the financial burdens that can be incurred from serious illnesses and are therefore likely to benefit from systems that reduce the financial risk from potentially catastrophic illnesses.

Addressing Market Failures

Governments must make choices about how to use their limited resources in addressing competing priorities. One area in which government intervention is a priority is with the financing of public goods, those public health services that protect many people simultaneously. Private markets are unlikely to exist for these services because people who do not pay cannot be excluded. In health, the principal examples of such goods and services are vector control, regulation and standardization, disease surveillance, and health education. Closely related to public goods are quasi-public goods—those goods and services that have benefits extending beyond the direct users of services. The most common examples are treatment of tuberculosis, sexually transmitted diseases, and other communicable diseases; administration of immunizations; and provision of safe water and sanitation. Quasi-public goods provide benefits—immunity, reduced exposure to illness, or alleviation of illness—to the direct users of services and at the same time reduce the risk of exposure to disease among the broader population. Those goods, although they may be provided privately, are unlikely to be provided at socially optimal levels. In contrast, private goods are those for which the benefits accrue entirely to the direct users of the goods. These include such services as acute curative care for chronic or incommunicable diseases.

In the absence of government involvement, public goods and goods with positive externalities are unlikely to be provided at all or are unlikely to be provided at levels that are socially optimal. Private providers will not be able to recoup the costs of their inputs in providing those services, and markets will not reveal the true value to consumers from providing those services. However, markets for private goods (in the absence of barriers to entry and other impediments) are likely to develop because providers can be remunerated for the value of their resources when they treat patients. But although markets are more likely to supply private health goods, the clinical quality of private services can be highly variable.

Although the concepts of public, quasi-public, and private goods may seem like esoteric economic jargon, they have considerable relevance for health services aimed at the poor. This is because many of the principal health problems faced by the poor involve public health concerns, requiring health services that may not be adequately supplied in the absence of government financing. In Sub-Saharan Africa, for example, more than 70 percent of the disability-adjusted life years (DALYs) lost are caused by communicable diseases—tuberculosis, sexually transmitted diseases and HIV/AIDS, diarrhea, vaccine-preventable childhood infections, and other public health problems (figure 6.2). In contrast, in the relatively wealthier countries of

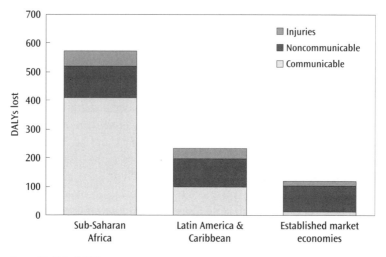

Source: World Bank 1993.

FIGURE 6.2 DALYs Lost per 1,000 Population by Cause

Latin America and the Caribbean, less than half of DALYs lost are caused by communicable diseases; in the established market economies, only 9 percent of DALYs lost are caused by public health problems.

Another area of public concern (addressed in greater detail later under "Equity and the Impact of Health Sector Financing") is with insurance market failures. A unique feature of the health sector is the uncertainty that exists regarding an individual's probability of illness and hence expected health care needs. Insurance markets can address this uncertainty by pooling the financial risks of catastrophic events across individuals or groups, thereby reducing the risk to any particular individual. However, private markets for insurance may not function properly under circumstances in which

- private insurers can deny coverage to whose who are most likely to need it (often the poor)
- less-healthy individuals drive healthy individuals out of insurance markets (adverse selection)
- having insurance encourages individuals not to avoid risk or to overconsume health resources (moral hazard)
- doctors, whose incomes may be tied to the levels of care they provide, overtreat patients and increase health care costs (supplier-induced demand)

The improper functioning of insurance markets is of particular importance to the poor, who are the least likely to be able to afford treatment of catastrophic illnesses or adverse health events (Gertler and Sturm 1997; Filmer, Hammer, and Pritchett 1998). Governments therefore have an important role: to regulate health insurance markets, to mandate social insurance, or to promote some other mechanism for managing the financial risks of catastrophic illnesses.

Improving Efficiency of Public Spending

Because of these market failures, governments generally provide a variety of interventions, often including low-cost clinical services with largely private benefits, to ensure that the poor have access to minimum levels of health care. The services may be free or subsidized. Such services are unlikely to be justified on the grounds of insurance—avoidance of catastrophic risks—but rather on the grounds of poverty alleviation (Pradhan 1996). But paradoxically, free or heavily subsidized health systems may actually be regressive in their subsidization of the poor and nonpoor since the nonpoor tend to benefit more from health services.

To address these market failure and poverty alleviation objectives, the *World Development Report 1993: Investing in Health* (World Bank 1993) advocated an essential package of public health and personal care services intended to improve allocative efficiency—allocating resources to those health services that have the largest overall benefit to society in improving health.[2] The recommended core package provides a guide for how countries can allocate their resources but requires adaptation to local circumstances and health conditions.

Appropriate methods for choosing among a variety of priorities generally involve analyses of social costs and benefits (Eastwood and Lipton 2000). Social cost-benefit analysis evaluates the total social health and nonhealth benefits and costs of health intervention. However, it requires making difficult choices about how to place a monetary value on health gains. Cost-effectiveness analysis is more straightforward—and frequently used—but it evaluates only the health gains from an intervention. However, cost-effectiveness analysis has strong limitations, most notably that it may prioritize activities that are already being addressed by private markets or activities that do not respond to the needs of poorer groups, for which providing appropriate services may be less cost-effective. In addition, cost effectiveness analysis, like cost-benefit analysis, makes implicit valuations of human lives.

From a poverty point of view, health spending would be considered more allocatively efficient if it corresponds well to the prevalence and incidence of conditions that cause serious ill health—the areas where the potential benefits of intervention are greatest—among the poorest groups. This is of course conditional on the interventions actually ameliorating those conditions. Spending would be considered less allocatively efficient if it is concentrated on services that provide care to richer groups and does not address the disease burden of the poor.

As a consequence, the core allocative issue in looking at health and poverty is the question of whether public health activities that benefit the poor are adequately funded by the government. This requires having information on expenditure patterns—by types of activities and by all actors in the health sector—and knowing the impacts of those expenditures on health. It requires having detailed information on the disease burden of the population and the expected use of services by different individuals—poor and nonpoor.

Analytic Approach to Evaluating Allocative Efficiency

To determine whether the government is providing those goods and services with the largest health impacts—net of what is being addressed by the private sector—the analyst can examine the distribution of government spending from recent budget years across the range of health services. A basic tool for doing so is the system of health accounts (also known as national health accounts), a method for classifying health sector activities and inputs in a standardized fashion. This methodology collects information on the sources of funds, the financing institutions, and the ultimate uses of those funds. Pioneered by the OECD, health accounts exercises have been conducted in many developing countries, and an adapted methodology for data-poor settings is emerging (Berman 1996). Similar methods have been applied at the subnational level.

Once data on government expenditures are collected, different methods can be used to evaluate the allocative efficiency of those expenditures. At the simplest level, analysts can look at the relative distribution of spending across services or levels of services to see what share of the pie is devoted to each. Different comparisons can be made, and spending can be disaggregated by function—curative care, preventive care, and public health goods. Expenditures can be further disaggregated into the core public health functions (that is, the pure public goods of communicable disease control, surveillance, and others); quasi-public goods (prenatal care, family planning services, and other goods with public health benefits); and purely private goods (acute curative care, chronic curative care).

Because of epidemiologic and demographic patterns, certain types of health services are used in greater proportion by the poor. Therefore, funds spent on those services are more likely to be directed to low-income populations. These include certain types of communicable disease control and treatment (for example, tuberculosis); prevention and treatment of nutritional deficiencies; prenatal and delivery care for high-risk pregnancies; and others.

An alternative method for assessing allocative efficiency is for the analyst to compare the pattern of government (and private) health spending with estimates of the burden of disease for the major categories of diseases. The drawbacks of this method are that it is extremely data intensive and, as noted earlier, it may ignore potential private sector supply-side responses to public sector changes in expenditures, as well as the distribution of the burden of diseases among income categories (Jha, Ransom, and Bobadilla 1996).

Two other dimensions of efficiency can also be related to reaching the poor:

- *Technical efficiency:* Lower levels of care may be more pro-poor. Typically, spending on primary care facilities is compared with spending on hospital and particularly tertiary care. A separate category is often used for non–facility-based public health programs. Spending on hospitals, as opposed to lower-level care or public health activities, tends to favor urban, higher-income populations and conditions with largely private benefits (Castro-Leal and others 1999).
- *Input efficiency:* The relative allocation for recurrent and capital spending may lead to services not being functional in poor areas. A common finding in many countries has been that countries disproportionately invest in new capital, such as health facilities, while underfunding—or underestimating—the recurrent expenditures associated with these investments. As a consequence, facilities aimed at serving the poor lack personnel and nonsalary inputs.

In almost all settings, the conclusion that is drawn from such analyses is that the government is not fulfilling its basic financing responsibilities optimally—in large part because of multiple competing demands on very limited resources. The implication is that substantial gains in health outcomes can be achieved by internal budget reallocations (Griffin 1992).

Key Indicators

- Per capita public expenditure for health, by region
- Percentage of public expenditure allocated among different health functions: acute curative care, chronic curative care, preventive care, and public health activities, by type of provider (public, private, nongovernmental) and by region

■ Percentage of public expenditures allocated to primary care, secondary care, tertiary care, and public health programs by type of provider (public, private, nongovernmental) and by region (in decentralized systems)

Reaching the Poor: Equity of Coverage for Interventions Addressing the Needs of the Poor

This section outlines a hierarchy of determinants affecting the likelihood that health services will meet the needs of the poor. It briefly examines methodologies and data necessary for evaluating each of the determinants. This analysis is particularly relevant for assessing a country's capacity to deliver a core package of health interventions that can address the principal health problems of the poor.

These determinants can be organized into eight simple steps (figure 6.3). The first five represent potential coverage (accessibility, availability of human resources, availability of material inputs, organizational quality, and social accountability), while the last three represent actual coverage (relevance and utilization of services, timing and continuity, and technical quality). Possible indicators for each of these determinants are discussed below. To the extent possible, analysts assessing each of these determinants should include information on all possible providers and sources of care—public, nongovernmental organization (NGO), and private services—in order to obtain a complete overview of health services delivery and to allow for comparisons of efficiency and quality.

Many of these determinants in the hierarchy are not specific to the supply of services for the poor, but rather reflect institutional features of government health care in general. However, because many of the nonpoor in developing countries opt out of the public health care system, or at least can afford to opt out, the burden of low quality or unavailable government care may fall disproportionately on the poor, who may have fewer modern medical alternatives to government care (Lasprilla and others 1999; Parker and Pier 1999).

Evaluating each component of the steps to effective coverage requires detailed information from a variety of sources, most of which exist or are in the process of being developed in the majority of developing countries. Assessing physical accessibility, for example, requires having information on both the distribution of medical services and the distribution of the population. Acquiring such information is likely to require combining data from ministries of health and national census bureaus. Health information systems often contain information on stocks and flows of drugs and equipment

Outcomes of the poor

Household factors

Other sectors

Health services coverage

Technical quality

Timing and continuity

Relevance and utilization

Social accountability

Organizational quality

Availability of material resources

Availability of human resources

Physical accessibility

FIGURE 6.3 Eight Steps to Effective Coverage for the Poor

and on levels of staffing, which can be used to evaluate the availability of human and material resources (although these data generally do not include information on nonpublic sources of care). Facility surveys, taken in a random sample of facilities, can provide a more detailed picture of these elements. Facility surveys can be combined with exit interviews and reviews of treatment behavior to evaluate organizational and technical quality.[3]

Ultimately, however, acquiring data will likely require collecting it from the intended beneficiaries of health services through population-based household surveys. Such surveys provide information on a random sample of the population, including both users and nonusers of services. In fact, population-based surveys have two main advantages over health information systems: they collect detailed information on background characteristics of households and their health care–seeking behaviors, and they collect information on households that may have limited contact with health systems, particularly the poor. Most importantly, data on household income or consumption patterns or on household ownership of basic assets can be used to categorize households into different wealth quartiles, thereby allowing comparisons of health care–seeking behaviors and health outcomes across different income groups. Common national household surveys include the World Bank's Living Standards Measurement Surveys, UNICEF's Multiple Indicator Cluster Surveys, and ORC/Macro's Demographic and Health Surveys, which are conducted regularly in approximately 100 countries. Some of the data collection instruments, and the steps in the hierarchy for which they may be pertinent, are listed in table 6.1.

An example of the hierarchy and its implications for evaluating a childhood immunization program, including the requisite inputs associated with the program, is given in table 6.2.

Physical Accessibility

A fundamental issue for many countries is physical access to essential health interventions and services for the poor, including community-driven health and nutrition activities. Access remains a key issue in most low-income coun-

TABLE 6.1   Sources of Data for Assessing Coverage

Stage	Poverty map	Health information systems	Facility surveys	Geographical information systems (GISs)	Exit interviews	Direct treatment observations/QIQ	Household surveys	Focus group discussions/ rapid assessment methods
Physical Accessibility	■	■	■	■			■	
Human Resources	■	■	■	■	■		■	
Material Resources			■	■	■		■	
Organizational Quality					■	■		■
Social Accountability					■			■
Utilization	■	■					■	
Timing and Continuity		■					■	
Technical Quality		■			■			

TABLE 6.2 Example of Determinants of Coverage with a
Core Package of Activities

Stages	Example of indicator for EPI	Example of inputs
Accessibility	Proportion of mothers of children 12–23 months who live less than 1 hour or 5 kilometers from a fixed health center with weekly immunization or less than 30 min. from a monthly outreach point	– Health Facilities and providers (public, NGO, private) – Outreach workers and mobile clinics – Transport (public and private) – Roads and communications
Availability of human resources	Proportion of mothers of children 12–23 months who live within 1 hour of a service delivery point where there is a qualified health technician providing immunization	– Personnel (public, private, NGO)
Availability of material resources	Proportion of mothers of children 12–23 months who have access to an immunization point with continuous availability of vaccines and syringes/needles	– Pharmaceuticals, supplies, stocks of consumables (public and private sources) – Equipment – Maintenance (e.g., functioning cold chain)
Organizational quality	Proportion of mothers of children 12–23 months having access to an immunization point where other key services are integrated: growth monitoring, ORT distribution, vitamin A supplementation	– Training, supervision, equipment, staff incentives
Social accountability	Proportion of mothers of children 12–23 months having access to an immunization point where communities conduct semestrial monitoring of immunization coverage and are involved in actively tracking defaulters	– Civil society representation – Involvement of users and communities in management, monitoring, etc.
Relevance and utilization	Proportion of children 12–23 months having received at least one shot of vaccine	– Outpatient and inpatient contacts – Facility deliveries – Management tools

(continued)

TABLE 6.2   Example of Determinants of Coverage with a
Core Package of Activities (*continued*)

Stages	Example of indicator for EPI	Example of inputs
Timing and continuity	Proportion of children 12–23 months having received the full course of vaccines at the appropriate dates in the first year of life and properly spaced	– Adequacy of record-keeping, outreach, follow-up. Incentives to personnel; knowledge of clients
Technical quality	Proportion of children having received the full course of vaccines with the appropriate technique	– Training, supervision, well-defined protocols – Availability of drugs and equipment

Source: Knippenberg and others 1997.

tries, in which the majority of the population—and the majority of the poor—often reside in rural areas at considerable distance from basic health services.

The effect of greater distance to health services is significant, since individuals are less likely to use services that are farther away or that involve greater amounts of time to access. Many studies have found that the distance to a health care provider influences the use of services more than other factors such as price. A study by Akin and others (1996) found that the distance to a provider was the most significant determinant of a person's use of curative care, more than price or other facility characteristics. Dor and van der Gaag (1988) in Côte d'Ivoire found that distance and time costs impede care-seeking behavior in a manner identical to that of monetary prices. The work leading up to the Poverty Reduction Strategy Paper (PRSP) in Burkina Faso, similarly, cited survey evidence that 40 percent of health center users had to walk more than one hour to reach the center. The work underpinning the Mozambique PRSP cited survey evidence that 38 percent of people who had been sick but had not sought care had not done so because their local facility was too far away.

A key indicator of health sector performance is therefore physical proximity to health services for the poor. This can be measured in several ways. The first is to measure the service supply in relation to the population served (for example, the number of hospitals for a given population) or as a proportion of facilities or service delivery points (for example, the number or percentage of facilities offering family planning, immunizations, or antenatal care). International standards (such as those developed by the World Health

Organization [WHO]) or local standards (determined through local operational research) can be used.[4] For comparison, this method can be used for different levels of aggregation or different regions within a country, such as districts or urban and rural areas. This method, however, may be limited because it may not account for the distribution of the poor within regions.

The second approach is to measure the proportion of the population living within a given distance of a particular type of health facility (for example, 10 kilometers) or of a particular type of intervention, preferably disaggregated by income level or by region. A third, closely related approach is to measure the time required for a client to reach a facility or service delivery point (for example, less than one hour).

Data Collection and Analysis

For the first method described above, detailed information is required on the basic inputs in the health sector—the number of facilities of different types and the services offered there, or the number of beds—by regions. This is then combined with information on the total population living in those areas, generally available from national census bureaus. Ratios of inputs to population sizes can then be compared across regions.

For the second and third methods, detailed information is needed on the locations of households and health services. An increasingly common mechanism for determining such locations is geographical information systems (GISs), which use global positioning systems to plot facility locations and a sample of households on digitized maps.[5] Distances can then be calculated either as Euclidean distances or, if combined with information on roads and road types, as the distances along principal thoroughfares. Standard calculations can be made using readily available software, such as the proportion of a sample of the population living within specified distances of health providers.

At the very least, such information on the locations of households and health services can be used to develop geographic representations of the distribution of health services relative to the distribution of the population. The maps should specify, if possible, the location of fixed facilities, outreach points, mobile clinics, and outreach workers for public and nongovernmental services, as well as major roads and natural barriers such as rivers. Many countries have developed or are in the process of developing health facility inventory and planning maps.

Information from household surveys can be used to calculate the percentage of poor with access to services, and to determine the extent to which limited physical access is a major constraint for the poor.[6] Because poverty is unevenly distributed, it is useful to assemble data on availability at the regional as well as the national level. These quantitative methods could be complemented by beneficiary surveys or participatory assessment approaches in poor communities, to assess whether physical access is perceived as a major problem by the poor.

Key Indicators

- Hospitals, health centers, dispensaries, or mobile clinics per 10,000 population, by region
- Percentage of population, by region, living within 5 kilometers or a 1-hour walk of a hospital, health center, dispensary, or mobile clinic

Availability of Human Resources

Low-income countries are beset by a variety of problems that constrain the supply of trained health staff. The main problems are often the public sector's inability to adequately remunerate and train health workers and the poor distribution of those health workers among urban and rural facilities or among different levels of facilities. Constraints on the supply of health staff, in turn, limit the ability of the public sector to supply basic health services to the poor.

In many countries, a scarcity of funds leaves the public sector unable to pay health workers at levels that are competitive with private practices or with salaries offered in other countries. A recent study conducted by the Antwerp Tropical Institute showed the actual remuneration of health staff in urban settings (public or private) to be approximately five times the public sector's average salary. For surgeons, this number could be as much as seven times higher (World Bank 2001).

Other problems relate to the inability to distribute personnel appropriately within a country. Rural areas, in particular, frequently face staffing shortages because workers tend to prefer living and working in urban areas, where family amenities and professional opportunities are greater. Many midwives trained in countries in francophone Africa consider themselves overqualified to work in rural areas and stay in the capital cities.

A final problem relates to the concept of technical efficiency—the idea that resources should be used to deliver the maximum level of outputs with the fewest inputs. This is particularly relevant for human resources management, because many health systems have workers who are either idle for a good proportion of their time or absent from their posts. The implication is that these staff members could be redeployed—or removed—with no decrease in the number of patients treated.

The extent of the problem is considerable. The authors of the *Voices of the Poor* report for Somaliland (Narayan and others 1999), for example, noted that "rural people said they rarely see health workers in their localities. If some people have been trained for the villages and other main grazing areas by international agencies, they are not now functional."[7]

For the poor, this means that while the physical structures for delivering care may be readily accessible, the absence or limited availability of health staff may reduce the overall availability of services, increase queuing, and ultimately reduce the likelihood that needed services are used.

Data Collection and Analysis

As with geographical access, the distribution of health personnel must be measured relative to the distribution of the population. A key indicator would be the number of doctors, nurses, midwives, or essential personnel per 10,000 population, by region. This information can be used to look at the geographical distribution of health workers, again with GIS information if possible, thereby revealing where there are serious deployment problems. Alternatively, as with physical accessibility, the proportion of the population living within a certain distance or time from a facility with a doctor, nurse, or specialist could be calculated with global positioning system information on the location of households and facilities.

Central health information systems may have data on the availability and distribution of personnel, although these data are often incomplete or unreliable. Conducting surveys of a sample of facilities or a group of health workers can provide more detailed and reliable information on the number of workers and the time spent delivering services. District or provincial officials could also be asked to compile tabulations of the availability of staff. In addition, qualitative surveys can be used to find out whether lack of staff is seen by the poor to be a major problem—and surveys are particularly useful for finding out whether staff absenteeism is an issue.

Key Indicators

- Doctors, nurses, and midwives per 10,000 population, by region
- Percentage of population, by region, living within 5 kilometers or a 1-hour walk of a facility with a doctor, nurse, or specialist

Availability of Material Resources

Health services also need to have the capacity to ensure the continuous availability of essential material inputs, including medicines, supplies, and equipment. Health, nutrition, and population facilities may be present and physically accessible in an area, yet essential consumable resources for the intervention may be lacking or frequently unavailable. A study conducted in Côte d'Ivoire (ICC 1997) showed, for example, that cotrimoxazole and four other essential drugs were not available in the public health clinics more than half of the time.

Even if drugs are available at facilities, they may be inefficacious because they either have expired or have not been properly maintained in controlled environments. These problems result from inadequate pharmaceutical and supply logistics and management.

Governments can also improve the efficiency of the markets for key inputs through a variety of mechanisms. These include improved procurement through competitive bidding, use of essential drugs lists, and promotion of low-cost, high-quality generic drugs. Such measures can reduce the costs of key inputs, thereby freeing resources for other activities.

An additional—and growing—problem is the emergence of fake drugs. Much of this problem stems from poor government regulation, but it is also related to a basic characteristic of health markets—the informational asymmetry between providers and consumers, who have limited capacity to verify the efficacy and contents of drugs and who thus rely upon government supervision to ensure appropriate quality.

Data Collection and Analysis

Developing indicators of the availability of critical inputs by level of service can help assess the extent of material resource inadequacies. These can be linked to data on the population distribution of the poor and nonpoor. Maps showing the distribution of drug and vaccine availability can be drawn and linked to poverty maps, to identify whether shortages are more common in poorer or more remote areas.[8]

Central health information systems may have data on the availability and distribution of equipment, drugs, vehicles, and other inputs, although these data are often incomplete or unreliable.[9] Conducting surveys of a sample of facilities can provide more detailed and reliable information on the availability of key inputs, and specific methodologies have been developed to do this (for example, essential drugs surveys). District or provincial officials could also be asked to compile tabulations of key inputs in their areas. Facility-level studies of the frequency of stock-outs of essential drugs can provide clues to the extent of these problems. If drug shortages are identified as significant problems, the more difficult challenge is to try to understand why these problems persist. Inadequate funding for inputs may be part of the problem but is rarely the only reason.

To understand how these failures affect poor populations, again surveys and exit interviews can be useful to find out whether the absence of drugs or supplies is seen by the poor to be a major problem and inhibits the use of health services. Household survey evidence was cited, for example, in the work underpinning the Mozambique PRSP. It showed that although a relatively small proportion of sick people not seeking care cited lack of drugs as the reason for their not seeking care, those who did seek care were almost all rural residents.

Surveys and inspections of health facilities are also useful. The work underlying the Burkina Faso PRSP reported that, when inspected, nearly 20 percent of facilities had run out of essential vaccines, and in 24 percent of health centers, the refrigerators for storing the vaccines did not function. The Mauritania PRSP reported that drug shortages were the most important reason for the low use of services.

Surveys can also provide useful information as to whether the poor purchase drugs from different sources than richer groups. In Africa (Benin) and India, for example, the poor were more likely to buy drugs in the market and less likely to buy them from a formal pharmacy.

Key Indicators

- Percentage of facilities—by level and region—having essential drugs, vaccines, supplies, and equipment

Organizational Quality and Consumer Responsiveness

Another key dimension of performance is the extent to which public, private, and NGO services are responsive to consumer concerns and the extent to which services are delivered in a way that encourages appropriate utilization of relevant interventions (WHO 2000). A number of factors influence the user friendliness of services, including the attitude of health staff members; hours of operation; space, cleanliness and comfort of the waiting area and of the wards; waiting time; gender of the service provider; modes of payment; and efficiency of referral. The poor, for example, may be forced to wait longer than paying patients or may be subjected to verbal admonishments by health staff members. These factors in turn strongly affect consumers' perceptions of quality and are important determinants of whether services are used—particularly since consumers are often not good judges of clinical quality.

Organizational quality is likely to vary among public, private, and NGO providers; by geographic location (they may be worse in poor areas); and possibly by the type and level of service (clinics versus district hospitals or antenatal care versus sexually transmitted infections treatment). It can be measured objectively (for example, average waiting times, time spent with providers), or qualitatively (for example, by asking the poor how they perceive the quality of different types of services).

Data Collection and Analysis

Measuring organizational quality relies on a mix of qualitative and quantitative tools. This type of information is rarely available through routine health information systems.

Qualitative surveys, focus groups, or exit interviews with the poor (and nonpoor for comparison) can be illuminating. Topics could include staff treatment, appropriateness of care, and perceptions of quality. Discussions should be conducted separately with men and women, and possibly adolescents and adults, since their concerns may differ. In many countries, for example, women report being treated rudely or even abusively during delivery at government clinics; or women or adolescents avoid seeking care for sexually transmitted infections at public providers because of privacy concerns. Exit interviews provide useful information on provider-client interactions, but they do not reach those not using services—for whom perceptions of low organizational quality may have prevented use of services in the first place. Collecting information from nonusers may therefore require household surveys and community-based approaches.

On-site assessment of various aspects of service organization can be compared with the problems identified by users. Direct observation of treatment by well-trained observers can be used to develop service-based objective measurements (average waiting times; observations of provider behavior; cleanliness of facilities) and then compared with consumer perceptions. The information collected can be used to build scales and indexes of quality, permitting comparisons of different types of services.

The family planning field has developed situation analysis methodologies that combine various methodologies to collect information from a sample of facilities and communities on the availability of inputs, provider behavior, process quality indicators, and the perception of community members.[10] The situation analysis approach can be adapted for other services.

Key Indicators

- Mean waiting time, by facility type (public, private, and nongovernmental) and by region
- Percentage of users of facilities, by level, by type (public, private, and nongovernmental) and by region, reporting staff treatment, drug availability, and quality of care as "good" or "excellent"

Social Accountability

The health system or particular health services are more likely to be responsive to the poor if the poor are able to exert influence over or have a voice in health systems and providers. Health staff in government clinics are often unresponsive to the poor because they are not directly accountable to them and because worker remuneration and career advancement are often not linked to performance.

There are several potential avenues for the poor to participate and have a voice. The first is the direct management of local clinical services, through community health centers or revolving drug funds, as experienced in the Bamako Initiative, supported by WHO and UNICEF and adopted by many countries in Africa and Asia (Knippenberg and others 1997; Gilson and others 1999). Second, the poor could be engaged in monitoring the performance of facilities or providers through representation on a district or facility board or committee, through an effective grievance system, or through intermediaries, such as local political leaders, religious organizations, or NGOs. Some countries have also developed and publicized a patients' bill of rights, to strengthen consumers' ability to demand quality care. A third avenue is through mobilizing communities for health promotion activities, such as malaria prevention or improved water supply.

It must be kept in mind, however, that even when formal mechanisms for participation exist, health providers often still dominate committees and participatory processes because of their greater education and expertise. Further, because of societal attitudes or cultural norms, women or certain ethnic groups may be excluded from decision making and may therefore have little voice in influencing the nature and quality of health services. An increasingly recognized problem in community participation processes is the possibility of local capture by local elites who influence decision making for their own gains rather than the greater good of the community.

Data Collection and Analysis

As with organizational quality, mechanisms to measure the level of participation of communities and the poor in health systems are likely to rely upon a mix of qualitative and quantitative sources, including community focus group discussions, household surveys, and rapid assessment mechanisms. This mix involves several steps. The first step is to assess the extent to which mechanisms exist for the poor to exert influence on services overall and on specific interventions. The next step is to determine whether those mechanisms actually influence the quality of services provided to the poor. Different categories of involvement can be used to measure the extent of participation by level and type of service, including information sharing, consultation, collaboration, and shared decision making.

Assessments of voice and participation in health services can be incorporated into an overall participatory assessment for the PRSP. Information would need to be collected through visits to a sample of communities and facilities. Relevant questions might include the following:

- What percentage of health facilities have some sort of community health committee or health board associated with them? Do these bodies meet regularly?
- Are health committees perceived as representative of the community and of the poor in particular, or are they dominated by local elites?
- Is there any measurable difference between the consumer-responsiveness of services for which the poor have some representation and those for which they do not? What factors explain the differences?
- Are local political leaders responsive to the poor, and is the quality of health services an issue of concern for local leaders?
- If the poor have relatively little influence, are there existing traditional or modern institutional structures that could be built upon to make their voice heard?

Key Indicators

- Percentage of facilities or communities with functioning community health management boards, by region
- Percentage of community health management boards with female members or members of minority ethnic groups, by region
- Percentage of local health officials who are elected, by region

Relevance of Production and Utilization of Health Interventions

Production of high-quality and accessible health services is of little value if they are not used by the people who need them, particularly the poor. As discussed earlier, many of the interventions in a core package of essential services address the principal health problems faced by the poor. Increasing the accessibility and availability of staff, supplies, and equipment—coverage steps one through four—will likely increase the quality and supply of services. However, the poor must also be sufficiently aware of the benefits of the services—their efficacy and long-term health gains—and value them relatively more than the other goods and services that they could consume with their limited resources and time. Time-series data on the utilization of health services—by category of service and by income group—are therefore essential to measure the impacts of any changes in service availability and quality.

Data Collection and Analysis

Utilization can be measured either in terms of the total volume of services provided, or as the percentage of a given target population using the intervention. These different ways of measuring utilization require different sources of data:

- Health information systems usually collect data on the use of services, including outpatient and inpatient visits, vaccinations, users of antenatal care, deliveries, family planning users, etc. These data are often under-reported, however, and therefore frequently cannot be used to calculate population-based utilization rates. Further, depending on the public sector market share for those services, they may represent only a fraction of total users in the population—with no information collected about nonusers, nor about the characteristics, including income levels, of users. However, they can still be useful for analyses of trends if compiled in a time series, with comparisons made across regions or across facilities, when information is available on the poverty level of the area they serve.
- Household surveys can provide more detailed information on the populations to whom health interventions are targeted, including both users and nonusers of services and poor and nonpoor households. From such surveys, the percentage of a target population making use of particular services (for example, percentage of facility deliveries, percentage of adults with a sexually transmitted infection seeking care) can be calculated, as can the distribution of users by types of providers—public, private, nongovernmental, or pharmacy. Users and nonusers can be stratified by income levels, which is an important step in benefit incidence analysis, discussed later. Further, such surveys can be used to examine reasons for use and nonuse of particular facilities by different income groups.
- The quantity of services produced in a specific area could be linked through a poverty map to the income level of the population of the area. Such a mapping of equity of output production is currently conducted routinely in Mozambique.[11]

Examining trends and patterns of utilization, particularly with respect to the poor, can help identify constraints on system functioning. Reasons for nonuse of health services cannot be assessed from the services side alone. Yet when utilization is low—despite high accessibility and availability of services—

analysts will need to explore survey data regarding the reasons why interventions are not used. These are likely to include aspects such as price, perceived quality, cultural acceptability, or household factors such as education.

Key Indicators

- Production of key services included in essential service packages, by region, ranked by poverty level
- Percentages of the poor and nonpoor using various health services included in essential service packages

Timing and Continuity

Many health services require not only that they be used, but that they be used at certain points in time or that repeated contacts be made in order for treatment to be effective. Several basic childhood vaccinations—polio and diphtheria, pertussis, and tetanus vaccinations—must come at certain points in a child's life, starting no earlier than six weeks of life, and must be followed by subsequent vaccinations at no less than four-week intervals. For tuberculosis, a single treatment under directly observed treatment, short course (DOTS), is ineffective. It requires repeated treatments for six months in order for a person to be fully cured and for drug resistance not to develop. For other interventions, such as emergency obstetric care, the timing is critical. Too often interventions are provided only in part, or at the wrong time, or too late.

Service continuity is a significant organizational challenge and an important indicator of system effectiveness because it requires the ability to track and follow up with consumers. For the poor, for whom utilization levels of basic services may already be low, timing and continuity of service use is an additional challenge to ensuring that they receive effective care.

Data Collection and Analysis

Analyses of the proper timing and continuity of health services delivery are similar to the analyses of service utilization outlined above. However, the focus instead is on those critical essential services for which timing is vital for effectiveness. Continuity can be assessed by looking at dropout rates and other indicators of follow-up, preferably using a combination of facility data and household surveys.

Key Indicators

- Diphtheria-pertussis-tetanus vaccination dropout rates for the poor and nonpoor

- Percentage of poor and nonpoor completing tuberculosis treatment programs or DOTS
- Percentage of pregnant women making the recommended number of antenatal care visits

Technical Quality

The final step in the hierarchy for improving health outcomes of the poor is ensuring that the health services are of a sufficient quality that, if they are used, will lead to an improvement in health outcomes. The capacity of the sector to provide the appropriate combination of technology and empathy at a given level of utilization is vital to ensure that interventions are translated into effective outcomes.[12,13] Technical quality depends on effective provider training and supervision, the existence of appropriate treatment protocols, and adequacy of critical inputs, as well as factors such as provider workload. Technical quality may be poor even when consumers express satisfaction with the services. This can be a particular problem in a poorly regulated private sector. For services for which a high proportion of the market supply is provided by private or nongovernmental sources, data collectors should strive to collect information on all types of providers.

Data Collection and Analysis

Assessing the capacity of the sector to produce outputs of good technical quality usually requires direct observation of provider behavior, to compare existing practices against standard protocols. In addition, a number of indicators are particularly sensitive to technical quality. They include perinatal mortality rates, malaria case fatality rates, tuberculosis cure rates, and maternal mortality. Follow-up studies of maternal or perinatal deaths can help shed light on whether shortcomings in clinical quality contributed to poor outcomes. More sophisticated instruments for assessing quality through facility surveys are available for some health, nutrition, and population outcomes. WHO's Topical List of Priority Indicators for IMCI (Integrated Management of Childhood Illnesses) at Health-Facility Level provides a useful instrument for assessing quality in the management of childhood illness.[14] Surveys undertaken using this instrument suggest some huge variations in quality across countries. These data could be linked to a poverty map or to a household survey to get a sense of how the poor fare in the country compared with the nonpoor.

Key Indicators

- Percentage of patients who receive treatment according to national standard treatment guidelines, by type of facility or by region

- Malaria or other disease-specific case fatality rates
- Tuberculosis cure rates
- Maternal mortality ratios

Equity and the Impact of Health Sector Financing

One aspect of health markets is similar to markets for other goods and services, namely that the nonpoor tend to benefit more from health services than the poor (Wagstaff, Paci, and van Doorslaer 1991; Van Doorslaer and Wagstaff 1992; Wagstaff 2000a; Whitehead 2000; Gwatkin 2000). As noted earlier, there are many reasons for higher health service utilization by the nonpoor, not the least of which is greater capacity to pay. Higher utilization is also likely to be associated with greater access (because the nonpoor tend to live in urban areas), as well as greater appreciation for the benefits of health services. To promote equity of health outcomes for the poor, governments must compensate for these factors (César and others 1999).

Governments have numerous options to ensure that out-of-pocket payments are not an insurmountable barrier to use of essential services by the poor. Typically, the poor in developing countries may have part of their health care subsidized by the government through general tax revenues. But both taxes (Kakwani 1977) and subsidies (Wagstaff and others 1999) may be regressive. When fees are charged, the poor may be exempted through fee-waiver schemes, but the evidence on the success of exempting the poor is mixed (Creese and Kutzin 1997; Leighton and Diop 1999).

Alternatively, governments can secure the conditions for proper functioning of risk-sharing strategies through a variety of mechanisms, including adequate regulation of private insurance markets, promotion of social insurance schemes, and development of local prepayment plans. Making these prepayment schemes pro-poor will, however, usually require some level of subsidy to the poor because premiums can be as regressive as user fees (Theodore and others 1999). The timing of such contributions may also help, by permitting the poor to pay small premiums at times when they have income from agricultural outputs, and then pay lower or no user charges when they use the services covered by the scheme.

In this section, we suggest ways to answer four basic questions related to the equity of health financing:

1. Does government spending on health benefit the rich or the poor?
2. Do the mechanisms for financing health services provide incentives or disincentives to health workers to respond to the poor?

3. Does the price of health services create or reduce barriers to the appropriate use of health services by the poor?
4. Does the system of financing health services protect the poor from—or expose them to—income shocks when they fall ill?

Question 1. Does Government Spending on Health Benefit the Poor or the Rich?

Several factors are likely to affect who receives the greatest benefit from health services. These include many of the factors described in the eight steps to effective coverage, including service mix, access, and quality.

Three main issues can be highlighted. First, many governments seek to provide universal coverage of a broad range of health services and, in that effort, find that the "big ticket" items such as large teaching hospitals absorb the largest share of the resources, leaving little for basic services, which do not have an organized constituency.

Second, hospitals tend to be located in urban areas, so that travel times are minimized for the largest number of people. Often this means that hospitals are closer to the nonpoor, who tend also to live in urban areas, than to the poor, who may live in greater proportions in rural areas. Health services in general may therefore be more accessible to the nonpoor than to the poor.

Third, the nonpoor will almost always consume more health services than the poor—both because they have greater resources to spend on health and because they often value good health or are more aware of the need for health services than the poor.

Analytic Approach

There are several ways to look at how government spending benefits different population subgroups, notably the poor and nonpoor. The most common approach is benefit-incidence analysis, which compares income groups in terms of the amount of the health subsidy that they receive (Castro-Leal and others 1999; Yaqub 1999). In addition to information on health spending by type of service and type of facility, benefit-incidence analysis requires information, usually from household surveys, about the utilization of health services by individuals of different income levels or of different geographical areas with various levels of poverty.

The first step in a benefit-incidence analysis is to estimate the amounts spent by the government on the main types of health services. This was discussed earlier in the context of allocative efficiency and expenditure reviews. The second step is to estimate the utilization of those same services by income quintile from household survey data on key services; for example, total annual visits by type of provider, use of curative care in the two weeks preceding the survey, use of antenatal care, delivery care, and childhood immunizations. The third step is to use the products of the first two calculations to estimate the amount of money being distributed to each of the income quintiles in the form of health services. This is usually done by dividing the total expenditures on each type of service by the numbers of users in each quintile, thereby producing the per capita subsidy to users in different quintiles. The final step is to translate these amounts into percentages of the total spending. The resulting estimates will indicate what share of total health spending is captured by each of the income quintiles. These estimates can be made separately for different classes of health services (for example, hospitals versus peripheral facilities).

Difficulties often occur with the analysis of public spending. Because public sector budgets are often organized according to inputs rather than outputs, some of the analysis may be cumbersome. In most countries, public spending is found to be disproportionately distributed through health services to better-off populations. As noted earlier, this is due in part to the urban-rural distribution of the poor and nonpoor and the concentration of more expensive care in urban areas, in addition to the greater willingness and capacity to pay for health services of the nonpoor. Breakdowns by type of health services usually show that hospital services, which are more costly on a per patient basis than lower-level primary care, are disproportionately used by urban, higher-income populations. In contrast, primary health services provided in peripheral facilities generally serve poorer, rural populations.

Key Indicators

- Per capita public, private, and nongovernmental expenditure, by region
- Per capita public, private, and nongovernmental expenditure, by income quintile

Question 2. Do the Mechanisms for Financing Health Services Provide Incentives or Disincentives to Health Workers to Respond to the Poor?

There are several ways to finance health services, each of which has implications for responsiveness to the poor. The main types of provider payment mechanisms are

- fee for service, in which the amount received by the provider depends only on the volume and unit prices of services

- case payment, in which providers are paid a fixed amount per standard diagnosis, based on assumptions about treatment protocols and their costs
- capitation, in which providers are paid a fixed amount on the basis of the number of patients under their care and general information about their case mix, without regard for the health care needs of those patients
- salary, in which the providers receive a negotiated salary (or, in the public sector, a salary based on a civil service schedule)
- fixed budget

Each of these payment mechanisms has distinct implications for efficiency, quality, and responsiveness to the poor. For example, payment systems in which the provider obtains a higher income when he or she provides higher-priced services (for example, fee for service) tend to be less pro-poor than systems in which there is no direct relationship between the price of the services and provider income. In contrast, under both case-based and capitation systems, providers are better off when the utilization of health services does not exceed the amount expected during a priori negotiations over per capita reimbursement. The downside to capitation systems is that they generally create incentives to limit treatment. To the extent that the poor have greater health needs, limiting care may disproportionately affect the poor, unless the capitation or case-based rates are adjusted by risk classification—and income is a criterion for that risk classification.

Key Indicators

- Percentages of the poor and the nonpoor using services in which providers are financed by fee-for-service, case-based, capitation, salary, or other financing mechanisms
- Mean expenditures, by type of service and type of provider, for the poor and non-poor

Question 3. Does the Price of Health Services Create or Reduce Barriers to the Appropriate Use of Health Services by the Poor?

In addition to those factors discussed earlier—quality, time costs, and preferences for health care—the demand for health care depends on the prices that the potential service users face relative to their incomes. Higher out-of-pocket payments, in the form of fee-for-service payments to health care providers, copayments that accompany insurance reimbursement, or user fees in government facilities, may affect the use of services by the poor.

Analytic Approach

An analyst interested in examining the impact of prices on the use of essential services by the poor may wish to use household survey data on health expenditures and income to estimate, for example, the proportion of discretionary income devoted to health services by income level or the ratio of average user fee per unit of utilization to household income. In a simple analysis, before-and-after comparisons can be made. Specifically, evaluators can look at the level of utilization by each income group before the introduction of user fees—or before a change in the level of user fees—and then look at how utilization changes for each income group after the price change (Diop, Yazbeck, and Bitran 1995; Litvack and Bodart 1993; Soucat and others 1997).

Before-and-after comparisons, however, must be considered with caution if they do not look at the full range of consumer reactions to a price change. Frequently, reductions in the demand for public services from a price increase are considered only as negative consequences. However, any increase in price is likely to be associated with two types of consumer behavior: demand diversion and demand reduction, both of which have different implications for evaluating changes in consumer welfare. For some individuals, an increase in price will mean that the value they place on public sector services—relative to the alternatives—no longer accords with the price being charged, and they will switch to using other medical providers—private or nongovernmental (demand diversion). For many services, those with private benefits, this diversion may be a good thing, because it frees government resources for concentrating on other, perhaps higher priority, public health services. Of greater concern, however, are those individuals who cease consuming health services at all in the face of price increases, or who switch to nonmedical providers with lower treatment efficacies. Even here, care must be taken in interpreting reductions in demand, as changes in the demand for essential services must be weighed differently than changes in demand for other health services. These considerations point to the need for distinguishing the impact of price on various types of services, weighted by quality measurement.

In the absence of before-and-after information, evaluators could look at whether households of different income levels are forced to borrow or sell household assets to meet health needs, particularly for catastrophic events. Alternatively, they could examine the share of health expenditures in total household expenditures.

More sophisticated analyses can use regression analysis to examine simultaneously the impacts of various factors affecting demand—including price—for different income groups and also different age categories (Grossman 1972). These analyses have the advantage of producing quantifiable measures of the impacts of various factors—price, income, education, quality of care, distance—on use and nonuse of health services. Elasticities of demand—the percentage change in use of services relative to a percentage change in price—can be calculated to determine the degree of responsiveness by the poor and nonpoor to changes in prices for different services or at different types of facilities (Schwartz, Akin, and Popkin 1988; Dor and van der Gaag 1985).

Regression analysis can also be used to estimate the effect of price and household income on the utilization of services. A large estimated effect of income for specific groups would suggest that low income is a serious barrier to proper health care seeking. From these measures, various policy scenarios can be simulated, including asking questions such as "how would service utilization (for different income groups) change if (a) the price were set to zero, (b) everyone lived within 5 kilometers of a health facility providing essential services, or (c) key drugs and supplies were available all the time?" From these simulations, policy makers and planners can prioritize different health sector reforms. Such analyses have been used in a variety of contexts to show that the potentially negative effects of price increases can be offset by quality improvements (Mwabu, Ainsworth, and Nyamete 1993; Alderman and Lavy 1996); that prices have different impacts on the poor and nonpoor (Gertler and van der Gaag 1990); that the effects of monetary prices can be outweighed by the time costs of using care (Akin and Hutchinson 1999); and that elasticity of demand can be higher for children than for adults (Sauerborn, Nougtara, and Latimer 1994).

Key Indicators

- Mean price of care relative to average monthly income, by income quintile
- Elasticities of demand for different income quintiles, by type of essential service and by level of care; that is, percentage change in use of service from percentage change in
  - Price
  - Quality indicator (staffing, drug and equipment availability)
  - Distance from household to provider
  - Education
  - Age

Question 4. Does the System of Financing Health Services Protect the Poor from (or Expose Them to) Income Shocks When They Fall Ill?

A separate issue is whether households are pushed into poverty or further into poverty through out-of-pocket payments. Evidence comparing households' living standards before and after out-of-pocket payments suggests, unsurprisingly, that for households without insurance coverage, out-of-pocket payments are a bigger financial shock, and that out-of-pocket payments can be large enough to make the difference between having a standard of living above the absolute poverty line or below it.

The impoverishing effects of illness can be traced to both the loss of income on the part of the individual who has become ill (and his or her caretakers), and to the expenses related to health care. A study in Indonesia, in fact, found that it was generally the loss of income from disability rather than the burden of medical expenses that led to household impoverishment (Gertler and Sturm 1997).

Analytic Approach

Assessing financial access and affordability requires comparing current prices of services with the capacity of households to pay and the patterns of utilization at given prices. This requires relating data on utilization of services and household expenditures to data on the prices of services. Government statistics can in principle provide data on the prices charged for different services, and the categories for which fee waivers exist, if any. In practice, facility surveys provide more accurate information on both, not least because fee waiver programs can be—and are often intended to be—subject to local interpretation and implementation.

More simple analyses can be conducted in comparing the average price for services or average annual medical expenditures to the average monthly or yearly income of a poor household. The latter can be particularly useful for assessing the potential dissavings impact of catastrophic illnesses. Willingness to pay can also be estimated from contingent valuation studies. These studies directly ask individuals through surveys the value they would place to particular types of services. Household surveys can be used to collect information on participation in insurance and prepayment schemes.

Key Indicators

- Percentage of average annual medical expenditures in total household expenditures, by income quintile
- Percentage of the population covered by insurance plans, by income quintile
- Percentage of clinics with fee waiver programs for the poor and other vulnerable populations
- Percentage of the poor exempted from paying fees

Conclusion

In this chapter, we have presented a method for assessing, in a stepwise fashion, whether the conditions are in place for the government health system to respond to the needs of poor households—or the population as a whole—and, if not, where the gaps lie. This strategy is summarized in table 6.3, which

TABLE 6.3 Summary of Major Questions to Be Answered in a Health Financing Assessment

Issues/question	Analytic approach	Data required
Step 1. Channeling Resources to the Poor and Addressing Market Failures		
Market failures	Identify public goods, market failures among the health services; prioritize based on costs & benefits; determine whether they are fully funded, given current budget allocations	Public sector expenditures, broken down by type of health service or by type of facility
Allocative efficiency	Compare public spending with burden of disease data to see if (a) there is a reasonable correspondence between spending and disease impact and (b) interventions are not fully addressed by other providers and (c) interventions are cost-effective	Public sector expenditures, broken down by type of health service • Burden of disease • Local costs • International estimates of cost-effectiveness for selected interventions
Step 2. Determine Obstacles to Coverage for Interventions Addressing the Needs of the Poor		
Technical efficiency, adequacy of inputs, and consumer responsiveness	Determine: (a) if services for the poor are accessible and adequate human and material resources are available (b) if communities have "voice" (c) if services are used by the poor at appropriate times and intervals	• Facility quality, location and service availability • Community participation and influence indicators • Health service utilization, income levels, and health outcomes

(continued)

TABLE 6.3 Summary of Major Questions to Be Answered in a Health Financing Assessment (*continued*)

Issues/question	Analytic approach	Data required
Step 3. Determine the Impact of Expenditures and Financing Mechanisms on the Poor		
Distribution of public spending to the poor	Benefit-incidence analysis	• Public sector expenditure data, broken down by type of health service • Household-level data on utilization of health services by income group
Impact of provider payment mechanisms on responsiveness to the poor	Identification of provider payment mechanisms, and qualitative assessment of their impact	• Information from key informants on provider payment mechanisms • International research on implications of provider payment mechanisms
Impact of price of health services on utilization by the poor	Assessment of prices for health services faced by poor households Estimates of price elasticity of demand	• Direct and indirect prices for private health services • Household-level data on utilization of health services by income group
Impact of the health financing mechanism on protection of poor households to economic shocks	Identification of extent of risk pooling with various financing arrangements	• Information from key informants on extent of risk pooling • Household spending per health event, relative to income • Household financing mechanisms when faced with catastrophic events, such as borrowing or selling assets

Source: Benin and Guinea." *International Journal of Health Planning and Management* 12 (supp. 1).

presents the basic questions to be asked by planners and policy makers in evaluating their health systems, describes the analytic approaches to addressing these questions, and suggests some possible data sources.

This diagnostic structure extends from how governments choose to allocate health resources, to the efficiency of the health systems in using those resources—including identification of potential impediments to an effective supply of health services, and finally to whether the health system has a measurable impact on health behaviors that affects the health outcomes of the poor. The value of this diagnostic structure is that it allows observers who see particular health outcomes—for example, that the poor have worse health than the rich—to understand precisely where and how the health system contributes to those differentials and to identify promising ways to correct the system's shortcomings. The diagnostic structure also makes use of data collection mechanisms that are already commonly available in many countries, requiring only that the data be put to the uses suggested here.

Notes

1. This chapter is adapted from the health, nutrition, and population chapter of the *Poverty Reduction Strategy Sourcebook,* which is available at www.worldbank.org/ poverty/strategies/sourtoc.

2. Some of the key health interventions that may have a significant impact on the health status of the poor include health education, micronutrient supplementation, integrated management of child illnesses (IMCI), immunizations, family planning, Safe Motherhood programs, malaria prevention and case management, tuberculosis case management, HIV prevention and basic care, community-based nutrition promotion, tobacco control, and other public health and personal care priorities.

3. A useful review of techniques and data collection procedures for facility surveys, including conduct of exit interviews and direct observation of treatment, is *Quick Investigation of Quality (QIQ): A User's Guide for Monitoring Quality of Care* (MEASURE Evaluation 2000).

4. One problem, however, is that these standards are rarely developed in the context of a realistic budget envelope for the sector. Reaching prespecified input targets should not substitute for carefully diagnosing the major constraints facing the sector, and the most efficient way to achieve outcome goals.

5. GISs allow the linking of a wide variety of information, but they require special equipment and trained staff to operate and sustain. An increasing number of health ministries are using GISs, however, and the actual GIS data entry and analysis could be done on contract with the private sector or a nongovernmental organization.

6. The Demographic and Health Surveys and the Living Standards Measurement Surveys, for example, include questions on household assets as well as the availability of essential services in the community, making it possible to compile tabulations for accessibility by income or asset levels.

7. See www.worldbank.org/poverty/voices.

8. Improving the quality and availability of pharmaceuticals and health staffing is difficult and often requires structural reforms. Refer to the PRSP toolkit for technical notes on pharmaceuticals and human resources.

9. Official statistics often provide information on the availability of drugs, medicines, growth monitoring and immunization programs, and so on. Aside from the fact that they are rather crude measures of quality, these statistics also may paint a rosier picture of quality than is warranted. A facility survey in Côte d'Ivoire found a substantial divergence between medicines that were supposed to be available, according to government records, and those that were actually available, according to the facility

survey. Despite the crudeness of the quality measure, the facility survey revealed some worrying gaps between poor rural areas and better-off urban areas in the proportions of facilities with immunization and growth monitoring programs.

10. The Population Council and the United Nations Family Planning Association have further information on these tools.

11. In Mozambique an index is constructed using services-based information on the proportion of children immunized, the proportion of women using antenatal services, and the number of inpatient and outpatient visits.

12. Striking examples of the impact of low quality of services are found in maternal health. Utilization of antenatal care is quite high throughout Africa, yet the relevance and the quality and efficacy of services is so low that despite high demand, maternal outcomes improve very little. In The Gambia, a traditional birth attendant program led to a major increase in utilization of obstetric services—yet had no impact on outcomes, since women reaching hospital services died there for lack of blood, material, and surgeons. In the same way for tuberculosis, we know that people seek health care when they have chronic cough and fever. Yet services often fail to recognize the diagnosis and to prescribe and follow up on appropriate treatments.

13. In Burundi, only 3 percent of children with diarrhea were correctly assessed and only 13 percent correctly rehydrated. In Vietnam, by contrast, the figures were 78 percent and 67 percent, respectively. In Indonesia, only 2 percent of pneumonia cases were managed correctly and only 4 percent of caretakers were correctly advised. The figures for China were 73 percent and 75 percent, respectively.

14. See http://www.worldbank.org/poverty/strategies/sourtoc, chapter 3.2 on health.

References

Acheson, Donald. 1998. *Independent Inquiry into Inequalities in Health.* London: Stationery Office.

Akin, John, and Paul Hutchinson. 1999. "Health Care Facility Choice and the Phenomenon of Bypassing." *Health Policy and Planning* 14 (2): 135–51.

Akin, John, David Guilkey, Paul Hutchinson, and Michael McIntosh. 1996. "Price Elasticities of Demand for Curative Care with Controls for Sample Selectivity on Endogenous Illness: An Analysis for Sri Lanka." *Health Economics* 7: 509–31.

Alderman, Harold, and Victor Lavy. 1996. "Household Responses to Public Health Services: Cost and Quality Tradeoffs." *World Bank Research Observer* 11 (1): 3–22.

Berman, Peter. 1996. "National Health Accounts in Developing Countries: Appropriate Methods and Recent Applications." Data for Decision Making Project, Department of Population and International Health, Harvard University, Cambridge, MA.

Castro-Leal, Florencia, Julia Dayton, Lionel Demery, and Kalpana Mehra. 1999. "Public Social Spending in Africa: Do the Poor Benefit?" *World Bank Research Observer* 14 (1): 49–72.

Cebu Study Team. 1991. "Underlying and Proximate Determinants of Child Health: The Cebu Longitudinal Health and Nutrition Study." *American Journal of Epidemiology* 133 (2): 185–201.

César, Juraci, Cesar Victora, Fernando Barros, Iná Santos, and José Flores. 1999. "Impact of Breast Feeding on Admission for Pneumonia during Postneonatal Period in Brazil: Nested Case-Control Study. *British Medical Journal* 318 (7194): 1316–20.

Creese, Andrew, and Joseph Kutzin. 1997. "Lessons from Cost Recovery in Health." In *Marketizing Education and Health in Developing Countries: Miracle or Mirage?*, ed. Christopher Colclough, 37–62. Oxford: Clarendon Press.

DFID (U.K. Department for International Development). 1999. *Better Health for Poor People.* London: DFID.

Diop, François, Abdo Yazbeck, and Ricardo Bitran. 1995. "The Impact of Alternative Cost Recovery Schemes on Access and Equity in Niger." *Health Policy and Planning* 10 (3). Special issue on Improving Quality, Equity, and Access to Health Services through Health Financing Reform in Africa.

Dor, Avi, and Jacques van der Gaag. 1985. "The Demand for Medical Care in Developing Countries: Quantity Rationing in Rural Côte d'Ivoire." Living Standards Measurement Survey Working Paper 35, World Bank, Washington, DC.

Eastwood, Robert, and Michael Lipton. 2000. "The Impact of Changes in Human Fertility on Poverty." *Journal of Development Studies* 31: 1–30.

Filmer, Deon, Jeffrey Hammer, and Lant Pritchett. 1998. *Health Policy in Poor Countries: Weak Links in the Chain.* Washington, DC: World Bank.

Gertler, Paul, and Jacques van der Gaag. 1990. *The Willingness to Pay for Medical Care: Evidence from Two Countries.* Washington, DC: World Bank.

Gertler, Paul, and Roland Sturm. 1997. "Private Health Insurance and Public Expenditures in Jamaica." *Journal of Econometrics* 77 (1): 237–58.

Gilson Lucy, Denny Kalyalya, Felix Kuchler, Sally Lake, Hezron Oranga, and Marius Ouendo. 1999. "Promoting Equity within Community Financing Schemes: Experience from Three African Countries." Department of Public Health Policy Publication 31, London School of Hygiene and Tropical Medicine.

Griffin, Charles. 1992. *Health Care in Asia: A Comparative Study of Cost and Financing.* Washington, DC: World Bank.

Grossman, Michael. 1972. *The Demand for Health: A Theoretical and Empirical Investigation.* New York: National Bureau of Economic Research.

Gwatkin, Davidson. 2000. "Health Inequalities and the Health of the Poor: What Do We Know? What Can We Do?" *Bulletin of the World Health Organization* 78 (1): 3–18.

Hughes, Gordon, and Meghan Dunleavy. 2000. "Why Do Babies and Young Children Die in India? The Role of the Household Environment." Working paper, World Bank, Washington, DC.

ICC (International Children Center). 1997. "Impact de l'Epidémie VIH sur le Système de Santé Ivoirien." Report of the European Commission.

Jha, Prabhat, Kent Ranson, and Jose Bobadilla. 1996. "Measuring the Burden of Disease and Cost-Effectiveness of Health Interventions: A Case Study in Guinea." Technical Paper 333, World Bank, Washington, DC.

Kakwani, Nanok. 1977. "Measurement of Tax Progressivity: An International Comparison." *Economic Journal* 87 (345): 71–80.

Knippenberg, Rudolf, Agnes Soucat, Kayode Oyegbite, Maria Calivis, Ian Hopwood, Reiko Niimi, Mamadou Pathe Diallo, Mamadou Conde, and Samuel Ofosu-Amaah. 1997. "Bamako Initiative Programmes in West Africa: An Assessment of 5 Years Field Experience in Benin and Guinea." *International Journal of Health Planning and Management* 12 (Suppl. 1): 29–47.

Lasprilla, Enrique, Carlos Obando, Eduardo Encalad, and Christian Lasprilla. 1999. "Health Sector Inequalities and Poverty in Ecuador." In *Health Systems Inequalities and Poverty in Latin America and the Caribbean,* ed. Edward Greene, José Vicente Zevallos, and Ruben Suarez. Washington, DC: Pan American Health Organization and World Bank.

Leighton, Charlotte, and François Diop. 1999. *Protection for the Poor under Cost Recovery.* Bethesda, MD: Abt Associates.

Litvack, Jennie, and Claude Bodart. 1993. "User Fees plus Quality Equals Improved Access to Health Care: Results of a Field Experiment in Cameroon." *Social Science and Medicine.* 37 (3): 369–83.

MEASURE Evaluation. 2000. *Quick Investigation of Quality (QIQ): A User's Guide for Monitoring Quality of Care.* MEASURE Evaluation Manual Series, No. 2. Chapel Hill: University of North Carolina.

Mosley, Henry, and Lincoln Chen. 1984. "An Analytical Framework for the Study of Child Survival in Developing Countries." *Population and Development Review* 10 (Supplement: *Child Survival: Strategies for Research*): 25–45.

Musgrove, Philip. 1996. "Public and Private Roles in Health: Theory and Financing Patterns." Discussion Paper 339, World Bank, Washington, DC.

Mwabu, Germano, Martha Ainsworth, and Andrew Nyamete. 1993. "Quality of Medical Care and Choice of Medical Treatment in Kenya: An Empirical Analysis." *Journal of Human Resources* 28 (4): 838–62.

Narayan, Deepa, Robert Chambers, Meera Shah, and Patti Petesch. 1999. *Global Synthesis: Consultations with the Poor.* Washington, DC: World Bank.

Panis, Constantijn, and Lee Lillard. 1994. "Health Inputs and Child Mortality." *Journal of Health Economics* 13: 455–89.

Parker, Susan, and Eduardo Pier. 1999. "Mexico." In *Health Systems Inequalities and Poverty in Latin America and the Caribbean,* ed. Edward Greene, José Vicente Zevallos, and Ruben Suarez. Washington, DC: Pan American Health Organization and World Bank.

Pradhan, Sanjay. 1996. "Evaluating Public Spending: A Framework for Public Expenditure Reviews." Discussion Paper 323, World Bank, Washington, DC.

Sauerborn, Rainer, Adrien Nougtara, and Eric Latimer. 1994. "The Elasticity of Demand for Health Care in Burkina Faso: Differences across Age and Income Groups." *Health Policy and Planning* 9 (2): 185–92.

Schultz, T. Paul. 1984. "Studying the Impact of Household Economic and Community Variables on Child Mortality." *Population and Development Review* 10 (Supplement: *Child Survival: Strategies for Research*): 215–35.

Schwartz, J. Brad, John Akin, and Barry Popkin. 1988. "Price and Income Elasticities of Demand for Modern Health Care: The Case of Infant Delivery in the Philippines." *World Bank Economic Review* 2 (1): 49–76.

Soucat, Agnes, Daniel Levy-Bruhl, Xavier De Bethune, Palicide Gbedonou, Jean-Pierre Lamarque, Ousmane Bangoura, Ousmane Camara, Timothee Gandaho, Christine Ortiz, Miloud Kaddar, and Rudolf Knippenberg. 1997. "Equity in Bamako Initiative Programmes in Benin and Guinea." *International Journal of Health Planning and Management* 12 (Suppl. 1): S81–108.

Theodore, Karl, Dominic Stoddard, Andrea Yearwood, and Wendell Thomas. 1999. "Jamaica." In *Health Systems Inequalities and Poverty in Latin America and the Caribbean,* ed. Edward Greene, José Vicente Zevallos, and Ruben Suarez. Washington, DC: Pan American Health Organization and World Bank.

Van Doorslaer, Eddy, and Adam Wagstaff. 1992. "Equity in the Delivery of Health Care: Some International Comparisons." *Journal of Health Economics* 11 (4): 389–412.

Vega, Jeanette, Rolf Dieter Hollstein, Iris Delgado, Juan Perez, Sebastian Carrasco, Guillermo Marshall, and Derek Yach. 2000. *Chile 1985–1996: A Multi-level Study of Education's Impact on Health Equity,* ed. Margaret Whitehead. Oxford, U.K.: Oxford University Press.

Wagstaff, Adam. 2000a. "Socioeconomic Inequalities in Child Mortality: Comparisons across Nine Developing Countries." *Bulletin of the World Health Organization* 78 (1): 19–29.

———. 2000b. *Unpacking the Causes of Inequalities in Child Survival: The Case of Cebu, the Philippines.* Washington, DC: World Bank.

Wagstaff, Adam, Pierella Paci, and Eddy van Doorslaer. 1991. "On the Measurement of Inequalities in Health." *Social Science and Medicine* 33: 545–57.

Wagstaff, Adam, Eddy van Doorslaer, Hattem van der Burg, Samuel Calonge, Terkel Christiansen, Guido Citoni, Ulf-G. Gerdtham, Mike Gerfin, Lorna Gross, Unto Hakinnen, Paul Johnson, Jürgen John, Jan Klavus, Claire Lachaud, Jorgen Lauritsen, Robert Leu, Brian Nolan, Encarna Peran, Joao Pereira, Carol Propper, Frank Puffer, Lise Rochaix, Marisol Rodriguez, Martin Schellhorn, and Olaf Winkelhake. 1999. "Equity in the Finance of Health Care: Some Further International Comparisons." *Journal of Health Economics* 18: 263–90.

Whitehead, Margaret. 2000. "William Farr's Legacy to the Study of Health Inequalities." *Bulletin of the World Health Organization* 78 (1): 86–87.

Wolfe, Barbara, and Jere Behrman. 1982. "Determinants of Child Mortality, Health and Nutrition in a Developing Country." *Journal of Development Economics* 11: 163–93.

Wong, Emelita, Barry M. Popkin, David K. Guilkey, and John S. Akin. 1987. "Accessibility, Quality of Care and Prenatal Care Use in the Philippines." *Social Science and Medicine* 24 (11): 927–44.

World Bank. 1993. *World Development Report 1993: Investing in Health.* Washington, DC: World Bank.

———. 2001. *Health Country Status Report Mauritania 2001.* Human Development Africa Region. Washington, DC: World Bank.

WHO (World Health Organization) 2000. *The World Health Report 2000: Health Systems.* Geneva: WHO.

Yaqub, Shahin. 1999. "How Equitable is Public Spending on Health and Education?" Background paper for WDR 2000/1. World Bank, Washington, DC.

7

Measuring Public Sector Performance in Infrastructure

HADI SALEHI ESFAHANI

Raising and maintaining the standards of living in any economy are contingent on the adequacy of infrastructure services in terms of quantity and quality.[1] Unlike many other products, infrastructure services such as water, electricity, transportation, and telecommunications are typically indispensable for households and businesses. Also, they often account for a sizable portion of living and business costs. As a result, when they are in short supply or costly to produce, production and standards of living are likely to suffer badly. This issue is particularly important from a public policy point of view because private markets for infrastructure services are subject to failures that call for regulation or public production. Under either form of government intervention, improving efficiency is contingent upon the availability of information about the quantity and quality of services produced and the cost of production. In this sense, measuring performance in infrastructure activities is a central factor in ensuring adequate provision of these crucial services and, ultimately, in supporting higher standards of living.

A key issue in the design of public policy toward infrastructure is that the information needed for performance measurement is costly to obtain, so the government has to decide how much and what type of information is worth gathering. The literature on performance measurement has focused on this issue and has tried to understand what sorts of conditions reduce the cost of gathering and using information for each type of service. The task has been difficult because the analysis has to take into account the fact that service providers and consumers have incentives to use the information under their control strategically. In this respect, the solutions for improving performance measurement must go beyond the simple choice of indicators and must pay attention to the ways in which tasks and roles in the provision of infrastructure services are organized. In this chapter, we review the problems of performance measurement in public infrastructure and examine the possible solutions.

The literature on performance measurement in public infrastructure is relatively small. But, there is a vast literature concerning public services in general that can be applied to the analysis of public infrastructure. In the past few decades, this literature has benefited from active research on performance measurement, especially in light of numerous experiments around the world in reorganizing bureaucracies based on performance criteria. There has also been steady fusion of the lessons from the studies of business practices and management. These aspects make the public services literature a rich source of ideas for our task. However, it should be pointed out that despite the recent advances, the public services literature is still mostly in the form of accumulated wisdom rather than a set of rigorous theoretical propositions supported by empirical observations and statistical tests (Wood and Marshall 1993).

One reason for this situation may be the fact that performance in public services is difficult to analyze because the outputs of many such services are hard to measure or even to define. For example, it is not clear how one can measure the output of a foreign ministry when the goal of the ministry (furthering the country's national interests around the world) is hard to define with any clarity (Wilson 1989). One manifestation of these difficulties is that in the public service literature a distinction is made between outputs and outcomes, with the former referring to what is done by carrying out tasks and the latter showing the consequences of outputs for the attainment of policy goals. For infrastructure services, the goals and outputs are, in principle, better defined, and once the output is measured, its outcome can be inferred easily. As a result, the key issue in assessing infrastructure performance is making information gathering more cost-effective.

Discussions and bibliographies of performance measurement in public services abound, both in print and on the Internet. We review a number of them below. For more extensive references and links, see the Web sites of the National Partnership for Reinventing Government (http://www.orau.gov/pbm/links/npr1.html), the National Center for Public Productivity (http://

www.ncpp.us/), the Governmental Accounting Standards Board (GASB) (http:// www.gasb.org/), the Organisation for Economic Co-operation and Development (OECD) Program on Public Management and Governance (PUMA)(http://www.oecd.org/about/0,2337,en_2649_34275_1_1_1_1_1,0 0.html), and the Inter-American Development Bank's Experiences on Peformance Measurement (http://www.iadb.org/roundtable/index_files/ex.htm).

The next section starts by analyzing the nature of the problem. The following section discusses the choice of indicators and organizational arrangements for more efficient information processing. The final section concludes.

The Nature of the Problem

On the surface, performance measurement in public infrastructure may seem straightforward. For example, in solving water supply problems, one may think of measuring the amount, quality, and cost of water services delivered. However, measurement is hampered by a number of factors, including those that cause market failure in the first place. For example, quality and cost have a variety of dimensions that may be hard to observe. In the case of water services, quality depends on the politeness of staff toward customers, and the promptness of responses to problems that arise at various parts of the system, and the likelihood of future breakdowns in the system in terms of health hazards as well as service interruption. On the cost side, it is difficult for observers (other than those who carry out the tasks) to determine whether the inputs are used efficiently and whether the managers and workers have been sufficiently innovative. Although the information about all these details may be known, at least in bits and pieces, to the production staff, gathering the information and summarizing it may be an extremely costly task. This is particularly the case because the individuals who have the necessary information can benefit from withholding or misrepresenting it. Similar problems exist in the case of all other infrastructure services and make the task of performance measurement difficult.

The factor that makes these problems particularly serious in the case of public infrastructure is the monopoly feature that such services commonly have. When a service is being offered to a competitive market, one does not have to know all the details of quality and cost. From the consumers' point of view, the poor quality or high cost of a particular service provider is an insignificant matter since other producers can meet their demands. This punishes the inefficient firms in terms of profitability, which is a good indicator of performance. Of course, when a publicly owned firm faces a soft budget constraint, the managers may not be very concerned with failure. But the government will have a reasonable yardstick with which to assess the firm and discipline the managers if it chooses to do so. This is not normally possible under monopoly conditions because, for the consumers, showing dissatisfaction with the service is not as easy as switching suppliers. The monopoly also makes the firm's circumstances unique and reduces the utility of profitability as a performance measure. For example, a local water company that experiences high costs may claim that the water supply conditions or the local geography are unfavorable, even though it may be possible to lower the costs with the investment of some managerial effort.

Why is monopoly a common problem in infrastructure services? The main factor is high fixed capital costs, especially in the networks delivering such services, which bring about economies of scale. For example, putting pipes or wires in place to bring water, electricity, or telecommunications to households in a locality requires a large capital cost. To create competition in such situations, often the network has to be duplicated, which in many cases is a very costly proposition. Of course, there are parts of infrastructure services that can be organized in a competitive fashion, and new technologies are making this increasingly possible. In those parts, naturally, the solution to the infrastructure performance problem is implementing competition and letting the market generate the relevant information and select the efficient operators. However, this option is not available or still far away for most infrastructure services, especially in smaller communities.

Given the difficulties mentioned above in using informative summary measures such as profitability or in obtaining direct indicators of quality and cost, the policy question regarding public infrastructure has to be focused on the selection of the most cost-effective indicators and the ways in which infrastructure activities can be organized to improve the flow of information and production incentives.

Choosing Performance Indicators

There is a wide range of indicators for measuring performance in any infrastructure service. In the literature on public services, such indicators are categorized in many different ways. One common form is to distinguish among measures of assets, inputs, process, outputs, and outcomes and then use them to define indicators of efficiency, effectiveness, and productivity (Boyle 1989; Ammons 1995; National Center for Public Productivity 1997). The definitions of the first set of variables are more or less similar to those used by economists. *Assets* are the capacity to provide services—for example, power generation and water processing capacity. *Inputs* are the resources (either financial, physical, or human) consumed for a particular activity—for example, staff time, materials, utilized assets, and the like. *Process* indicators refer to the steps taken in the provision of a service—for example, the tasks performed and the extent to which they follow the required procedures. *Outputs* refer to the services actually provided or performed—for example, electricity generated, faults repaired on telephone lines, etc. *Outcomes* are the impacts of a service on its recipients—for example, the contribution of water and sanitation systems to the health of the population.

The indicators of assets are not emphasized much in the public service literature. In fact, there is an opposite emphasis that the advocates of performance measurement should distance themselves from the traditional concerns with inputs and focus on outputs and efficiency. Attention to performance is, of course, crucial. However, the development and maintenance of assets should be an important part of selected performance measures because assets indicate potentials for delivering a high stream of output in future times. Examining both assets and current performance is common practice in evaluating private businesses.

The similarities with economic definitions are much less for the second set of variables—efficiency, effectiveness, and productivity. In the public service literature, *efficiency* is defined as the amount of output per unit of an input used in the process—for example, the number of road repairs per employee-days involved in the task. *Effectiveness* is the degree to which the outcomes achieve the goals set for the activity—for example, the percentage of roads maintained in good condition relative to policy goals. Finally, *productivity* is the combination of efficiency and effectiveness: the outcomes achieved per dollar of cost—for example, the percentage of roads maintained in good condition per dollar of cost. The most conspicuous difference of these definitions from those in economics is the reversal of the efficiency and productivity concepts. To avoid confusion in this chapter, we will be mostly concerned with outputs rather than outcomes and define productivity as the output-input ratio and efficiency as the total cost per unit of output.

The public service literature also differentiates between quantitative and qualitative indicators. *Quantitative indicators* are direct cardinal measures of output such as the number of phone calls completed in a telephone network. *Qualitative indicators* are ordinal measures based on opinion surveys and subjective assessments—for example, customer satisfaction rates and expert opinion surveys. Both types of indicators are important because while quantitative indicators can be used as objective and hard evidence, they cannot capture many aspects of product quality. To obtain data on the latter type of variables, one has to rely on qualitative measures that may be subjective and imperfect, but nevertheless informative.

Tables 7.1–7.5 provide examples of indicators for assets, outputs and processes, and efficiency and productivity in typical infrastructure services. The indicators listed in these tables are mostly aggregate ones. There are many more detailed indicators that one can specify for each of these services. For example, in water services, the numbers of meters read or repaired properly are also output indicators. Also, one can specify more detailed measures of the process of production. For example, in sanitation services, one can build

TABLE 7.1   Examples of Performance Measures for Power Infrastructure

Outputs/processes	Productivity/efficiency	Assets
KWhs generated	Cost per KWh	Generation capacity
KWhs delivered	KWhs generated per employee (or labor hour)	Number of employees
Days without power for various types of customers	Capacity utilization rate	Employee education and experience
Response time for repair requests	System loss (percentage of power generation lost in transmission)	Expert rating of asset quality (technology, maintenance, reliability, etc.)
Percentage of repairs that do not fail within a year	Consumer satisfaction rating and other quality measures relative to cost per KWh	
Number of user complaints per 1,000 households served per month	Expert rating of productivity/ efficiency	
Percentage of operational procedures followed correctly		
Consumer satisfaction rating (survey)		
Employee and other stakeholder satisfaction rating (survey)		
Expert rating of service quality		

TABLE 7.2 Examples of Performance Measures for
Telecommunications Infrastructure

Outputs/processes	Productivity/efficiency	Assets
Telecom traffic: Number and minutes of calls	Call completion rate	Length of installed cables (various types)
Completed calls: Number and minutes of calls	Number and minutes of calls processed per employee	Capacity of circuits and exchange switches (various types)
Days without service for various types of customers	Telephone lines per employee (or labor hour)	Number of employees
Line fault rate	Total cost per line	Employee education and experience
Restoration rate	Consumer satisfaction rating and other quality measures relative to total cost per line	Expert rating of asset quality (technology, maintenance, reliability, etc.)
Percentage of repairs that do not fail within a year	Expert rating of productivity/efficiency	
Number of user complaints per 1,000 lines per month		
Percent of operational procedures followed correctly		
Consumer satisfaction rating (survey)		
Employee and other stakeholder satisfaction rating (survey)		
Expert rating of service quality		

an indicator of the kinds of treatment applied to wastewater and the procedural details followed in those treatments. As we will see below, such indicators are more important in services where the quality or quantity of the product is difficult to measure and one has to rely on how a task is performed to ensure a minimum level of service (Boyle 1989).

A third type of variable that is important to consider but has received little attention in the literature is *flexibility.* Flexibility can be assessed based

TABLE 7.3   Examples of Performance Measures for
Transportation Infrastructure

Outputs/processes	Productivity/efficiency	Assets
Traffic (car miles per day)	Traffic per dollar of total (capital and maintenance) cost	Length of roads and railroads (various types)
Days with limited or no service for various types of roads/railroad	Traffic per employee (or labor hour)	Width and quality of roads (various types)
Road and railroad damage per 1,000 kilometers per year	User satisfaction rating and other quality measures relative to cost per traffic unit	Number of employees
Length of restoration time	Expert rating of productivity/efficiency	Employee education and experience
Percentage of repairs that do not fail within a year		Expert rating of asset quality (pavement, maintenance, reliability, etc.)
Number of user complaints per 1,000 lines per month		
Percentage of operational procedures followed correctly.		
User satisfaction rating (survey)		
Employee and other stakeholder satisfaction rating (survey)		
Expert rating of service quality		

on the type of assets and skills available in an organization and through the extent of training and research and development that is regularly performed (Maskell 1994). Such indicators are important because the demand and supply conditions are subject to change. Infrastructure service providers should be able to cope with such changes and constantly take advantage of new knowledge and technology.

Given the list of possible variables for measuring performance, the questions are which ones are more appropriate and worth focusing on, and should

TABLE 7.4 Examples of Performance Measures for
Water Infrastructure

Outputs/processes	Productivity/efficiency	Assets
agCubic meters of water processed	Unaccounted for water	Length of installed pipes (various types)
Cubic meters of water delivered	Cubic meters of water delivered (or processed) per employee (or labor hour)	Water processing capacity (various types)
Water substances and organisms controlled for	Cost of a cubic meter of water delivered	Number of employees
Outbreaks of health hazards in the water system per year	Cost of a cubic meter of water delivered, including the costs of health hazards in the water system to the population	Employee education and experience
Days without service for various types of customers	Consumer satisfaction rating and other quality measures relative to cost per cubic meter of water delivered	Expert rating of asset quality (technology, maintenance, reliability, etc.)
Number of system breaks per kilometer of pipeline	Expert rating of productivity/efficiency	
Restoration rate		
Percentage of repairs that do not fail within a year		
Number of complaints per 1,000 customers per month		
Percentage of operational procedures followed correctly.		
Consumer satisfaction rating (survey)		
Employee and other stakeholder satisfaction rating (survey)		
Expert rating of service quality		

TABLE 7.5   Examples of Performance Measures for
Sanitation Infrastructure

Outputs/processes	Productivity/efficiency	Assets
agCubic meters of liquid waste processed	Cubic meters of liquid waste (or tons of solid waste) processed per employee (or labor hour)	Length of installed pipes (various types)
Tons of solid wasted processed	Cost of a cubic meter of liquid waste (or a ton of solid waste) processed	Waste processing capacity (various types)
Outbreaks of environmental and health hazards from the sanitation system per year	Cost of a cubic meter of liquid waste (or a ton of solid waste) processed, including the environmental and health hazards costs	Number of employees
Waste substances and organisms controlled for in the system's discharge	Consumer satisfaction rating and other quality measures relative to cost per cubic meter of water delivered	Employee education and experience
Days without service for various types of customers	Expert rating of productivity/efficiency	Expert rating of asset quality (technology, maintenance, reliability, etc.)
Number of system breaks		
Restoration rate		
Percentage of repairs that do not fail within a year		
Number of complaints per 1,000 customers per month		
Percentage of operational procedures followed correctly		
Consumer satisfaction rating (survey)		
Employee and other stakeholder satisfaction rating (survey)		
Expert rating of service quality		

one keep track of all possible measures. Ideally, one would like to come up with a few measures or a single measure that summarizes all information relevant to performance. Economists, for example, commonly assume that private enterprises measure their performance based on long-term profitability. Although this is a reasonable theoretical assumption, in practice even private firms have difficulty coming up with a single indicator of this type, because there are no clear ways of measuring expected future profitability. This is why private firms constantly ponder their business strategy and joggle indicators such as market share, superior value for chosen customers, and the like as possible indicators of their long-term profitability. In the context of public services, the matter is made more complicated by the fact that financial profitability is not necessarily a good indicator of performance. This means that one has to choose a group of indexes and ensure that their combination provides sufficient information for assessing the extent to which policy goals are fulfilled.

Given that a multiplicity of variables must be selected, a key issue is the choice of the number and range of indicators. One approach has been to restrict the measures to a very limited, but crucial, set of indicators. The argument behind this approach is that with too many variables to consider, one may lose sight of what really matters to the public. Focusing on a few measures may also distort the incentives of service providers and encourage them to concentrate on what is being monitored to the detriment of everything else. An important side effect of such a development is that those who monitor and manage the incentive system for public services may miss some early signals of performance failure because the producers will have an incentive to mask failures by shifting their shortcomings toward service aspects that are not monitored.

This concern has led to the idea of a *balanced scorecard* in recent years (Kaplan and Norton 1996; National Partnership for Reinventing Government 1999). The argument here is that while one focuses on a few crucial indicators, one also should keep an eye on a variety of gauges, much the same way that drivers develop the skill to keep an eye on dashboard indicators while concentrating on the view ahead. The details of most dashboard indicators may not be important within a certain range. But a good system of dashboard signals ensures that the driver receives a quick warning whenever a problem starts to arise. This is what a properly designed balanced scorecard is supposed to do (Kaplan and Norton 1996). Significant attention may be paid to a few key indicators, but minimum standards for a variety of other measures must also be met. The resource cost of the latter set of indicators can be kept low because a very limited amount of data is needed on their details.

Whether one uses the balanced scorecard or a more focused set of variables, the question still remains as to the nature of the criteria that need to be used for selecting the indicators for what should be monitored for performance. The recent public services literature has mostly adopted Ammons' (1995) criteria, which can be summarized as follows.

- *Valid:* The indicators should reflect what is supposed to be measured.
- *Reliable:* The indicators should be accurate and objective as much as possible.
- *Understandable:* Each indicator should have a clear meaning.
- *Timely:* It should be possible to compile and use the indicators promptly, to be of value for incentive and policy purposes.
- *Resistant to perverse behavior:* The indicators should not be easy to manipulate and should not distort the incentives of operators to focus on the observed variables to the detriment of less observable, yet more valuable, objectives.
- *Comprehensive:* The indicators should capture the most important dimensions of performance from the point of view of policy objectives.
- *Nonredundant:* The indicators should be parsimonious and avoid duplication so that the time required for analyzing and responding to them is minimized.
- *Focused on controllable facets of performance:* While outputs are always influenced by factors other than those controlled by the service providers, using indicators that better highlight the controllable aspects is more desirable for performance measurement.
- *Sensitive to data collection cost:* Among the set of indicators that generally meet the above criteria, it is more practical and less costly to obtain data for some than for others. The selection of indicators should balance the value of the indicators against their costs.

To these criteria, some sources (for example, Governmental Accounting Standards Board 1994) have added *comparability* and *consistency.* These mean that performance indicators for a public service project should be systematic and consistent over time and comparable with the same services elsewhere, some other similar services, or externally established norms or standards. Of course, performance measures may need to be reviewed and modified or replaced to reflect changing circumstances. But it is important to make sure that the indicators can be put to effective use by building a history for them or making them comparable with the information generated in other entities.

Another consideration is the nature of the clients, consultation mechanisms, and uses for which the data are collected (for example, rewarding service providers and providing information to citizens). When the clients are well organized and well educated (for example, formal enterprises), qualitative measures that provide feedback from them can be more sophisticated and informative. The uses of the indicators also matter because if the data are to be reported to citizens, one may want to feed them data that can be best assessed and refined by their reactions. Naturally, such data may not be of much use if they are only reported to a bureaucratic agency (unaccompanied by citizen reaction) for setting service provider rewards.

While all of these criteria are important, they mainly provide a checklist of considerations for indicator selection, rather than strategies for appropriate choices under various circumstances. This limitation is to some extent inevitable, given our limited knowledge of what works best in different situations (Wood and Marshall 1993). However, there are some service aspects that seem to lend themselves to systematic analysis regarding the choice of performance criteria. In particular, outputs and inputs in some services can be measured with less accuracy than in other services. This may call for the use of procedural indicators in place of quantity and quality measures that ultimately matter for the outcome (Boyle 1989). For example, output quality in telecommunication services lends itself to measurement much more easily than in sanitation services, where the extent of environmental and health risks caused by mishandling of tasks are difficult to measure and usually only observable when there are outbreaks of pollution or epidemics. As a result, while cost per unit may be a good indicator of performance in telecommunications, sanitation services may have to be judged by the procedures followed in the treatment of waste.

Given our limited knowledge of which indicators work better than others in each situation, there is a clear need to allow for some experimentation in the choice of performance measures. As suggested by the National Partnership for Reinventing Government (1999), one should adapt, not adopt. A best practice generally cannot be adopted exactly the way it was done in another organization, but it can be adapted to fit the organizational needs of each type of service. One needs to maintain flexibility and experiment with alternative sets of measures.

To conclude, a host of indicators can help one assess performance in each type of infrastructure service. There is also a host of criteria for selecting among them. Our knowledge of how to apply those criteria in specific situations is still quite limited, and the selection of indicators remains largely an art. It is, therefore, important to maintain a broad view of the options and to remain open to experiments that can help improve the match between indicators and service characteristics.

Evaluating Performance

Given a set of indicators available for outputs and inputs of a project, the question becomes how one should evaluate the information offered by them. Since financial measures such as profitability are not sufficient for assessing performance in infrastructure services, one has to look at other efficiency and productivity measures. But to assess whether a given level of a measure indicates good or bad performance, one has to rely on comparisons. For this purpose, one has to establish benchmarks based on the history of an enterprise and the experience of others.

Benchmarks can reflect efficiency and productivity or best-practice procedures, depending on what types of indicators are more appropriate for performance assessment. Also, benchmarks can be best-practice standards defined by experts or the performance of actual enterprises that are comparable with the one under review. There is a large literature that discusses how benchmarks should be selected and reviews the experience of various countries.[2] However, as in the case of indicator choice selection, the existing knowledge is still more in the form of checklists rather than systematic relationships (Helgason 1997).

A key issue in comparisons against benchmarks is the role of exogenous factors that affect the production process and outputs. This issue is important because service providers may not be able to bear much of the risks that the exogenous factors pose. As a result, if performance measures are to be used for incentive purposes, one has to discern, as much as possible, service providers' deeds from their luck. This task is, of course, not an easy one and may require a great deal of knowledge about the process and the ways in which circumstances matter. Systematic analysis of the role of exogenous noise in each specific situation is a desirable approach, but may prove too costly. One solution to this problem is to use expert judgment for evaluating performance indicators.

There are at least three ways of doing this. First, evaluation of an enterprise can be referred to peer enterprises in the same way that academic articles are refereed for publication. For example, water companies in different locations can be asked to review each other, preferably in anonymous ways. When the number of separate entities engaged in similar infrastructure tasks in the same country is small, one can make the exercise international and involve service providers across countries (Helgason 1997).

Second, infrastructure services can be endowed with boards that are responsible to the customers and stakeholders of the enterprise. The task of monitoring and assessing performance can be delegated to the judgment of such a board. Of course, to ensure that the task will be done properly, there must be mechanisms that ensure that individuals with appropriate expertise are involved in the boards.

Third, independent rating agencies can be engaged in evaluating infrastructure service activities. When such agencies do not exist, the government can offer benefits and encourage them to enter and develop the necessary expertise for the purpose. Consumer advocacy groups and nongovernmental organizations may be eager to take on such tasks. However, such groups are often effective advocates of stakeholders and provide valuable information about public services (Paul 1999), and it may be best if they maintain that role and let the judgment be carried out by an independent third party. This is confirmed in reviews of water and sanitation utilities by the World Bank's Operations Evaluations Department (1994), which show that such utilities are most successful in countries with strong but arm's-length regulation of the sector.

All three arrangements can improve assessment and help raise the incentive effects that such performance indicators can have on service providers. But some may be more costly than others and some may fit some situations better than others. Based on the extent of specialization that can be achieved with a given level of effort, rating agencies are likely to be least costly and peer evaluations are likely to be most costly. However, when the service providers are scattered and very diverse, service boards may be in a better position to take account of local information. In such situations, one can enhance the role of service boards by creating information clearinghouses that provide benchmark information to the boards and enable them to make more informed decisions. The United Nations Development Programme (UNDP)–World Bank Water and Sanitation Program (2000) offers a detailed discussion and useful suggestions for this purpose.

Conclusion

Large parts of the population in many countries, especially the poor, bear substantial economic and human costs because of serious shortages in infrastructure services, both in quantity and quality terms (World Bank 1994). To remove these shortages and improve the standard of living in these countries, governments need to create incentives for private and public service providers to invest and perform. We have argued that improving performance measurement is a crucial step in this endeavor. For this purpose, the problem that needs to be solved is efficient and systematic collection and processing of information about performance in infrastructure services. Since the nature of infrastructure services limits the relevance of simple productivity and profitability measures, one has to collect data on a variety of measures, both quantitative and qualitative. In this regard, involving communities to provide information about outputs and feedback on other performance measures can be very helpful. To put the collected data to effective use, one has to make a choice of which indicators are more important than others. Recent experience suggests that it may be better to focus on some key indicators and ensure that the others meet some minimum criteria.

Evaluating and using performance indicators poses problems of their own. One needs to have appropriate benchmarks and, as much as possible, to distinguish between the effect of exogenous factors and the consequences of actions taken by service providers. This cannot be achieved easily through quantitative analysis and, inevitably, one has to rely on judgment. Ensuring that the judgment is well informed and widely accepted requires appropriate institutional arrangements that can ensure that experts are involved in the process and act independently.

Finally, it is evident from a review of the existing literature that the existing knowledge about the selection of performance indicators and evaluations mechanisms is rather cursory. There is a lot of folk wisdom about what works and what does not. But these ideas are not generalized and cannot be systematically transferred from one case to another. There is a clear need for further research in these areas.

Notes

1. The relationship between infrastructure capital and economic growth has been controversial. A number of empirical studies have found high returns to infrastructure investment (Aschauer 1989; Easterly and Rebelo 1993; Canning, Fay, and Perotti 1994; Sanchez-Robles 1998; Esfahani and Ramirez 1999). But the robustness of the results has been questioned in other empirical studies and surveys (Munnell 1992; Tatom 1993; Gramlich 1994). Nevertheless, it seems hard to deny that maintaining higher standards of living is unlikely without well-performing infrastructure services.
2. For reviews and references see the Web site of the OECD Program on Public Management, go to http://www.oecd.org, then type in PUMA.

References

Ammons, David, ed. 1995. *Accountability for Performance: Measurement and Monitoring in Local Government.* Washington, DC: International City/County Management Association.

———. 1996. *Performance Measurement of State and Local Government.* Public Policy Analysis, Management and Methodologies Seminar and Workshop Series, Dissemination Paper 3, Inter-American Development Bank.

Aschauer, David A. 1989. "Is Public Expenditure Productive," *Journal of Monetary Economics* 23: 177–200.

Boyle, Richard. 1989. *Managing Public Sector Performance: A Comparative Study of Performance Monitoring Systems in the Public and Private Sectors.* Dublin: Institute of Public Administration.

Canning, David, Marianne Fay, and Roberto Perotti. 1994. "Infrastructure and Growth." In *International Differences in Growth Rates*, ed. Mario Baldassarri, Luigi Paganetto, and Edmund S. Phelps, 285–310. New York: St. Martin's Press.

Easterly, William, and Sergio Rebelo. 1993. "Fiscal Policy and Economic Growth: An Empirical Investigation." *Journal of Monetary Economics* 32: 417–58.

Esfahani, Hadi Salehi, and Maria Teresa Ramirez. 2003. "Institutions, Infrastructure, and Economic Growth." *Journal of Development Economics* 70: 443–77.

Governmental Accounting Standards Board (GASB). 1994. *Service Efforts and Accomplishments Reporting.* Concepts Statement 2. Norwalk, CT.

Gramlich, Edward M. 1994. "Infrastructure Investment: A Review Essay." *Journal of Economic Literature* 32 (3): 1176–96.

Helgason, Sigurdur. 1997. "International Benchmarking: Experiences from OECD Countries." PUMA Working Paper, Organisation for Economic Co-operation and Development, Paris.

Kaplan, Robert S., and David P. Norton. 1996. "Using the Balanced Scorecard as a Strategic Management System." *Harvard Business Review* (January/February): 75–85.

Maskell, Brian. 1994. *New Performance Measures.* Portland, OR: Productivity Press.

Munnell, Alicia H. 1992. "Infrastructure Investment and Economic Growth." *Journal of Economic Perspectives* 6 (4): 189–98.

National Center for Public Productivity. 1997. "A Brief Guide for Performance Measurement in Local Government." Rutgers University, Newark, NJ. http://newark.rutgers.edu/~ncpp/cdgp/teaching/biref-manual.pdf.

National Partnership for Reinventing Government. 1999. *Balancing Measures: Best Practices in Performance Management.* http://www.npr.gov/library/papers/bkgrd/balmeasure.html.

Operations Evaluations Department. 1994. "Managing Urban Water Supply and Sanitation: Operations and Maintenance." World Bank, Washington, DC.

Paul, Sam. 1999. "Making Voice Work: The Report Card on Bangalore's Public Services." Public Affairs Center, Bangalore, India.

Sanchez-Robles, Blanca. 1998. "Infrastructure Investment and Growth: Some Empirical Evidence." *Contemporary Economic Policy* 16: 98–108.

Tatom, John A. 1993. "The Spurious Effect of Public Capital Formation on Private Sector Productivity." *Policy Studies Journal* 21: 391–1395.

UNDP (United Nations Development Programme)–World Bank Water and Sanitation Program. 2000. *Water and Sanitation Services for the Poor: Innovating through Field Experience Program Strategy: 1999–2003.* Washington, DC: World Bank.

Wilson, James Q. 1989. *Bureaucracy: What Government Agencies Do and Why They Do It.* New York: Basic Books.

Wood, Robert, and Verena Marshall. 1993. *Performance Appraisal: Practice, Problems, and Issues.* OECD Occasional Paper, Organisation for Economic Co-operation and Development, Paris.

World Bank. 1994. *World Development Report 1994.* Washington, DC: World Bank.

Index

Africa, health financing in, 171, 173
Ahmedabad, local government performance in, 77
Alberta, Canada, performance measures, 6–7, 23, 34
Alcoholics Anonymous, 138
allocation decisions, level of local political influence on, 72–73
allocative efficiency
evaluation, analytic, 160–61
improvement of, 159–60
annual budget, core businesses measurement, integration in preparation of, 7
anticorruption effort measurement, 42, 57, 59, 98–99, 107–8
Asia, health financing in, 173
Australia, performance planning, 22

Bamako, local government performance in, 76, 173
Bangalore, local government performance in, 72
Bangladesh, local government performance in, 67
Belo Horizonte, local government performance in, 73–74
benchmarking movements, parallels, 10–11
benchmarks, infrastructure, public sector performance, 206–7
benefits of drafting governmentwide plan, 3

Benin City, Nigeria, local government performance in, 79
Benin, poverty reduction in, 171
Bolivia, local government performance in, 67, 72
Brazil, local government performance in, 73–74
budgetary planning, 13–14, 19–20, 24
core businesses measurement, integration, 7
Buenos Aires, local government performance in, 77
bureau level identification of performance measures, 2–3
Burkina Faso Poverty Reduction Strategy Paper, 166, 171

California
local government performance in, 66
service delivery in, 130
Canada, 120, 144
service delivery in, 120, 144
Canadian government. *See also* specific province
draft outcome measures for, 37–38
economy, 37
environment, 37
governance, 38
society, 37
federal performance reporting exercises, U.S., performance planning, distinguished, 22–23

211

Canadian government (*continued*)
  Improved Reporting to Parliament
    Project, 2
  performance planning, 8–9, 14–17, 21,
    23
    business planning reforms, 2
  service delivery, 130–32, 136, 139–40
Cape Town, local government performance in, 70
catalysts for change, 46–47
causality, 52–53
Cebu City, Philippines, local government
  performance in, 65–67, 71, 77, 79
Cebu People's Multi-Purpose Cooperative, 67
central bank independence, 42, 50
centralized fiscal systems, 50–51
Chiles, Lawton, Jr., 5–6
citizen dissatisfaction with government,
  1–2
citizen participation in fiscal decentralization, 47–48
citizens' participation index
  political freedom, 41
  political stability, 41
Colombia, local government performance in, 73
Commission for Government Accountability to the People, 6, 12–14, 19
  ambivalence of state legislature, 13
  mandate of, 6
communication with nongovernmental
  stakeholders, governmental, 2
contracting out, service delivery, 128–33
  competitive tendering system, 129
  in California, 130
  in Canada, 130–32
  in Dunedin, 130
  in New Zealand, 128, 130
  in United Kingdom, 128
  privatization, local public services,
    128–33
  unions opposed to contracting out,
    133
core businesses, measurement of, 7
correlation coefficients, governance
  index, 45

corruption, measurement of, 42, 57, 59,
  98–99, 107–8
Costa Rica, local government performance in, 73
credibility of statistical agencies, 18
credible outcomes information, availability of, 16–18
Critical Benchmarks Goals, 6
customer feedback surveys, 94–96

data quality controls, 100
debates of public, shaping of, 20–23
debt
  expansion, 1–2
  ratio to gross domestic product, eco-
    nomic management, 42
decentralization
  fiscal system, 50–53
  proponents of, democratic context, 72
  quality of governance, 52–54
definition of governance quality, 54
definition of performance measures,
  14–16
developing countries, 63–116. *See also*
    specific country
  centralization in, 46
  donor organizations in, 95
  obstacles to outcome measurement in,
    86–87
Dhaka, local government performance in,
  67
dissatisfaction with government, 1–2
Dunedin, service delivery in, 130
Durban, local government performance
  in, 70

economic liberalization, 51
economic management, 52
economic management index, bias of,
  42–43
Economic Report of President, 10
economies of scale, advantage of savings,
  139
efficiency of public spending, improving,
  159–62
efficiency, defined, 86

elementary school systems, outcome
    indicators for, 88
equity of coverage for interventions
    addressing needs of poor, 162–78
executive, legislative branches, separation
    of powers between, 12–13
exercise of power, impact on quality of
    life, 40
expenditure decentralization, correlations
    positive, 48–49

federal–provincial relations, tensions in,
    16
fiscal decentralization, 46–52
    citizen participation, 47–48
    government orientation, 48–49
    impact on governance quality, 46–52
    macroeconomic management, 49–52
        economic management, 52
        fiscal policy, 50–51
        monetary policy, 50
        outward orientation, 51
        positive correlation with, 52
        social development, 49
fiscal federalism, economic framework of,
    46
fiscal policy, 50–51. *See also* Budgetary
    planning
Florida
    outcome measures in, 31–33
        economy, 32
        environment, 33
        government, 33
        health, 32
        learning, 31–32
        safety, 31
    performance monitoring in, 5–6
    performance planning in, 12–17
Florida Commission for Government
    Accountability, 21–22
focus groups, use of, 96–97
franchise, service delivery, 133–34
    items of franchise agreement, 134

General Accounting Office, 15, 22–23
Ghana, local government performance in,
    73

Goldschmidt, Neil, 4, 21
Gore, Al, 1
governability threats, 23
Governance and Development, 40
governance index
    components of, 41
    composite indexes, 40
governance quality measurement, 39–62
    adjustments to indexes, 58–59
    causality, 52–53
    omissions, 53–54
    quality of indexes, 58
    reservations, 53
    Sources of Data, 57–58
        Political Freedom, 57
governance quality, decentralized expen-
    ditures, relationship between level
    of, 52
Government Accountability Act, 7
government orientation in fiscal decen-
    tralization, 48–49
Government Performance and Results
    Act, 2, 8, 19, 22
Governmental Accounting Standards
    Board, 64, 67
governmental indebtedness, expansion
    in, 1–2
governmentwide performance plans
    benefits of, 3
    current efforts, 4–11
    implementation of, 3–4
gross domestic product, ratio of debt to,
    economic management, 42

health insurance, 158, 178
    private, 178
    social, 178
health outcomes, poverty and, 153–92
health personnel, distribution of, 169
health services, 153–92
Hong Kong, local government perfor-
    mance in, 78
household questionnaires, 103–6
housing, low-cost, development of, 66
human resources, availability of, 168–69

identification of quantifiable outcome
    measures, 24–25

Ilo, Peru, local government performance in, 73
improved Reporting to Parliament Project, 2
indebtedness, expansion in, 1–2
independent body, outcome selection by, 4
index trade policy, 42
India, health financing in, 171
Indonesia, local government performance in, 64
infrastructure, public sector performance, 193–209
   benchmarks, 206–7
   boards, 206–7
   effectiveness, defined, 197
   efficiency, defined, 197
   evaluation of performance, 206–7
   fixed capital costs, 196
   independent rating agencies, 207
   indicator selection, 196–205
      clients, nature of, 204–5
      comparability, 204
      consistency, 204
      consultation mechanisms, 204
      flexibility, 199–200
      inputs, 196–97
      outcomes, 197
      outputs, 197
   monopolies, 195–96
   National Partnership for Reinventing Government, 205
   peer enterprises, 206
   performance, criteria to be monitored, 204
   power infrastructure, performance measures for, 198
   process indicators, 197
   productivity, defined, 197
   quantitative, qualitative indicators, distinguished, 197
   range, 203–4
   sanitation infrastructure, performance measures for, 202
   systematic analysis, service aspects of, 205
   telecommunications infrastructure, performance measures for, 199
   transportation infrastructure, performance measures for, 200
   uses for which data are collected, 204–5
   water infrastructure, performance measures for, 201
insurance, health, 158, 178
   private, 178
   social, 178

judicial systems, 47
jurisdictional realignment, 47

Kenya, local government performance in, 71
Klein, Ralph, 7
Korea, local government performance in, 66
Kumasi, Ghana, local government performance in, 73

legislation, conformance to, 65–71
legislative branch, executive branches, separation of powers between, 12–13
legislative review of proposed outcome measures, 13
legitimacy issues
   choices of indicators, mechanism, 11–12
   political, 14
   transference of policy influence to unelected body, 13–14
Leon, Nicaragua, local government performance in, 73
local government enterprise, 118–27
   accountability, 125–26
   competition with private sector, 119
   coordination of inter-related activities, difficulty of, 125
   governance, 127–28
      local councils, 127–28
   individual enterprise, 118
   nepotism, 124
   public sector monopolist, 119
local government performance, developing countries, 63–83. See also specific country
   accountability, criteria, 64–65

efficiency, 75–77
fiscal health, 69–71
legislation, conformance to, 65–71
responsiveness, 72–75
lowest level of government, assignment of
    responsibility to, 46

macroeconomic management in fiscal
    decentralization, 49–52
economic management, 52
fiscal policy, 50–51
monetary policy, 50
outward orientation, 51
Mali, local government performance in,
    71
market failures, 157–59
Mauritania Poverty Reduction Strategy
    Paper, 171
measurement of governance quality,
    39–62
adjustments to indexes, 58–59
causality, 52–53
fiscal decentralization, 46–52
    citizen participation, 47–48
    government orientation, 48–49
    macroeconomic management,
        49–52
    economic management, 52
    fiscal policy, 50–51
    monetary policy, 50
    outward orientation, 51
    social development, 49
omissions, 53–54
quality of indexes, 58
reservations, 53
Sources of Data, 57–58
Political Freedom, 57
Measuring Up, 7
medications, fake, emergence of, 170
monetary policy, 50
monetary policy index, 42
monitoring of governmentwide perfor-
    mance, 1–38
developing countries, 63–83
early outcome measurement, 85–116
health service, 153–92

infrastructure, 193–209
measurement, 39–62
service delivering, 117–52
monopolies, public sector performance
    infrastructure, 195–96
Mozambique Poverty Reduction Strategy
    Paper, 171

Nairobi, local government performance
    in, 66, 69
narrow performance measures, difficulty
    in defining, 14–16
National Partnership for Reinventing
    Government, 205
national statistical systems, limitations of,
    17–18
nepotism, with local government enter-
    prises, 124
New Zealand
    performance planning in, 22, 25
    service delivery in, 128, 130
Next Steps Initiative, of United Kingdom,
    2
Nicaragua, local government perfor-
    mance in, 73
Nigeria, local government performance
    in, 79
North America, service delivery in,
    144–45
Nova Scotia
    outcome measures in, 7, 35–36
    economic growth, 35–36
    fiscal stability, 36
    responsive government, 36
    social responsibility, 35
Nova Scotia Counts, 7

observer assessment, key physical condi-
    tions, 97–98
obstacles to outcome measurement,
    developing countries, 86–87
Olson, Mancur, 9–11, 23
Ontario, Canada, service delivery in, 120,
    144
open federal systems, financing of sub-
    national governments, 51

Oregon
  benchmarks, 17
  outcome measures in, 30
    communities, 30
    health, 30
    quality of jobs, 30
  performance planning in, 4–5, 12–24
Oregon Benchmarks, 5
  exercise, 13–14
Oregon Progress Board, 5, 12–13, 21–23
Oregon Shines, 5
outcome measure selection, 11–16
  by independent body, 4
outcome measurement, defined, 85–86
outward orientation in fiscal decentral-
    ization, 51

parliamentary models, 14–15
Performance and Results Act, 2, 8, 19, 22
performance targets, stipulation of, 15–16
performance, governmentwide, monitor-
    ing of, 1–38
  early outcome measurement, 85–116
  health service, 153–92
  infrastructure, 193–209
  local government, in developing coun-
    try, 63–83 (*See also* specific coun-
    try)
  measurement, 39–62
  service delivering, 117–52
Peru, local government performance in,
    73
Philippines, local government perfor-
    mance in, 65–67, 71, 77–79
photographic scales, trained observation,
    111–12
planning exercises, public consultations,
    13
political contention, plan as object of, 16
political freedom index, 41
political stability index, 41
politicization of statistics, 18
Porto Alegre, Brazil, local government
    performance in, 73–74
poverty
  channeling resources, 156–92
  equity of coverage for interventions
    addressing needs of, 162–78

health outcomes and, 153–92
  interventions addressing needs of,
    162–78
Poverty Reduction Strategy Paper
  Burkina Faso, 166, 171
  framework-determinants of health
    outcomes, 154
  Mauritania, 171
  Mozambique, 171
power infrastructure, performance
    measures for, 198
price regulation, 142–44
private goods, 158
  defined, 157
private sector provision
  grants for specific services, 134–35
  self-help, 137–38
  volunteers, 136–37
  vouchers, 135–36
private sector service delivery, 128–39
  Alcoholics Anonymous, 138
  contracting out, 128–33
    California, 130
    Canada, 130–32
    competitive tendering system, 129
    Dunedin, 130
    New Zealand, 128, 130
    privatization, local public services,
      128–33
    unions opposed to contracting out,
      133
    United Kingdom, 128
  economies of scale, advantage of sav-
    ings, 139
  franchise, 133–34
    items of franchise agreement, 134
  grants for specific services, 134–35
  mix of delivery systems, 138–39
  private nonprofit agencies, 138
  Salvation Army, 138
  self-help, 137–38
    "block parent" programs, 137
    "neighborhood watch," 137
  United Way, 138
  volunteers, 136–37
    Canada, 136
    United States, 136

vouchers, 135–36
  effectiveness of information network among voucher holders, 136
  incentive for diversity, 136
procurement processes, local government, 66–67
product, defined, 86
production of health interventions, relevance of, 174–76
production, local government performance, 76–77
productivity, defined, 197
program level identification of performance measures, 2
proponents of decentralization, democratic context, 72
proposition 13, 66
public debate, shaping of, 20–23
public goods, 157–58
  defined, 157
public sector service delivery, 117–28
public–private partnerships
  Canadian, 139–40
  service delivery, 139–45
    asset ownership, 139
    Canadian, 139–40
    forms of, 140
publication of performance information, reaction of legislators, 22
publication of targets, 20–24

quasi-independent commissions, 12–15
quasi-public goods, defined, 157

ranking of countries on governance quality, 44
reallocations, budgetary, decisions regarding, 24
relevance of health intervention, 174–76
representatives, local-level, in decentralization theory, 78
republic of Korea, local government performance in, 66
response time, measurements of, 99–100
results orientation within government, initiation of, 2–3

revenue-raising activities, 66
Roberts, Barbara, 12, 21
Rothenbacher, Franz, 10

Salvation Army, 138
San Diego, local government performance in, 76
sanitation infrastructure, performance measures for, 202
school systems, outcome indicators for, 88
secondary school systems, outcome indicators for, 88
sectoral basis, development, publication of outcome measures on, 25
selection of outcome measures, 11–16
separation of powers between executive, legislative branches, challenges, 12–13
service delivery, 117–52
  criteria for evaluation, 121–22
    accountability, 121–22
    ease of administration, 122
    economic (allocative) efficiency, 121
    transparency, 122
  governance, local government enterprises, 127–28
    local councils, 127–28
  local government, 118–27
    accountability, 125–26
    competition with private sector, 119
    coordination of inter-related activities, difficulty of, 125
    individual enterprise, 118
    nepotism, 124
    public sector monopolist, 119
    role, 141–44
  monitoring, 144–45
  North America, 144–45
  Ontario, Canada, 120, 144
  price regulation, 142–44
  private sector provision, 128–39
    Alcoholics Anonymous, 138
    contracting out, 128–33
      California, 130
      Canada, 130–32
      competitive tendering system, 129

service delivery (*continued*)
    Dunedin, 130
    New Zealand, 128, 130
    privatization, local public services, 128–33
    unions opposed to contracting out, 133
    United Kingdom, 128
    economies of scale, advantage of savings, 139
    franchise, 133–34
        items of franchise agreement, 134
    grants for specific services, 134–35
    mix of delivery systems, 138–39
    private nonprofit agencies, 138
    Salvation Army, 138
    self-help, 137–38
        "block parent" programs, 137
        "neighborhood watch," 137
    United Way, 138
    volunteers, 136–37
        Canada, 136
        United States, 136
    vouchers, 135–36
        effectiveness of information network among voucher holders, 136
        incentive for diversity, 136
    public sector, 117–28
    public–private partnerships, 139–45
    asset ownership, 139
    Canadian, 139–40
    forms of, 140
    unions, public sector, criticism of, 146
social consensus, plan as instrument for building, 16
social development, 43, 49
social planning, encouragement of, 10
social reporting movement, 9–11
social statistics systems, development of, 9–10
solid waste collection, outcome indicators for, 91–92
South Africa, local government performance in, 66, 68–70, 72, 74
South African Local Government Transition Act of 1993, 68

staff members skilled in performance measurement, shortage of, 20
standard of living, measurement of, 9
statistical agencies, credibility of, 18
statistical systems, national, limitations of, 17–18
statistics, politicization of, 18
steps in implementing outcome measurement process, 88–93
subjective nature of indexes, 43
subnational expenditures, governance quality indicators, correlation, 48
systematic analysis, service aspects of, 205

Tanzania, local government performance in, 68–69
technical efficiency, 168–69
telecommunications infrastructure, performance measures for, 199
time-specific nature of fiscal health evaluation criteria, 70
Toronto road condition rating scale, 112
trained observer assessment, 109–13
    advantages, 110
    disadvantages, 110
    implementation of, 114–15
    outcomes examples, 109–10
    photographic scales, 111–12
    physical conditions, 97–98
    rating scale, 113
    ratings applications, 109
    Toronto road condition rating scale, 112
    types of trained observer rating system, 110–12
    visual scales, 112
    written descriptions, 110–11
transference of policy influence to unelected body, legitimacy issues, 13–14
transportation infrastructure, performance measures for, 200
types of trained observer rating system, 110–12

unelected body, transference of policy influence to, legitimacy issues, 13–14

unions, public sector, criticism of, 146
United Kingdom
  Next Steps Initiative, 2
  performance planning in, 18–20, 22
  service delivery in, 128
United Nations' Human Development
    Index, 42
United States. *See also* specific state
  Canadian, federal performance report-
    ing exercises, difference between,
    22–23
  local performance, 64–65, 67–68
  performance planning, 8, 17, 19–20, 23
    structural changes in government,
    20
  service delivery, 136
United States Government Performance
    and Results Act, 2, 8, 19, 22
  state, provincial governmental plans,
    distinguished, 8
United Way, 138
universal health coverage, 179
utilization of health interventions, rele-
    vance of, 174–76

visual scales, trained observation, 112
Voices of Poor, 169
volunteers
  in Canada, 136
  in private sector, 136–37
  in United States, 136
vouchers, 135–36
  effectiveness of information network
    among voucher holders, 136
  incentive for diversity, 136

waste collection, outcome indicators for,
    91–92
water infrastructure, performance meas-
    ures for, 201
World Bank index, 51
*World Development Report 1993: Investing
    in Health,* 159
written descriptions, trained observation,
    110–11

youth welfare, outcome indicators for,
    89–90